Ticket Operations
AND
Sales Management in Sport

TITLES IN THE SPORT MANAGEMENT LIBRARY

Case Studies in Sport Marketing

Developing Successful Sport Marketing Plans, 3rd Edition

Developing Successful Sport Sponsorship Plans, 3rd Edition

Economics of Sport, 2nd Edition

Ethics & Morality in Sport Management, 3rd Edition

Financing Sport, 2nd Edition

Foundations of Sport Management, 2nd Edition

Fundamentals of Sport Marketing, 3rd Edition

Law in Sport: Concepts and Cases, 4th Edition

Media Relations in Sport, 3rd Edition

Sport Facility Management: Organizing Events and Mitigating Risks, 2nd Edition

Sport Governance in the Global Community

Sport Management Field Experiences

Ticket Operations AND Sales Management in Sport

James T. Reese, Jr., Editor
Drexel University

Fitness Information Technology
A DIVISION OF THE INTERNATIONAL CENTER FOR PERFORMANCE EXCELLENCE
262 Coliseum, WVU-CPASS
PO Box 6116
Morgantown, WV 26506-6116

Library of Congress Card Catalog Number: 2012941393

ISBN: 978-1-935412-20-5

Cover Design: 40 West Studios

Cover Photos: Stadium image © Rpernell | Dreamstime.com; tickets image courtesy of Joe DiFazio

Typesetter: 40 West Studios

Production Editors: Matt Brann and Rachel Tibbs

Copyeditors: Erica Reib and Rachel Tibbs

Proofreader: Matt Brann

Indexer: Rachel Tibbs

Printed by: Data Reproductions Corp.

10 9 8 7 6 5 4 3 2 1

Fitness Information Technology
A Division of the International Center for Performance Excellence
West Virginia University
262 Coliseum, WVU-CPASS
PO Box 6116
Morgantown, WV 26506-6116

800.477.4348 (toll free)
304.293.6888 (phone)
304.293.6658 (fax)
Email: fitcustomerservice@mail.wvu.edu
Website: www.fitinfotech.com

Contents

Foreword

The sports landscape at every level and in every sport has evolved in many ways during the past 35 years since I had the privilege of breaking into sport management.

Back in the mid-1970s sport teams and organizations were typically small. Everyone multi-tasked and the level of business expertise and sophistication was not a particularly high bar. For the most part, sport properties were operated as a "Mom and Pop" businesses and many were indeed owned and operated by family members.

But the increased value of sport franchises and amateur organization properties has changed the level of performance for everyone connected with sports.

As players grew bigger, more agile, and more skilled, the financial rewards for professionals exploded. Coinciding with that, the value of professional and amateur sport properties grew exponentially as well. As a function of that growth, an evolution took place in which owners, operators, media partners, and the fans themselves began to demand more from sport organizations at all levels.

A by-product of this evolution was the need for academia to fill the void of trained sport administrators. This burgeoning educational field developed sport management degree programs in order to prepare students for careers in sport administration.

Sport administration educators in the first wave had little practical experience in sport; rather, they applied the marketing, administrative, and business principals to the business of sport. As those first sport administration graduates matriculated, they entered the work force and rose in the ranks of sport organizations, teams, and leagues. Then the real revolution began, and former students returned to school and brought practical field experience to the educational programs.

That revolution continues with top educators sharing practical experience with students that will enable them to contribute to sport management in greater depths than ever before, as many educators now have years of highly successful careers and accomplishments. One of those educators is Dr. James Reese, who has edited this book on arguably the most ignored aspects of sport—ticket operations and sales management.

In sports where admission fees to attend are charged, ticketing is the financial life blood of the organization. It is a fascinating, ever-changing aspect of sport administration that is perhaps the most entrepreneurial of all departments, utilizing technology, marketing, finance, advertising, sales, customer service, and a strong work ethic.

I hired Jim Reese as a paid intern for the Denver Broncos while he was working on his doctorate at the University of Northern Colorado. Jim experienced an intoxicating time with the Broncos as he joined a group of dedicated ticketing professionals that achieved some of the following accomplishments:

- brought a state-of-the-art technology online
- helped the organization win an election to build a new stadium
- prepared new ticket policies and shed old ones
- built a new sales and service-oriented culture
- relocated a sold-out venue to another sold-out venue after the new stadium was completed

There were some misses, but mostly successes, and our ticket group learned to enjoy and grow from them both. Among the greatest achievements was being part of two National Football League World Championships and having the Super Bowl rings to prove it! Based on that invaluable work experience, Jim continues to be part of the revolution that brings a wealth of experience to students of the business of sport.

Obviously Jim is part of another great team, as he and fellow educators and professionals collaborated to write the content of this book, which presents information that will help students become instant contributors and sport organizations to continue to reach new heights of success and sophistication.

This book is the "how to" book on ticket operations and sales management. Students utilizing this book will be prepared to sell and operate one of the most important revenue streams in sport—ticketing. This book should be required reading for every aspiring or current ticketing and marketing professional in sport and entertainment.

— *Rick Nichols,* owner of Admissions Sport Consulting

Acknowledgments

Thank you to all of the talented co-authors who worked so hard on this book project. I am so grateful to each of you for your contributions. Thank you Shelley Binegar, Dr. Dexter Davis, Dr. Joris Drayer, Mark Dodds, Peter Han, Flavil Hampsten, Dr. Kevin Heisey, Katelyn Jacobs, Dr. Jim Kadlecek, Dr. Vicky Martin, Don Rovak, Dr. Kristi Schoepfer, Derek Thomas, and Mark Washo. You provide an amazing collection of real world experience and theoretical knowledge to share with future generations of sport leaders. Thank you for helping to advance the impact of ticketing in the discipline of sport management.

Bekah Jarman, a former graduate secretary in the Department of Sport Management at Liberty University, assisted in completing many of the PowerPoint files for the book. Bekah did a wonderful job and we are extremely grateful for her support and contribution toward the success of the text.

A special thank you to Rick Nichols, former Vice President of Ticket Operations and Business Development for the Denver Broncos, and my former boss, for the honor of writing the forward for this book. Everything I know about ticketing is because of Rick's leadership during our time together in Denver. I am extremely thankful Rick took such an interest in my personal development. I can never thank him enough for the enormous impact he has had on my professional life.

We appreciate the support of Tim Wiles, Director of The National Baseball Hall of Fame and Museum's A. Bartlett Giamatti Research Center in Cooperstown, for graciously providing a photo of the oldest ticket in their archives to be used in this text. In addition, Jeff Sherrat and the staff at Ballena Technologies were kind enough to provide graphics and a number of screenshots for inclusion in the book.

I am especially grateful to Matt Brann at Fitness Information Technology (FiT), who has shown an incredible amount of patience during this process. Because of my poor health recently, the completion of this project means more to me than you might imagine. Thank you for your patience and understanding. Also, thank you to Rachel Tibbs at FiT for the great communication and editorial support.

Finally, thank you to my wife, Candace, and son, Nathan, for the support they provided during this process. Many hours were spent writing, and away from family time and activities, in order to finish this project. Thank you for your love, prayers, and support during this process. I love you and am blessed to have such a wonderful family.

1

Ticket Operations History and Background

James T. Reese, Jr. and Derek Thomas

LEARNING OBJECTIVES

Upon completion of this chapter, students will understand the discipline of ticket operations, how the need for ticket operations developed, and how the discipline satisfies the needs of spectators in sports and entertainment.

KEY TERMS

amphitheater, Colosseum, customers, Olympic Games, ticket history, ticket markets, ticket operations

HISTORICAL BACKGROUND

History credits a variety of cultures with originating sport, including the Chinese, Egyptians, Babylonians, and the Greeks (College Sports Scholarships, 2001; Graham, Goldblatt & Delpy, 1995; Mint Museum of Art, 2001). Examples include horse racing, traced to central Asia as early as 4500 B.C.; bowling, identified in Egyptian tombs as early as 3200 B.C.; and wrestling, documented in China as early as 2697 B.C. (Shuai jiao, 2008), and around 2600 B.C. in Khajafi, Iraq, near Baghdad. A Mesoamerican sport/religious ritual called the Ballgame is promoted as the first team sport in history ("Mint Museum," 2001), with origins as early as 3500 B.C.

No one knows for sure when the first ticket in history was issued. It is logical to assume that ticketing was introduced as a result of the effects of supply and demand. When the demand for attending a religious event, theatrical production, or sporting event exceeded the supply of seating, the need to create a system for limiting attendance was likely born. However, the implementation of ticketing may be more cynical. Assigning exclusivity to different socio-economic classes of people is documented throughout history (Masteralexis, Barr, & Hums, 2009; Pearson, 1973). It is possible that ticketing originated as a way to separate the wealthy or important from the common or less fortunate within the population.

The oldest known sports arena is the site of the ancient Olympic Games in Olympia, Greece. However, research differs as to when the ancient Olympic stadium was actually constructed. It is possible that some sort of primitive ticketing system was in use during the ancient Olympic Games. At the opening of the Ancient Olympic Games in 776 B.C., no seating was available for fans. Other than judges, those watching the games stood in the sun all day, without shelter, if they wanted to take in the action (Ryan, 1996; Swaddling, 1999). The date of the ancient Olympic stadium's construction is estimated at 350 B.C. (Swaddling). Seating capacity for the ancient stadium is estimated at 45,000-50,000 (Kieran & Daley, 1973). However, there is no archeological evidence to indicate that any sort of primitive ticketing system was used. Seating in the stadium may have been open to everyone without the use of assigned seat locations.

Some historians suggest that ticketing and assigned seats were invented in Rome (Ryan, 1996). Archeological evidence suggests that the earliest use of a ticket to gain entrance to a facility was documented in Rome in the first century (Tessera, 2008). In addition, most archaeologists agree that the first amphitheater, likely made of wood, was built in Rome (Pearson, 1973). Other ticketing language, such as sight lines, defined as the quality of a spectator's view at an event, was first used in early Roman amphitheaters (Pearson, 1973). Therefore, significant scientific and historical evidence exists to support the link between Roman innovation and the establishment of the field of ticket operations. As the number of spectators increased from hundreds in amphitheaters to thousands in the Roman Colosseum in approximately 80 A.D., it is logical to assume that functional ticketing practices were necessary in order to provide for efficient traffic flow and to successfully manage large crowds.

From a practical perspective, anything can be used as a ticket as long as the availability of the item can be controlled and not easily reproduced. For example, in ancient Rome, tessera were used to gain access to events at amphitheaters and arenas including the Colosseum (Tessera, 2008). The word tessera is a broadly defined term as applied to ancient Rome. Tessera included many different items, including pottery shards, colored stones, glass, ceramic, and mosaic tiles, as well as pieces of marble and limestone cut into small cubes (Futrell, 2006; Tessera, 2008). As applied to use as a ticket to gain entrance to amphitheaters and arenas, the word tessera likely refers to either small ceramic tiles or pottery shards.

At the Colosseum, arguably one of the best-designed facilities in history, 80 arches and staircases called *vomitoria* were used to efficiently allow traffic flow in and out of the building (Oxford Dictionaries, 2011; Pearson, 1973). At least 66 of these arches were numbered. Arches, landings, and staircases in the Colosseum were all identified with Roman numerals (Pearson, 1973; Quennell, 1971; Ryan, 1996). Tickets were labeled with the arch number and staircase (vomitoria) closest to the seat location, as well as the section (maenianum), subsection (cunens), row number (ordo), and seat number (locus). This allowed spectators to enter and depart the facility at the ideal arch and locate their seat in a timely and efficient manner (Futrell, 2006; Tessera, 2008). Experts estimate the seating capacity of the Colosseum at anywhere from 45,000 to 87,000 (Futrell, 2006; Kohne, Ewigleben, & Jackson, 2000; Pepe, 2008; Quennell, 1971). Reports also indicate that the Colosseum could be filled or emptied of full capacity quickly, perhaps in as little as 3-15 minutes (Pearson, 1973; Pepe, 2008; Ryan, 1996). If true, this statement is a testament to the brilliant planning and design of the ancient facility. Evidence may also indicate the concept of Will Call, a location where tickets may be picked up in advance of an event, was in place at the Colosseum (Ryan, 1996).

The Colosseum was also years ahead of its time in regard to safety. A safe environment for fans is a basic requirement for successful ticket sales. The Colosseum used archers on catwalks and nets above certain sections of the facility to protect dignitaries and spectators from animals. These safeguards were in addition to the 10-foot wall with railings around the perimeter of the arena floor (Pearson, 1973). Another interesting Colosseum fact is that there is no written evidence to suggest any riots ever occurred at the facility. One could argue that such written evidence would make Roman authorities look weak. That may be the case. Spectators may have behaved well due to fear of a violent response by Roman soldiers, or perhaps adequate security staff was provided by the government to portray a strong security presence to deter inappropriate behavior. No ancient written code of contact or policies for fan behavior have ever been discovered. Regardless, from a crowd control perspective, events at the Colosseum appear to have been managed with diligence and efficiency.

ORIGINS OF TICKETING IN THE UNITED STATES

Although specific references to tickets and ticketing are absent, and some disagree as to which sport was the professional forerunner in America, it is clear that the first sport for which admission was charged in the United States was horse racing (Adelman, 1986; Masteralexis, Barr, & Hums, 2009). The earliest known racetrack existed in Long Island, New York, as early as 1665 (Driscoll, 2008).

On May 27, 1823, at the Union Course in Long Island, New York, an estimated 50,000 fans gathered to watch a horse race (Adelman, 1986). Although attendance figures during a 50-year period from 1820-1870 were thought to be exaggerated, the fact that fans were said to have overflowed the seating capacity of the facility and were forced to stand along the track is a sign that it was a well-attended event (Adelman, 1986). Although racetracks in that period were not fully enclosed, premium seating and bleacher seats were exclusive. Though not officially documented, it is logical to conclude that some sort of admission fee or membership was charged to gain access to premium seating (Adelman, 1986).

The Union Course was renovated in 1829 and was financially ahead of its time by incorporating a groundbreaking innovation into the upgraded facility. New proprietor Cadwallader R. Colden decided to fully enclose the entire track and force any spectator that wanted to attend a race to pay an entrance fee. This was done to generate additional revenue to offset the facility upgrade, pay off existing debt, and increase purses, or prize amounts, to attract the finest horses in the region. Higher-profile horses would result in more fans interested in coming to the track. Attendance fees ranged from a quarter for general admission with no assigned seat to $3.00 for a four-horse carriage (Adelman, 1986). Although not specifically referenced, the separate fee for the four-horse carriage also may indicate another innovation considered standard today, premium facility parking. Colden's plan may have been innovative, but fans did not respond well. Since admission was previously charged only for those fans interested in the best seat locations, not everyone attending the event, less affluent fans decided to stay home rather than pay for standing room or less than optimal seating (Adelman, 1986).

By 1845, horseracing was in need of reform. A lack of standardized rules resulted in favoritism, partisanship, and corruption that affected the perceived character of the sport. Subsequently, attendance started dwindling and the popularity of horseracing sharply declined (Adelman, 1986; Driscoll, 2008; Parker, 1996). Harness racing had long been in the shadow of the thoroughbreds. However, as the popularity of horseracing decreased and the perception of prestige began to wear off, race fans and the media looked to harness racing as an affordable alternative wherein anyone that owned a horse could now be a jockey.

NASCAR Hall of Fame legend Richard Petty once said, "There is no doubt about precisely when folks began racing each other in automobiles. It was the day they built the second automobile" (Goldberg & Wincer, 2004). Though average middle class Americans did not have the resources to own thoroughbred racehorses in the mid-1800s, the preferred method of transportation for the middle class was a horse and buggy. If we apply Richard Petty's philosophy to the horse and buggy, harness racing likely began shortly after the second buggy was constructed. In fact, Masteralexis, Barr, and Hums (2009) suggest that harness racing was "an early precursor of stock car racing" (p. 9). Harness racing was the sport of the people because the same horse that was used for work during the day could be used to race in the evening (Adelman, 1986; Masteralexis, Barr, & Hums, 2009). In fact, harness racing was without doubt the first successfully commercialized sport and by the mid-1850s was the leading spectator sport in America (Adelman, 1986). However, in the period leading up to the Civil War, a new sport, baseball, was also attracting large numbers of fans and challenging harness racing in terms of popularity.

Baseball is considered the oldest organized "team" sport in America. The earliest known reference to baseball in the United States is a 1791 bylaw in Pittsfield, Massachusetts. Known as the "Broken Window Bylaw," the document was uncovered in an 1869 book about the history of Pittsfield by historian John Thorn. The bylaw reads as follows: "...for the Preservation of the Windows in the New Meeting House ... no Person, an Inhabitant of said Town, shall be permitted to play at any Game called Wicket, Cricket, Baseball, Batball, Football, Cat, Fives or any other Game or Games with Balls within the Distance of Eighty Yards from said Meeting House" ("Pittsfield's," 2006, para. 3).

Baseball expanded rapidly in the Northeast and Midwest parts of the United States in the 1800s. "By 1858, trains were being run to the Fashion Race Course on Long Island to witness games. It was there that 4,000 spectators watched the New York All-Stars defeat Brooklyn two games out of three. The owner of the fields charged each

At a legal Meeting of the Inhabitants of the Town of Pittsfield qualified to vote in Town Meetings, holden on Monday the fifth day of Sept. 1791 —

Voted, The following Bye Law, for the Preservation of the Windows in the New Meeting House in said Town — viz,

Be it ordained by the said Inhabitants that no Person an Inhabitant of said Town, shall be permitted to play at any Game called Wicket, Cricket, Base ball, Bat ball, Foot ball, Cats, Fives or any other Game or Games with Balls, within the Distance of Eighty Yards from said Meeting House — And every such Person who shall play at any of the said Games or other Games with Balls within the Distance aforesaid, shall for every Instance thereof, forfeit the Sum of five shillings to be recovered by Action of Debt brought before any Justice of the Peace to the Use of the Person who shall sue and prosecute therefor —

And be it further ordained that in every Instance where any Minor shall be guilty of a Breach of this Law, his Parent, Master, Mistress or Guardian shall forfeit the like Sum to be recovered in Manner and to the Use aforesaid —

Original 1791 Bylaws.
Courtesy of the Berkshire Athenaeum.

50 cents admission—the first time spectators paid to watch the game" (Burns, 1994). However, since the contest in 1858 was an all-star game, it is possible that the first paid admission to a baseball game actually occurred in 1857 (Light, 1997).

Union Grounds, constructed in the Williamsburg section of Brooklyn, New York, across the East River from Manhattan, is credited as being the first fully enclosed baseball park in America (A&E, 1996; Lowry, 1992; Ross & Dyte, 2010b). The facility was built by William Cammeyer and opened on May 15, 1862 (Lowry, 1992). Although it is known that admission was charged to watch baseball games prior to the opening of Union Grounds, just as at the Union Course horse racing facility before it, Union Grounds represents the first time a baseball park was totally enclosed in order to ensure that all fans paid an admission price. According to A&E (1996), "That very act of enclosing the park is really the beginning of pro sports in America." Such a statement

Earliest known baseball ticket. *Courtesy of the National Baseball Hall of Fame and Museum.*

is debatable since Union Course was said to have accomplished the same feat more than three decades earlier. However, the opening of the fully enclosed Union Grounds in 1862 was surely the beginning of professional team sports in the United States.

An early ballpark constructed in Brooklyn, New York, to rival Union Grounds was Capitoline Grounds (Ross & Dyte, 2010a). Capitoline Grounds was on the same street as Union Grounds, Marcy Avenue, and was in use from 1864 until 1880 (Lowry, 1992). The Atlantic Club, also referred to as the Brooklyn Atlantics and the Atlantic Base Ball Club, of the National Association of Base Ball Players was the first tenant. The Atlantic Club used the facility from 1864 until 1871 (Lowry, 1992; The Capitoline Grounds, n.d.). The first baseball game at Capitoline Grounds was played on May 5, 1864, between the Atlantic Club and a group of nine players from a variety of Brooklyn baseball clubs. The earliest known ticket to a baseball game is housed at the National Baseball Hall of Fame and Museum in Cooperstown, New York. The ticket is from a July 1, 1869, Cincinnati Red Stockings game played at Union Grounds, also known as Lincoln Park Grounds, in Cincinnati, Ohio. Admission to the game was fifty cents.

TICKET OPERATIONS DEFINED

According to Reese (2004), ticket operations is a twofold process of granting access to events and servicing fans. More specifically, Johnson and Reese (2011) define sport ticketing as "the discipline of granting access and serving those who have purchased a ticket to a sporting event." (p. 1,556)

TYPES OF MARKETS: PRIMARY AND SECONDARY

The primary ticket market continues to be the main focus for NFL teams (i.e., season ticketing, advance and onsite single game sales, and group ticketing), but the growing need for secondary markets is undeniable. One important function a secondary market partner can provide a team is the ability for season ticket holders to resell unwanted seats. Many teams allow season ticket holders to post individual game tickets for resale on a team-approved and authorized website. This provides a safe and secure way to sell tickets and gives the buyer peace of mind that tickets are authentic. Ticketmaster was already providing primary ticket services to most NFL teams, but in December of 2007 the NFL selected Ticketmaster as their official online secondary ticket exchange provider and offered "TicketExchange" to the teams. This new agreement allowed Ticketmaster to compete in a growing new business category. The Denver Broncos Football Club reached a secondary market partnership with Ticketmaster a year earlier (October of 2006) and was already offering this added value service to season ticket holders and fans.

TYPES OF CUSTOMERS

Season Ticket Accounts

Reese (2004) and Johnson and Reese (2011) identify season ticket holders as the financial foundation of any sport organization since they purchase tickets for an entire season. The first known references to season tickets were in baseball during the late 1870s. The first reference appeared in the *Morning Herald* of Titusville, Pennsylvania, which referred to the White Stockings, now the Chicago Cubs, having 150 honorary members for the 1870 season. According to the article, each paid $10.00 for the year and received a season ticket ("Chicago Cubs," 2010; Morris, 2006). In 1871, The Cleveland Forest Citys announced two season ticket price levels—$10.00 for the possessor with a lady and carriage, or $6.00 for the ticket bearer alone ("Cleveland," 2010; Morris, 2006).

Mini Plans

Mini plans, also referred to as multi-game plans, are a valuable ticketing option since many fans either cannot attend all games or cannot afford tickets for the entire season (Johnson & Reese, 2011). Mini plans may be constructed in a variety of ways based on the type of sport, number of home games, etc., in order to maximize revenue.

Premium Seating

Premium seating typically refers to luxury suites and club seats. These seating options have become one of the primary sources of revenue for sport organizations (Reese & Johnson, 2011). Both suites and club seats may be sold on a season or individual games basis. Both seating options offer more amenities than general season tickets, including improved sight lines, upscale food and beverages, private concourses and restrooms, and convenient parking, to name a few (Johnson & Reese, 2011).

Individual Game Tickets

According to Reese (2004) and Johnson and Reese (2011), any seat locations that remain after completion of season ticket sales and the seat improvement/upgrade process are offered to fans on an individual game basis.

Group Tickets

Group tickets are individual game tickets that have been packaged to attract groups of people such as youth sports leagues, churches, and local businesses. Group packages may also include themes such as certain dress, costumes, etc., to gain entrance at a discount. Amenities such as concerts, fireworks, etc., are also used to attract groups (Johnson & Reese, 2011).

TICKET OPERATIONS FUNCTIONS

In order to properly serve ticket customers, there are a variety of different functions routinely provided in a professional ticketing environment. These functions include, but are not limited to: facility relocations, season ticket transfers, the opportunity to upgrade seat locations, the ability to be placed on a season ticket waiting list in locations where demand exceeds supply, the use of ticket lotteries for post-season tickets, ticket forwarding, ticket replacement, and the ability for season ticket holders and guests to pick up tickets at a Will Call.

Facility Relocations

Each facility relocation is unique, so several factors are taken into consideration: architectural features, seating capacity, introduction of increased premium seating, and season ticket holder base, for example. The Denver Broncos were the first modern day professional football team to relocate approximately 72,000 season ticket holder seats into a new stadium with approximately the exact same capacity, in this case around 76,000 seats. This necessitated a very small margin of error, as each piece had to fit into the overall puzzle. Most new NFL stadiums have a larger seating capacity than their predecessors. Relocation into INVESCO Field at Mile High (the new stadium) from Mile High Stadium (the former stadium) was affected by architectural design and other design characteristics of the new stadium, including a Club Level and an increased number of luxury suites. The primary goal of the Denver Broncos' new stadium relocation was to relocate season ticket holders to the most similar area/location in the new stadium to their seats at Mile High Stadium. Final determination regarding the relocation of season ticket holders took into account the following:

- Desire of current season ticket holders to upgrade to Club Level seating (Club Seating did not exist at Mile High Stadium)
- Current seat location of the season ticket account holders and the availability of seats in their preferred areas
- Relative priority numbers of season ticket holders
- The location of seating for disabled patrons and the needs of disabled patrons
- Seating capacity of approximately 76,000—all seats in the new stadium have seat backs and cup holders (Mile High Stadium had several thousand bleacher seats)

The final determining factor was a questionnaire each season ticket holder was given the opportunity to complete in order to include more specific information relative to his/her specific situation (i.e., seats in separate locations, aisle seating, ADA [disability] seating, sitting next to other account holders, etc.).

Season Ticket Transfer Policy

Season ticket transfer policies vary by team in the NFL . For many organizations season ticket accounts are nontransferable with a few exceptions. If the account is held in a business name the account in its entirety can be transferred to a business affiliate, partnership, corporation, or LLC. The other transfer exception is to an immediate family member, defined as parent, spouse, child, or sibling.

Season Ticket Holder Seat Improvements

Seat improvement requests from account holders are accepted and based on account priority number and seat availability. Account priority numbers are assigned when the account is first established with the organization. The priority number may be a numerical number or the date and time the account was established. Season ticket holders requesting a seating location change are queued by priority number and given the opportunity to exchange seat locations based on availability (Reese, 2004).

Season Ticket Waiting List

Season ticket account holders are the life blood for professional teams (Reese, 2004). In the NFL monies generated by season ticket holders (reserved and premium seating) rank as a top three revenue stream for most if not all teams. Some teams are fortunate enough to have several thousand, if not tens of thousands, in queue to purchase season tickets. Each season after the seat improvement process is complete, tickets teams will begin contacting those first in line on the waiting list for the opportunity to purchase season tickets. More often than not, the only seats available are all located in the upper level of the facility.

Ticket Lotteries

Ticket lotteries usually only occur when ticket demand will outweigh ticket supply. Lotteries are typically held for high-profile events for which tickets are scarce, such as post-season events. If a team participates in a post-season contest for which there is more ticket demand than supply, a lottery is typically held to distribute tickets in a fair manner based on account priority. All season ticket account holders are automatically eligible and entered into the lottery. The lottery is "weighted" so that season ticket account holders with the lower priority numbers (those with the highest seniority) have a greater opportunity to be selected. The timing of lotteries, if they are needed, is determined by the respective governing body in conjunction with the sport organization.

Ticket Forwarding

Ticket forwarding is sometimes offered by a sport organization as a season ticket holder amenity. It allows the season ticket holder to cancel an original "hard ticket" and forward a virtual ticket to another fan. The virtual ticket cancels the original barcode and generates a new barcode. The new ticket is formatted as a printable file and may be printed at the respective ticket office or even on a home or office printer to be presented for admission at the facility.

Stolen and Lost/Destroyed Tickets (Duplicate Tickets)

To accommodate season ticket holders, if tickets are stolen, destroyed or lost, the season ticket account holder of record can notify a sport organization and request duplicate tickets. Duplicate tickets must be picked up in person with a valid photo identification.

Will Call

Will Call is an important fan amenity for any stadium, arena, or event facility. Will Call is viewed as an important customer service "touch point" and opportunity for face-to-face direct fan interaction. Tickets for any event hosted at a facility can usually be left at one central Will Call location. An envelope will be filled out for each person picking up tickets at Will Call. Individuals picking up tickets at Will Call must present a valid photo identification and will be asked to sign for the envelope. Individuals leaving tickets at Will Call assume all risk of loss or incorrect ticket redistribution.

CHAPTER SUMMARY

Tickets of various types have been used throughout history for a variety of purposes. Whether to provide exclusivity, limit attendance, manage traffic flow, or generate revenue, tickets have been a steadfast part of sport event experiences for centuries. Their presence provides a constant historical reminder of where sport has been. Ticketing has also come a long way since pottery shards and tessera were used to gain access to ancient facilities. Many modern sports facilities now register driver's licenses or credit cards to provide a "ticketless" system for fans to access facilities. In the years to come, it will be interesting to see how the discipline of ticket operations continues to evolve.

LEARNING ACTIVITY

In this activity, your task is to select your favorite professional sports team and do some research on season ticket sales. Many teams offer media guides for sale or for free on their respective websites. You should attempt to answer the following questions:

1. In what year was the team established?
2. How many season ticket holders (or total seats) has the team had for each year since inception?
3. What percent of total facility capacity is comprised of season ticket holders as compared to seats offered for sale individually?
4. Do season ticket holders receive a per-game discount as compared to seat locations offered on a per-game basis?

Answering these questions may provide an interesting perspective on the financial stability of the sport organization. Generally, the more season ticket holders an organization has, the more financial secure it becomes.

2

Ticketing Technology

James T. Reese, Jr., Dexter Davis, Katelyn Jacobs, and Don Rovak

LEARNING OBJECTIVES

Upon completion of this chapter, students will have an understanding of the value and benefits of a technology-based ticketing system for a sport organization, as well as how technology may be used as a learning tool for sport organizations.

KEY TERMS

alumni development, database, incentives, loyalty, relocation, rewards, targeted marketing, technology, tracking

INTRODUCTION

The purpose of this chapter is to discuss how technology can enhance a sport organization not just financially by selling additional tickets, but also on a customer relations level by improving communication and building long-term relationships with season ticket holders and fans. From the perspective of learning, sport organizations and some educational institutions have access to affordable and portable technology that fosters learning in the classroom, in the boardroom, or on the field of play.

The proper use of technology has the ability to enhance the relationship the sport organization has with fans. The strength of this relationship, known as fan identification, may impact a variety of factors important to a sport organization, such as attendance, sale of concessions and licensed merchandise, tailgating before events, participation in fan clubs, travel to events held in different cities, etc. (Reese & Moberg, 2007). As current and future fans embrace the incorporation of technology into their daily lives, sport organizations must also move forward technologically to keep pace. The following topics are discussed in this chapter: online ticket management, benefits of a ticketless system, loyalty and incentive programs, use of technology to reach transplant fans, collection of fan data, strategies for marketing to sports fans, and use of technology as a learning tool. Finally, the ways in which all of this information may be used are addressed.

ONLINE TICKET MANAGEMENT

Implementation

In the late 1990s, technology advanced to the point where ticketing software provided more than merely a resource to print tickets. The Denver Broncos Football Club was one of the first professional sports teams to work with a new company called ARCHTICS to establish an advanced ticketing management system. Rather than just providing a seating chart and printing function, ARCHTICS allowed the archiving of historical data; customization of tickets; and the reprinting of tickets, which to that point had been written by hand. Most importantly for the organization, the software provided a much-needed reports function that improved decision-making and enhanced customer service. The benefits were just as drastic an improvement for season ticket holders. Season ticket holders now had an opportunity to manage their customer accounts online. This was a significant convenience for fans since previously, many made payments in person at the ticket office to ensure that the tickets arrived on time. Those who mailed payments would (understandably) call the ticket office to confirm receipt. In addition to being an inconvenience for fans, the constant phone calls created a work overload for staff during the seasonal account renewal period. As the functionality and benefits of the software continued to improve with updates, fans could begin to complete tasks online that had previously been done through the mail or that had required a trip to the stadium. Examples include requesting additional seats, applying for seat improvements, requesting tickets for away games, and purchasing tickets for the post-season (Reese, 2005).

Ticket Redistribution

One of the benefits of an online ticketing system is the ability to redistribute tickets to a third party in an efficient, user-friendly way. Ticket software technology now allows sport organizations to tap into the billion-dollar secondary ticket market by providing a way for fans to resell tickets on their own websites (Smith, 2011). Tickets that used to go unused because there was not enough time to get them into the hands of a potential user can now be redistributed in a matter of minutes as long as the respective sport or entertainment facility scans bar-coded tickets at entry points(Smith, 2011). The ticketing software simply cancels the original barcode on the ticket(s) and issues a new barcode to the new user for a designated number of seat locations. The new ticket and barcode are emailed to the new user to be printed (Smith, 2011). In cases of short notice, redistributed tickets may be printed automatically at the facility and placed at Will Call.

Real-Time Live Attendance and Traffic Flow

Technology has advanced to the point where ticket administrators can better understand and monitor real-time attendance and traffic flow into a facility as well as fan movement during an event (Reese, 2005). This enables sport administrators to reallocate staff to and from gates to better serve the needs of fans. Sensors strategically placed throughout a facility can also monitor traffic flow during an event. These data

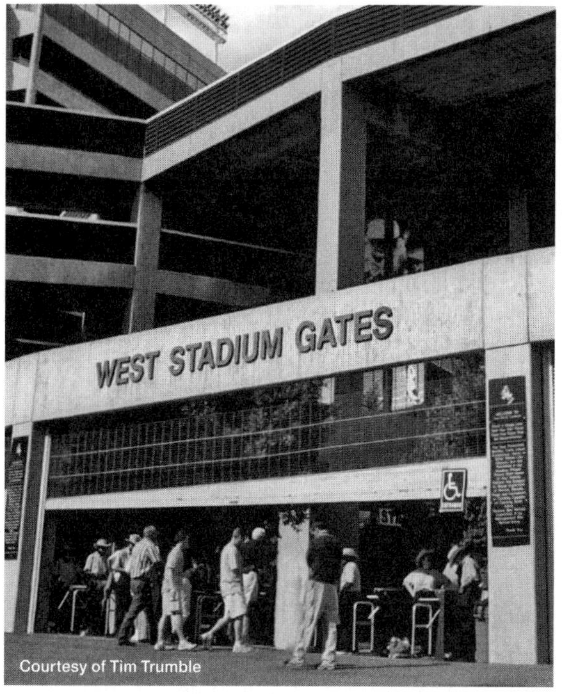

Courtesy of Tim Trumble

are extremely valuable in regard to the placement of sponsorship signage, merchandise carts, and concession stands (Reese, 2005).

Ticket Lotteries

For sports teams that advance to post-season competition, the distribution of a limited number of playoff tickets can be a daunting task. In most cases, the post-season ticket allocation is far below the demand from a variety of constituents such as players, coaches, premium seats holders, season ticket holders, administrators, staff, and the general public (Reese, 2005). Pre-programmed, computerized ticket lotteries provide an opportunity for a fair and efficient ticket distribution process.

Seat Improvements and Fan Parking

One of the most time-consuming tasks for ticket administrators in the offseason is the seat improvement process. After season ticket renewals are complete, teams offer relocation opportunities to season ticket holders interested in moving to more favorable seat locations. For more than a century, this process has been done by hand in professional sports and college athletic departments.

In the late 1990s, the Denver Broncos had approximately 22,000 season ticket holders representing around 72,000 seats at the old Mile High Stadium. The Broncos normally received about 5,000 seat improvement requests per year. Seats turned back to the organization during the season ticket renewal process were used to improve the seat locations of existing season ticket holders. Although effective, completing the seat improvement process by hand is a painfully slow process, taking approximately three months to complete. Although seats could be offered in a relatively efficient manner, the most inefficient part of the process was the amount of time it took for season ticket holders to complete the selection process. This included mailing proposed seat upgrade information to fans on index cards. Many organizations are now able to utilize email for this process. Regardless, in many organizations, the relocation process still creeps along a less than idealistic timeline. It is also a less than ideal experience for fans when the process is completed by hand. In order to expedite the process, fans are typically offered only one option to consider for a new seat location. This sometimes left fans feeling unappreciated by the organization.

Technology has finally solved the efficiency problem and allows the fans to feel that they now have more options. The seat relocation process, as well as preferred parking renewals, may now be done completely online. Previously, after administrators would mail or email possible upgrade locations to season ticket holders, they would still need to wait days to receive a response. California-based Ballena Technologies now offers a software package that assigns season ticket holders a window of opportunity for the seat improvement process. The length of the window may be adjusted based on the needs of the respective organization, but is normally 20-30 minutes in duration per season ticket holder. What makes the process so efficient is that different season ticket holders are granted access every five minutes. Having others selecting seats at the same time encourages efficient seat and parking selections. This allows the same process that used to take three months to be completed in approximately three weeks. The ability to conveniently upgrade seats online will become the future norm rather than the exception (Ballena Technologies, 2012).

Unlike the one seat relocation option fans may have received in the past when the process was completed by hand, the new online system allows fans to see all available inventory. This has two significant benefits. First, not only does this provide an increase in options, it also provides fans with a certain level of transparency that did not exist in the past. Available inventory was never a matter of keeping a secret from fans, but a matter of reassigning inventory in the most efficient way possible. Allowing 5,000 fans multiple options in the old system would have added months to an already slow process. Fans that may have felt unappreciated in the past are now able to connect with their respective sport organization in a way they never could before. Second, from a financial perspective, this new level of transparency and the ability to view available inventory allows fans to view other, more expensive seat options. Since lower-priced seat locations typically sell out first, most of what fans will be viewing will be equal to or more expensive as compared to their current seat locations. Some fans will inevitably justify an increase in price for seats with better sight lines or more amenities.

The University of South Carolina implemented the Ballena Technologies software at Williams-Brice Stadium for the 2009 football season. According to Jeff Crane (personal communication, April 15, 2010), Director of Revenue Development for Gamecock Athletics, the technology paid immediate dividends since the old system of managing relocations by hand was vague and cumbersome, especially with so much ticket inventory. South Carolina has approximately 13,000 football season ticket holders that represent approximately 55,000 seats at the 80,000-seat facility. "The new software streamlined the seat relocation process and put donors in the driver's seat in regard to locating seats," Crane said. Crane also indicated that fans have had minimal problems or complaints with the new software. South Carolina added the Ballena Technologies software option that provides the same service for stadium parking in 2010.

This new technology option allows ticket operations staff to better manage the seat relocation process. The hands-on process that used to take months can now be completed in weeks completely online without the need for fans to even visit the stadium. This is another example of how technology can enhance internal efficiency while providing fans with superior customer service.

TICKETLESS SOFTWARE SYSTEM

Just a decade ago, most ticket administrators would have laughed at the possibility of utilizing a ticketless system for a sporting event. However, Flash Seats, a Cleveland-based subsidiary of Veritix, has already had a ticketless system in place for a number of years. Flash Seats is an electronic ticketing system that allows fans to enter an event by swiping an electronic ID, such as a driver's license, credit card, or any other form of identification that utilizes a magnetic strip or barcode ("Flash Seats FAQs," 2011a). This event access system, similar to an electronic ticket (e-ticket) used by the airline industry, also allows users to manage season tickets online, and provides the ability to sell, buy, and transfer seats through a virtual marketplace endorsed by the respective team or venue ("What Makes Flash Seats Different?," 2011a). Specific benefits of a ticketless system include:

a) *Lower Printing Costs and No Shipping Fees.* Since existing personal forms of identification are used for event access, sport organizations eliminate ticket printing costs and fees previously used to ship tickets to season ticket holders (Flash Seats, 2011b). The airline industry adopted this system of saving in 1996 (Rovell, 2011).

b) *More Efficient Facility Access.* Season ticket holders and guests simply register a form of identification that utilizes a barcode or magnetic strip (e.g., driver's license, credit card, etc.) with the respective facility to be scanned at entry points (Flash Seats, 2011b).

c) *Accurate Attendance.* With a traditional ticketing system, season ticket holders may occasionally give unused tickets away to friends, family, or colleagues. Though sport organizations benefit when tickets are used, they may not actually know who may be sitting in seats at any given time. Flash Seats helps to reduce this issue since personal forms of identification are rarely shared with others. This provides a more accurate snapshot of the true fan demographics at any given event (Flash Seats, 2011b).

d) *Increased Security.* The possibility of lost, stolen, or forgotten tickets is significantly reduced since personal forms of identification are usually carried at all times (Flash Seats, 2011b).

LOYALTY AND INCENTIVE PROGRAMS

Student Ticketing

The challenge of involving the student body in athletic events in a positive and meaningful way is one that is faced on college and university campuses across the country. However, as technology has continued to advance, and interest on the part of students in their peers' athletic pursuits is on the rise, athletic departments and ticket offices at various levels of athletic competition are beginning to examine new options for student ticketing. While long lines and preprinted tickets on a first-come, first-served basis are still common practice on many campuses, there are many new and exciting options available that will enable students to be incorporated into the fabric of the world of collegiate athletics, and can potentially secure them as lifelong fans of a program.

Implementing student ticketing options requires a consideration of the goals of the student ticketing system, technique of ticketing students, and also incentives for students to buy in to the program that will be put in place (Jacobs, 2010). In the case of the goals of the student ticketing system, is the school looking to simply boost attendance at its major revenue sports such as basketball and football? Or is the goal to smooth attendance out across the Olympic sports that are ticketed as well? Examining these and other questions will enable the decision maker to determine the ultimate direction for the student ticketing operation. In regards to the technique that will be utilized in ticketing students, it was previously mentioned that students have often been required to stand in long lines and wait for preprinted tickets for each and every athletic event that they hope to attend. This practice risks alienating students and leaves much room for improvement. One such possible improvement is the use of student ID cards as a replacement for actual tickets. With the increased use of technology as a means of safety and communication throughout the college experience, it only makes sense for the collegiate athletic community to utilize this resource as well (Jacobs, 2010). At many colleges and universities, student IDs are already coded with barcodes specific to that student, and the potential is there for this barcode to be utilized as a means of game entry for athletics events as well. Each student could be provided the option to sign up for an account that provides access to game tickets, as well as the chance to switch tickets with other account holders, and also track loyalty points. Such an account system already exists at the University of South Carolina and has resulted in increased team spirit and loyalty to the athletics on campus ("University," 2009b).

Incentives for students to attend events are an extremely important aspect of any student ticketing initiative. Not only must students see the benefits of changing the way they access a sporting event or tickets to the event, but schools that have not previously ticketed students must understand that this adds value and legitimacy to athletics programs. Perhaps one of the best ways to involve the student body in this type of system is to put in place a loyalty points system, which rewards students for attending all events, not just the hallmark games that everyone wants to see. Each program is run differently and points can be awarded according to the goals of each school's athletic department, but the idea is to reward those who have consistently attended events throughout the season with access to either priority seating, merchandise, or tickets based on accumulation of points ("University," 2009a). For example, the University of Pittsburgh made the decision to revamp their student ticketing system in 2005, after their previous system of selling season men's basketball tickets to students resulted in empty seats throughout the majority of the season's early games and then a packed arena once the team reached Big East Conference play. By instead switching to a loyalty points system, again using the TicketReturn software, Pittsburgh sold tickets to students through a lottery system based on the number of early season games students had attended ("Basketball," 2005). With this type of system in place, schools such as

Pittsburgh can enjoy increased guaranteed attendance, seek to prevent no-shows if they deduct loyalty points after the purchase of a ticket and its non-use, and also attract fans who want to be at events, all of which create a more dynamic event atmosphere.

For colleges and universities that are enjoying growing popularity and success rates with their athletics programs, the emergence of resources that will enable these organizations to take their student ticketing programs to the next level is an exciting prospect. Not only will new technology and methods of student ticketing make these programs more effective, they will also contribute to a committed fan base that remains loyal long after the last class is in session.

Priority Based on Giving

Used primarily in college athletics, access to tickets and hospitality is sometimes based on the amount of money donated to a respective educational institution or its athletic department ("Basketball," 2005; Reese, Dodds, & Snyder, 2009). Driven by higher demand than available inventory, priority-based giving is typically used in high-profile Division I athletic programs.

Fan Loyalty Programs

Similar to the priority program used to attract students to sporting events, fan loyalty programs in professional or college sports are an excellent way to stimulate repeat attendance through the use of incentives. Demographic data captured through the ticket purchase process may be used to target specific fans based on a variety of characteristics such as age, gender, income, geographic residence, race and ethnicity (Reese, 2005). Examples of incentives include special ticket offers, hospitality opportunities not available to the general public (e.g., access to secure facility areas, access to coaches and players, autographed memorabilia, etc.), and coupons for free or discounted merchandise and concessions.

USING TECHNOLOGY TO REACH FANS

Advertising

Ticketing technology now allows fans to print tickets at home. Print-at-home tickets are simply an 8.5" x 11" sheet of printer paper that includes a barcode, which provides facility access. Not wanting to miss an opportunity to reach fans, sport organizations have the ability to add coupons or sponsor advertising to print-at-home tickets.

Direct Messages from Coaches and Players

Ticketing software offers some very creative ways to make an impression and generate a tremendous amount of discussion among fans. Imagine being a season ticket holder for your favorite sports team. For whatever reason, you miss a few events. You then receive an email from your favorite player stating how much the organization values you and how much you were missed at the last few events (Reese, 2005). Included in the email is a coupon for a free concessions item at the next home game. Most of us would immediately understand that our barcoded tickets' not being scanned at the last few games triggered an automated email. Regardless, how much discussion do you think that simple email message would generate among fans?

Payment Options

Advances in technology now allow a variety of computerized payment programs not available just a decade ago. Sport organizations understand the competitive environment in regard to securing disposable income. Fans may now set up monthly payment plans for ticket packages that may also include parking and concessions (Reese, 2005).

Data Transfer After Graduation

Academic institutions have the ability to use one ticket system across their entire campus. A ticket system used seamlessly across multiple institutional departments provides a unique opportunity to share data. Some ticket systems allow any points earned while a student to be transferred to a new alumnus account created upon graduation. This is a creative way to try and create a lifetime connection with students after they leave campus.

© iStockphoto.com/iTobi

TECHNOLOGY AS A LEARNING TOOL

In its broadest sense, the use of technology is as old as human civilization. Definitions of the term "technology" include phrases such as "application of knowledge," and "application of science to industrial or educational objectives" (*American Heritage Dictionary,* 1982). Out of necessity, the earliest forms of education involved the application of knowledge gained through experience and the use of tools to ensure survival. Today, it may not be the survival of the species for which the application of knowledge and the use of these tools are needed, but there is growing evidence (Geraghty & Johnson, 1997; Smith, Leimkuhler, & Darrow, 1992) that organizational survival might well be the result of the smart use of technology.

Over the past few decades, the use of technology as a learning tool has evolved in response to the rapid evolution of technology itself. Gone are the days of technology being equated to a single desktop computer in the back of a classroom. Today, students have access to affordable and portable technology that allows learning to occur in almost any environment. Technology allows us to find, gather, and transfer learning material from nearly anywhere on the planet. The Internet allows anyone to "Google" information on any topic. Email provides an opportunity for sharing information instantly. CD-ROMs and DVDs are means by which information can be stored and transmitted from one spot to another (Noe, 2010).

The Internet serves as the foundation for what has become known as online learning or e-learning, a learning method where the learner and teacher are separated by distance and possibly time, but are able to carry out the teaching-learning process through the use of network technology (Bebawi, 2011). There are numerous advantages to this use of technology as a learning tool, including

- Flexibility with regards to time and place of learning,
- Reduced cost for both partners (learner and educational institution),
- Quicker dissemination of material, and
- Ability to align material with specific organizational goals (Paulsen, 2009).

Numerous organizations have used e-learning as a means of differentiating themselves and their workforce in the marketplace. Many sales-driven organizations have used e-learning as a means of training their staff and providing them with the knowledge needed to be successful in a highly competitive environment. One such program was developed by Nike, a leading sport retailer that relies on large number of part-time, transient employees (Marquez, 2005). In this program, labeled Sports Knowledge Underground, employees work through a program that is laid out to look like a subway map, with different stations indicating different training programs. Each training session is delivered through an online platform and lasts three to five minutes. These sessions introduce basic product knowledge so that the sales associate can pass that information on to the consumer. As products and seasons change, the training program can also be changed, and the content can be customized to meet the specific needs of individual retail outlets ("Welcome," 2011).

This program has had an impact on Nike's bottom line, as stores using the program have reported an approximately five-percent increase in their sales. Other sales organizations, large and small, have seen success from the use of e-learning programs as well. Organizations ranging from a crop-seed dealer employing 250 people, to large international banking establishments employing thousands, have successfully used Internet-based training programs to increase sales and lower their training costs (Flandez, 2007). It is evident that this use of technology as a tool for learning has a positive impact on the success of an organization and its individual members.

Recently, however, technology has become even more sophisticated than the use of the Internet and e-learning. Today, advances in technology allow for learning in the form of simulations and their even more realistic successor, virtual reality. Simulations are learning activities in which the learner is immersed in a computer-generated decision-making activity, where the consequences of those decisions resemble what would happen in the workplace (Sitzmann, 2011). In this form of learning, the individual's decisions result in an outcome they would experience if they were to make that decision in an employment situation. This allows them to experience the impact of their choices. However, it is done in an artificial environment, where poor decisions are relatively risk free, and the trainee has the opportunity to learn from less than desirable outcomes.

Numerous industries use simulations as a component of their employee training programs. In organizations as divergent as Cold Stone Creamery (Sitzmann, 2011) and

Time Warner Cable (Noe, 2010), simulations have been used to prepare employees for the situations they are likely to encounter in the course of performing their daily tasks. A leader in the use of simulation for sales training is American Express and SIMON (Simulator Online Network) (Dolezalek, 2004). In this program, sales staff use a lab that replicates their call center in every fashion, including any reference material they might use throughout their day. From this lab, SIMON generates simulated live calls; the trainee must field these calls and respond to questions. SIMON has the ability to give feedback and track performance so that management can see if a learner is falling behind.

As with the e-learning program at Nike, American Express has seen the results of this training in their bottom line. What once took 12 weeks to accomplish is now done in approximately four. Turnover rates have dropped significantly, saving millions of dollars in recruitment and hiring costs. In addition, performance has increased since employees are more comfortable with the work environment after experiencing a workplace replica of the call center in their training (Dolezalek, 2004).

Virtual reality takes simulation to an even more realistic level. In this form of activity, the learner interacts with a simulated environment in which technology is used to activate multiple senses of that learner. Headsets, gloves, and motion platforms provide environmental information for the learner, while the same equipment can be used to provide the computer with information regarding the learner's movements. These technologies function to allow the learner to feel as though he/she is actually in that particular environment (Patel & Cardinali, 1994). The potential applications of virtual reality to sport and entertainment are limitless. Imagine yourself as a new cornerback on a football team who uses virtual reality to improve defensive skills by guarding a Jerry Rice avatar. Perhaps you are a baseball player looking to improve at the plate by using virtual reality to hit against C. C. Sabathia, Josh Beckett, or Justin Verlander. Could you imagine using virtual reality to try and return a world-record 155 mile per hour serve from Andy Roddick? Sport organizations could create a new revenue stream by allowing fans to participate in these virtual reality experiences at stadiums and arena across the country.

In an article outlining the potential of virtual reality, Briggs (1996) lays out a scenario where a beer company invites consumers to take a virtual tour of its brewing facilities to experience the beer-making process. Replace the brewery with a sport facility, and one can envision potential ticket buyers being led on virtual tours of that facility, experiencing the sight lines, the crowd noise, perhaps even the lines at the concession stand prior to purchasing their seat. Sales personnel could be trained on nearly every aspect of the game-day environment, enhancing their ability to explain the features and benefits of each seat in the facility to the consumer. This application of virtual reality technology to the learning process could have as much impact as the SKU and SIMON systems have for their respective organizations.

A variety of factors influence the acquisition of knowledge, and technology has been shown to have an impact on learning (Davies, Lavin, & Korte, 2009). Engagement, interaction, and even experimentation are crucial components of any learning situation. The proper use of technology can assist in attaining these goals, but we must not forget that, just as its definition implies, technology is a tool and should be used to enhance the learning process. As technology advances, we must find ways to incorporate those advances into our training-learning programs, but only as a means of enhancing the ability of our personnel; technology is truly is a tool for learning.

CHAPTER SUMMARY

This chapter highlights specific ways technology can be used as a tool to enhance a variety of ticketing functions such as season ticket account management, traffic flow, fundraising, advertising, branding, database creation and management, fan loyalty, and marketing for sport organizations. The chapter also demonstrates how technology may be used as a tool to improve the administrative skills of staff, or the physical skills of athletes in a variety of sports. When properly implemented and managed, technology has the ability to transform a sport organization into a powerful resource for connecting with sport fans.

LEARNING ACTIVITY

1. A midsized NCAA Division II university with 8,000 total students currently manages all ticketing for its intercollegiate athletic department by hand. This includes ticketing for 23 sports: 10 men's sports and 13 women's sports. Based on the information contained in this chapter, please create a list of reasons why the athletic department should consider investing in a Web-based student ticketing system.

3

Customer Service and Customer Relationship Management (CRM)

Jim Kadlecek and Flavil Hampsten

KEY TERMS

customer-centric, customer relationship management (CRM) system, data collection, Fan Loyalty Tracker (FLT), incentive program, Microsoft Dynamic CRM, renewals, retention, season tickets, ticket sales

LEARNING OBJECTIVES

Upon completion of this chapter, students will understand the importance of customer service, as well as the need to collect and manage consumer data to make sound strategic management decisions.

INTRODUCTION

In a book focused on ticket sales and operations in sports, it may be redundant to state that most sport industry executives will identify ticket sales as the engine that drives the sports machine. For professional teams and sport events, ticket sales affects many aspects of the organization, even the product on the field or court. Strong ticket sales enhances the value of sponsorship inventory, generates more concessions revenue, provides leverage for media broadcast rights, and contributes to the organization's ability to sign free agents. Therefore, of all the individuals who purchase tickets, the most valuable sport customer to a team has been the season ticket holder. According to noted sport sales trainer Charlie Chislaghi, President of Sport Sales Consulting, in recent years, depending on the sport, as much as 75% of a team's ticket sales revenue has come from full season tickets.

As a result, one would assume that sport organizations have a dedicated customer service staff to address the needs of ticket holders and concentrate on retaining them as customers. Many businesses have seen enormous success with an attitude that the customer always comes first, but the sport industry has been slow to adopt a customer-centric approach. While difficult to imagine, many sport organizations still operate with very limited interaction between the sports team and the season ticket holder. Surprisingly, there are still organizations where the only contact between the sport organization and the season ticket holder consists of a once-a-year mailing of the invoice to purchase next year's season tickets.

Considering that consumers have so many choices regarding how to spend their money and time, as well as other factors that may affect their purchasing decisions, such as team performance and the economy, a concerted effort needs to be made to build a strong relationship between the organization and the account holder in order to communicate the value and benefits of the sport product—in this case season tickets. Bernie Mullin, principal at The Aspire Group consulting firm, former CEO of the Atlanta Hawks/Thrashers, and senior vice president of team marketing at the NBA, states, "It's all about relationships. If you didn't build the relationship with a sponsor or season ticket holder or fan back when things were good, it's very hard to all of a sudden do it now. You can. But it's very hard" (King, 2010).

The goal of a commitment to service is to provide account holders with a positive experience and interaction with the product, resulting in the customers' renewing their tickets for the following year. This is extremely important on a number of levels but foremost is that most marketing literature indicates that the cost of acquiring new customers can be five to ten times more than satisfying and retaining current customers (Fenn, 2010).

For years, the model used by sport organizations placed the responsibility of customer service on the sales executive who sold the ticket to the account holder. The benefit of this approach was the familiarity between the sales executive and the account holder and the rapport that existed, which could be particularly useful when renewing the account. However, the time spent servicing and renewing the account hindered the sales executive from spending time on developing new sales. Even the team with a consecutive sell-out streak needs to actively seek new customers as there is no team in the market that has 100% of its seats sold out as part of a season ticket plan, with a 100% renewal rate. There is always a need for new customers, and sales executives need to constantly be prospecting and following through on leads.

Unlike other products in the marketplace, the purchase of season tickets requires the sport consumer to invest on three levels—money (price of the tickets as well as parking, food, etc.), time (number of home games, which may be as few as 10 in the NFL, 41 for the NBA or NHL, or as many as 81 for MLB), and emotion (avidity for the team, players, or event)—so servicing the account must effectively address all three (Sutton, 2011). This requires the sport organization to commit the resources necessary to provide a high level of proactive customer service.

When Derrick Hall, appointed president of the Arizona Diamondbacks, compared his sales department to others that were highly regarded, he realized the need to be more progressive with the team's approach to sales and service. The Diamondbacks increased the staff from 15 to 50 and implemented a sales and service model that assigned a service representative to each season ticket account. The result was an increase in new season ticket sales, revenue, and renewals.

NEW BUSINESS VS. RETENTION

Retention is the most important aspect of ticket sales; however, it is often the most overlooked and underfunded. The reasons for this vary but revolve around a few key principles of belief.

Some teams believe that retention is money in the bank. They consider these accounts as renewed until proven otherwise, often deciding to concentrate on renewing these accounts well after it is too late. Other teams do not invest in the proper amount of staff, leaving each staff member with a too-large account base that is unmanageable. Having an unmanageable account base leads to neglected accounts, and neglected accounts lead to non-renewed accounts. The internal consulting division of the NBA, Team Marketing & Business Operations, provides teams with information to assist with all of their sales and marketing efforts. The NBA considers the optimal amount of accounts that a service representative should handle to be approximately 300. Anything more makes it difficult to manage and hinders the service representative's ability to build a relationship with the season ticket holder. Lastly, other teams may believe that there is nothing that they can do to influence a renewal, and that the decision is made based on the product on the field alone. Regardless of one's stance on service and retention, the fact that it sets the tone of the off-season cannot be denied.

According to the NBA, in 2010-2011 the average renewal rate was 81%. If a team has 10,000 season ticket holders (STHs), this means that only 8,100 will renew, leaving the team with 1,900 new full season tickets to sell just to break even. In that same season, the NBA average in new full season ticket sales was 1,958, which means that a team with 10,000 season ticket holders that renewed at 81% had a small bump in full season tickets sold. However, only 50% of the teams actually renewed at 81% and higher. The remaining half of the league renewed at an average of 62%. This means that those teams need to replace 38% of their full season base just to break even, which is no easy task. While an entire book could be written about renewal tactics alone, following are a few successful tactics that teams use to better their renewal rates:

Understanding account base tenure – Tenure matters. First-year season ticket holders renew at a rate 10% lower than second-year season ticket holders, and a rate 20% lower than fifth-year season ticket holders, according to the NBA. It is important to understand the risk associated with the younger accounts and dedicate resources to retaining those accounts.

Understanding account base objections – The Charlotte Bobcats have done this by ranking their accounts from 1-5, with five (5) being definitely renewing and one (1) being not renewing at all. They have found that $5M of business falls into a 3, which means that the account holders have not made up their minds about renewing. They also understand, through a combination of surveys and conversations, the major objections of each account.

Targeting fence sitters with a retention plan – When the organization understands where the accounts fall and what their objections may be, it can engineer a plan targeted to resolve the accounts' objections and increase the retention percentage.

Since the Charlotte Bobcats finished the 2011-12 season with a 7-59 record, the team understands that a majority of objections fall into the team performance bucket, the "waiting" bucket, or a value-based bucket, and the team has designed a plan for each. The team has 60 events in 60 days, hosted by the basketball operations department that will advise on the direction of the product. The Bobcats have also designed a strategic renewal incentive program that rewards STHs for renewing early by entering them in a drawing to win prizes. Lastly, the team has launched an innovate program titled "Cats 365" that enhances the value of the season ticket package by adding up to 60 events annually to the package.

At the time of publication, the Bobcats are sitting at $1M above their renewals from the 2011-12 season.

COLLECTION OF DATA

It is apparent that the collection of data is the lifeblood of an organization. Every action that a team will take comes back to data. Who should be targeted with this offer? How many pieces of direct mail should be sent? How many people are going to renew their season tickets? The answers to all of these questions can be determined if the team is collecting enough data. The data can be gathered by conducting focus groups, posting online surveys, conducting fan questionnaires at games, or a combination of all three. Regardless of the method(s) used, the teams that collect the most data will understand their fans better and thus operate more efficiently.

Collecting data should provide a means of making educated business decisions and completing economic forecasts. An organization should gather the data it needs to make these decisions as easy as possible. In order to do so, a short list of information is essential to capture. This is not a complete list and can be expanded based on the needs of each organization. As a point of reference, the Charlotte Bobcats capture more than 50 points of data on each buyer; however, we will keep to the basics with the information below and look at how to use this information to make business decisions.

Sex

Age

Marital Status

Number of Children

- Age of Children

Employment Status

- Title/Responsibilities

Income

Where media is consumed (print, television, Web)

Are the tickets used for business or personal use if season ticket holder [STH])

Attendance rate (if STH)

How many years this account has had seats (if STH)

Renewal intent (if STH)

Once the organization has basic information on the buyer, decisions can be made. The majority of the decisions fall into three categories: new business, retention, and individual game tickets.

New Business:

Identifying lead sources and establishing call priority

Marketing to the appropriate amount of leads

Targeting leads with the appropriate marketing resource

Understanding why people are not buying

Recognizing why people are not buying more

Knowing the buyer before the first phone call

Group sales – Understanding to what groups a buyer could belong

Retention:

Forecasting the retention rate

Understanding why some accounts will not renew

Gaining the ability to address concerns prior to asking for renewal

Obtaining insight into the service team's performance

Gathering information on the team's customer service performance

Individual Ticket Sales:

Knowing what segment to target with specific offers

Understanding buying behaviors

Learning which marketing mediums the organization's buyers consume

Let us look more closely at a few examples of the above categories:

Identifying lead sources and establishing call priority – If an organization's personnel understand what its current buyers look like, they can then go find similar lead sources. For example, if you know that your typical club seat buyer is male, 35–40 years old, earns $100,000+, and is married, you can identify all similar leads in the database and continue to search for more leads in this category.

Forecasting retention rate – Each winter, the National Basketball Association (NBA) surveys each team's season ticket holders. The survey, Fan Loyalty Tracker (FLT), measures a variety of aspects, but the biggest factor it measures is renewal intent. The survey has been surprisingly accurate within a few percentage points each season. This is a good benchmark when starting yearly revenue budgets.

Understanding why people are not buying – Another useful aspect of the FLT survey is that it allows the organization to see why some people do not intend to renew. This allows the organization to address those issues before asking customers to purchase again, often resulting in hundred of thousands of dollars generated because the team has made adjustments.

Understanding why people are not buying *more* – In 2010, the NBA conducted its first-ever partial plan buyer survey. The results indicated that partial plans are purchased because of time commitment and not financial commitment. In other words, a partial plan is purchased instead of a full season ticket because the buyer does not have the time to attend 40+ games per season, not because he/she cannot afford to do so. The league also learned that buyers would spend up to 250% more and attend more games if there were more flexibility in partial plan options. One team that put this system in place was the Charlotte Bobcats. The Bobcats typically had a menu of partial plans that consisted of set games with a variety of opponents and days. However, in the 2010 offseason, the Bobcats switched to a pick plan menu, which allowed buyers to choose the games that worked for them, at a premium price. The results? A million dollar increase in partial plan sales. If the information obtained through the survey was unknown, the team may never have adjusted its strategy.

Selling individual game tickets – This is a tricky task for most teams, as buyers of individual game tickets generally have different buying motives than season ticket holders. If the team can gain insight into what drives a buying decision, they can find other buyers with similar habits to target with a message. See Figure 3.1 for an example from

When did you purchase your ticket or tickets to the game?

How many Bobcats games do you plan to attend during the 2011-12 season?
(Please include any previous games you have attended this season in your answer.)

Please rank the reasons why you chose to buy tickets for the Heat game (as opposed to other Bobcats games)?

	1 - Least Important Reason	2	3	4	5	6 - Most Important Reason
The giveaway/promotional item of the night (no giveaways on this game)	○	○	○	○	○	○
This was the best time my friends/family/guests could accompany me to the game	○	○	○	○	○	○
The price of the tickets for this game were attractive to me	○	○	○	○	○	○
Wednesday nights are the best nights for me to come to a game	○	○	○	○	○	○
I wanted to see the stars of the opposing team (LeBron James, Dwyane Wade, etc.)	○	○	○	○	○	○
I am a big fan of the Miami Heat team	○	○	○	○	○	○

How did you hear about this Heat game? (Please select all that apply)

- [ ] At a Bobcats Game
- [ ] Billboard Advertisement
- [ ] Bobcats Delivery Truck Ad/Billboard
- [ ] Bobcats Email
- [ ] Bobcats Ticket Sales Executive
- [ ] Bobcats.com
- [ ] Community Event with Bobcats Presence
- [ ] Daily Deal Websites (GroupOn/LivingSocial)
- [ ] Direct Mail
- [ ] Facebook
- [ ] Internet Website Advertisement (not Bobcats.com)
- [ ] Listening to Bobcats Game on Radio
- [ ] Newspaper Advertisement
- [ ] Newspaper Article
- [ ] Picked Up A Schedule
- [ ] Radio Advertisement
- [ ] Radio Interview/DJ Mention
- [ ] Television Advertisement
- [ ] Television News/Interview
- [ ] Twitter
- [ ] Watching Bobcats Game on Television
- [ ] Word of Mouth

FIGURE 3.1. Bobcats IG Buyer Survey (Post Game)

the Charlotte Bobcats' individual game ticket buyer survey. This survey is completed after the event and attempts to gain insight into the buyers' motives in purchasing, where the buyers consume media, and why they do not attend more games. Adjustments are then made based on feedback from the customers. This feedback dictates what marketing elements are incorporated into each campaign and what product is offered.

STORING AND USING THE DATA

Once the data is aggregated, it is typically stored in a Customer Relationship Management (CRM) system. There are many CRM systems, but for our example we will assume the data is stored in Microsoft Dynamic CRM. From this screen, the user can access various pieces of demographic information about anyone in the database. Figure 3.2 is a shot of an account in the Bobcats' CRM system. Notice that there are 11 tabs at the top of the screen.

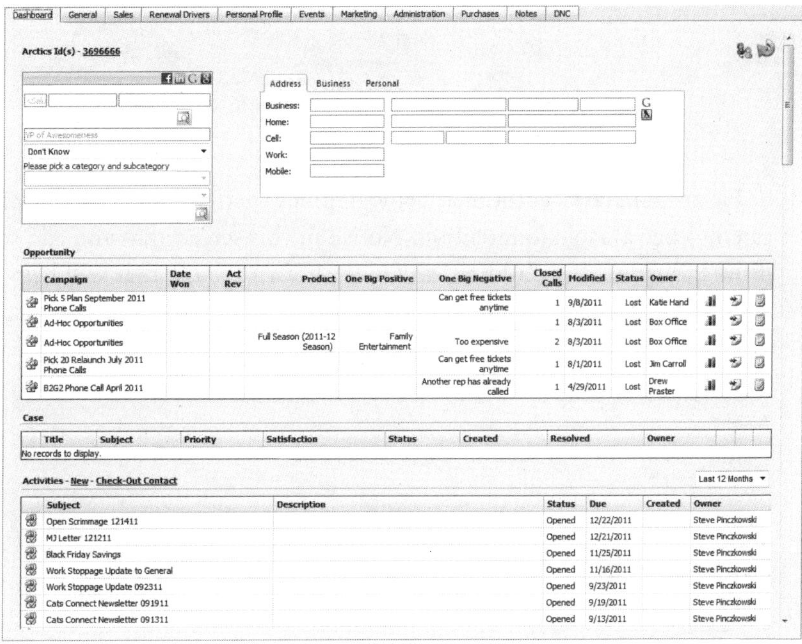

FIGURE 3.2. Bobcats CRM Home Screen

Each tab hosts information that is helpful to the sales function. Take a look at the retention tab in Figure 3.3—you can now see various fields that will help predict whether this person will renew. By looking at the attendance percentage, how the individual uses the tickets, if there are partners, and most importantly if there is an objection to renewing the seats, the organization will have a good idea of whether this person is likely to renew. By storing this in one place in the CRM system, a salesperson or manager can be knowledgeable when speaking to this person on the phone. Moreover, the system will provide an overview of total items in the entire system to know how many people have a common objection. If 45% of a team's customers have a common objection, the organization can address that objection immediately to ensure that the renewals can occur.

Dashboard | General | Sales | Renewal Drivers | Personal Profile | Events | Marketing | Administration | Purchases | Notes | DNC

Contract Expiration Date

Computed Renewal Score (Fence Sitter)

Attendance STH 2010-11		Computed Renewal Score	
STH Tenure		Current Renewal Expectation?	

Renewal Expectations

Desired Future Location		Primary Renewal Objection	
In-Game Renewal Driver		Secondary Renewal Objection	
		Lockout STH Option	

Event Information

Event STH - Community Involvement	No / Yes	Event STH - Athletic Events	No / Yes	Event STH - Family	No / Yes
Event STH - Guys-Girls Night Out	No / Yes	Event STH - Date Night	No / Yes	Event STH - Business	No / Yes
STH Stereotype					

How are tickets used?

Percent Business		Percent Personal	
Business Reason for Buying		Personal Reason for Buying	
Does account holder attend when business?		Does account holder attend when personal?	
Usage Clients?	No / Yes	Usage Spouse?	No / Yes
Usage Employees?	No / Yes	Usage Kids?	No / Yes
Usage Prospects?	No / Yes	Usage Friends?	No / Yes
Usage Vendors?	No / Yes		

Share Partners

Usage Share Partners?		Share Partner 1	
Share Partner Desired Location		Share Partner 2	
Share Partner Has-Needs		Share Partner 3	
		Share Partner 4	

FIGURE 3.3. CRM Renewal Intention Screenshot

Figure 3.4 shows additional demographics that are used primarily for new sales but can also be valuable to retention. Notice in this screen that you can see marital status, if the individual has children, and several other factors that will help to identify a potential customer.

Dashboard | General | Sales | Renewal Drivers | Personal Profile | Events | Marketing | Administration | Purchases | Notes | DNC

PersonicX

PersonicX Cluster	Married Sophisticates	PersonicXChildren	
Prospector Star Rating	4		

Marital Status

Spouse/Partner Name	Ashlee	Marital Status	Married
Spouse Birthday		Anniversary	
SpouseOccupation			

Children

Child Name 1		Child Birthday 1	
Child Name 2		Child Birthday 2	
Child Name 3		Child Birthday 3	
Child Name 4		Child Birthday 4	

Basketball/Sporting

Favorite NBA Team 1	Charlotte Bobcats	Favorite NBA Player (non-Bobcats)		Favorite Other Sports Team	
Favorite NBA Team 2	Cleveland Cavaliers	Favorite Bobcats Player		Favorite NCAA School	Ohio State

Entertainment

Favorite Restaurant		Favorite Movie Genre		Favorite TV Show		Favorite Charity	Make-A-Wish
Favorite Fast Food		Favorite Music Genre		Favorite Radio Station			

Education

High School		College/University (Bachelors)	Mount Union University	College/University (Master/Doctorate)	Arizona State University
HS Graduation Year		Graduation Year	2,001	Master/Doctorate Graduation Year	2,009
Hometown		College Degree		College Master/Doctorate Degree	

FIGURE 3.4. Personal Profile CRM Screenshot

CHAPTER SUMMARY

Though ticket sales are an important part of any sport organization, this chapter demonstrates the need for a highly interactive, customer-centric approach in order to properly service and ultimately retain the business of sports fans. Accomplishing this requires that sport consumers receive a positive experience on multiple levels of interaction. Achieving such a goal required a change in thinking for many sport organizations, including the implementation of a staff solely dedicated to serving ticket account holders. Sales staff previously responsible for selling and service could now focus on acquiring new customers. Since it is much more expensive to secure new customers than to renew existing ones, customer retention is the key to financial success in the sport industry. A successful retention plan is based on understanding the wants and needs of customers, collecting relevant data, and the ability to overcome any reasonable objections to renewal.

LEARNING ACTIVITY

In this activity, your task is to select a partner for the exercise and collect as much sales-related data about your partner as possible in the time allotted by your course instructor. You should attempt to answer the following questions to determine if your partner is a potential season ticket holder for any respective sport selected for the activity. If your partner consumes sports via the media, your goal is to persuade him/her to purchase tickets and attend a sporting event. If your partner already attends sporting events, your goal is to increase attendance. Possible questions include:

1. Does your partner watch or attend any college or professional sporting events?
2. If yes, what are your partner's areas of interest and favorite players, and how often does he/she watch and/or attend? What motivates attendance?
3. Is your partner interested in saving money on tickets?
4. Where does your partner live geographically in relation to the respective athletic facility?
5. When your partner attends sporting events, who usually attends with him/her? In addition, are there any additional friends or family who may be interested in attending in the future?

Collecting data from these questions will allow a sales associate to determine if the person is a viable sales candidate, and if so, what event package (games, number of tickets, etc.) would be the best fit personally, socially, and financially.

4

Priority Systems

James T. Reese, Jr.

KEY TERMS

facility relocations, post-season tickets, preferred parking, priority, seat relocations, seniority, special functions, transfers, waiting lists

LEARNING OBJECTIVES

Upon completion of this chapter, students will have an understanding of why a priority system is necessary in ticketing, as well as how it may be implemented and executed.

INTRODUCTION

As the number of season ticket holders in the sport and entertainment industry continues to expand, so does the need for a way to determine levels of seniority among fans. A method to track seniority, commonly referred to as a priority system in the ticketing industry, allows ticketing administrators to distribute resources and services by using the method most acceptable to fans—account seniority. In addition to being accepted by consumers as a fair process, a priority system rewards fans for loyalty to an organization, not for how much money people or corporations have in their bank accounts. The level of association with and commitment to a team, artist, or institution is considered a badge of honor among many fans. A policy that equitably rewards fans for loyalty through tenure of association is one of the few systems that allows blue collar and white collar fans to be placed on somewhat of a level playing field. That is the remarkable thing about using account seniority to make decisions—almost all fans respect the process. This makes the customer service aspect of running a ticket office a much smoother process. A priority system based on seniority even works well when distributing tickets and services to six-foot five-inch, 300-pound athletes in the locker room. A seniority based priority system is a simple but extremely effective management tool for ticket administrators.

Because they belong to different economic classes, all fans may not be able to afford the same sight lines in a stadium, arena, or theater. However, blue collar season ticket holders with longer seniority may actually receive greater benefits than their more financially advantaged counterparts with more expensive seats. The key to properly managing a priority system is to implement the process from the very beginning, at the inception of the organization, facility, event, etc., regardless of current demand. The Denver Broncos made this mistake in the early years of the franchise because demand was scarce and it was hard to foresee sellouts. When the Broncos were established as part of the American Football League in 1960, few executives, staff, or administrators could envision eventually selling out the almost 76,000 seat Mile High Stadium for more than four decades with a waiting list for tickets. When first occupied by the Broncos in 1960 and prior to numerous renovations and expansions, Mile High Stadium was originally called Bears Stadium and only seated approximately 34,000 (Denver Broncos, 2001). Not documenting the exact dates of the first 5,000 season ticket holders' ticket purchases created priority problems for ticket administrators when the popularity of the team finally caught on and ticket sales exploded. When the team finally implemented a priority system and tracked when season ticket accounts were created, there was no way to distinguish seniority among the first 5,000 season ticket holders. The team was forced to create a seniority category for those earliest accounts and treat them all the same. This was the best solution to the problem at the time, but it did not best serve the season ticket holders or the organization.

Although it may appear complicated on the surface, a priority system is actually a rather simple process and can work effectively in several ways. When ticket administrators create a new season ticket account, in addition to collecting important personal information from the customer, they should assign the new account either 1) a sequential priority number or 2) a sequential priority date. "A priority number is a numerical representation of the duration of a season ticket account. Typically, the lower the priority number, the longer the season ticket account has been active" (Reese, 2004, p. 170). A priority date works the same way. When an account is established, the date and exact time, down to the second, is entered into the office's computer system. As with a priority number, a priority date provides a clear record of when accounts were created so that they may be sorted oldest to newest when necessary.

Because low priority numbers or older priority dates represent fans that have been account holders with an organization the longest, they may receive benefits not available to season ticket account holders with less seniority. Some of these benefits are significant and become more pronounced as the account continues to gain seniority over time. Season ticket priority typically relates to the following ticketing functions: seat relocations, season ticket transfers, facility relocations, ticket waiting lists, preferred parking options, special functions, and post-season tickets. Each of these areas will be defined and addressed in depth.

SEAT RELOCATIONS

Seat relocations are defined as the process by which season ticket holders are assigned different seat locations in a stadium, arena, or theater. Most organizations implement a supply and demand based model for what is classified as a "better" seat location. This is used to create and maintain ticket price points. In the simplest terms, the more popular a specific seat location (e.g., lower level, 50-yard line in football; lower level

Courtesy of Arizona State University

center court/ice in basketball and hockey; lower level front rows in theaters), the more expensive the seat will be. However, some fans do not share the same supply and demand based perspective on which location is considered best. For example, some fans prefer seat locations with a view from an end zone in football, rather than the more popular lower level location close to the 50-yard line. These football "purist" fans suggest that an end zone view in football allows fans to better watch plays develop. Fans willing to select a less popular seat location have a much better chance of securing the seats they want during the seat relocation process. In addition, because most accounts contain an even number of seats, fans with an odd number of seats typically have more relocation options. This occurs because single seats occasionally open up throughout the stadium and are difficult to sell. Specifically, fans with three seats in their accounts have the easiest opportunity to relocate. Selling these single seats as an add-on to existing season ticket accounts is one of the primary responsibilities of ticket sales people.

Even with an abundance of ticketing software packages, few have determined an efficient way to properly manage the seat relocation process. Therefore, the overwhelming majority of organizations currently execute seat relocations individually on a case-by-case basis. Typically, season ticket holders request to be relocated during the annual ticket renewal process. Some organizations process online requests, while others place mailed requests in priority order and process them manually. For the manual process, Figure 4.1 illustrates a sample season ticket relocation card (Denver Broncos Ticket Office, 1998).

DEAR SEASON TICKET HOLDER,

We are pleased to offer you a new seat assignment based on your relocation request. The location we are offering to exchange is as follows:

Section: Row: Seat(s):

Please call 433-7466 before the close of business on ________ to confirm your acceptance of the above mentioned seats and to release your current seats. The ticket office business hours are 9:00 a.m. - 5:00 p.m., Monday thru Friday.

If you requested additional seats, your name has been added to the waiting list and you will be contacted in the near future.

Thank you again for your continued support. We look forward to an exciting season!

Sincerely,

DENVER BRONCOS TICKET OFFICE

FIGURE 4.1. Denver Broncos Season Ticket Relocation Postcard, 1998

New technology has been introduced that can now manage the seat relocation process in a more efficient manner, reducing the process from months to weeks, depending on the size of the customer base. Once the season ticket renewal period has ended, seats from non-renewed season ticket accounts are used to process seat relocations. Any prime seats obtained during the renewal process may be transferred to the organization's "house account." The house account is used to service tickets for administrators, players/talent, coaches, staff, and visiting teams, performers, etc. of the organization. The house account is also used to resolve difficult seating problems throughout the year. An example of a seating problem may be a fan that has an obstructed sight line and wishes to be relocated. The best remaining seats available through the renewal process are offered to season ticket holders with the highest level of priority as a seat relocation opportunity. This creates a domino effect because every time one fan changes location, their seats become available for other fans. In essence, a handful of non-renewed seat locations can allow hundreds of fans to change or improve their seat locations. In order to facilitate the process in a timely manner, fans have a designated time period in order to respond before seats are offered to the next person on the list. Organizations may have thousands of requests to process, depending on the size of the season ticket holder base. Even with time management controls in place, it is not uncommon for the seat relocation process, done manually, to take several months to complete. New ticketing software now allows seat relocations to be completed in weeks rather than months. However, fans have much less time to make a decision. If using online software, fans may have minutes rather than days to decide whether to accept a seat relocation opportunity. Each method—manual or online—has benefits and drawbacks.

From a fan perspective, the seat relocation process can either be an extremely easy decision or an agonizing one, depending on a variety of factors. Anyone who has ever attended a sporting or entertainment event knows that much more than the seat location contributes to the overall experience. For example, some fans prefer aisle seats over seats in the middle of a seating area. There are advantages and disadvantages of each. Fans that possess aisle seats have easy access to restrooms and concessions areas, and they can exit the facility more efficiently at the end of an event. Unfortunately, fans with aisle seats also may have to stand often to let other fans out of the seating area. This creates a significant number of sight line interruptions throughout the event. This is just one of many factors to consider when deciding to relocate. Other factors may include the level of happiness with the personality and behavior of other season ticket holders in the immediate vicinity; proximity to restrooms, other amenities, and concourses; and sight lines. For season ticket holders in outdoor facilities, there are other concerns as well. For example, design characteristics may create more wind in certain sections of the facility. Whether seats are covered by upper levels of the stadium or open to the elements may also impact the desire to relocate. The quality of the sound system may vary in different areas of a facility due to acoustics and the age of the equipment. The location of the sun at different times during an event can also impact vision and temperature for fans.

It may be virtually impossible to create a software package that takes all of these factors into consideration. The decision of a fan to relocate is typically non-revocable. Once the change is made, the fan's former seats will likely be selected by another fan that may retain them for decades. Ticket administrators have the responsibility to properly service the needs of the fans, while still balancing the need of the office to complete the seat relocation process in a timely manner. Until all fans have secured seats, final ticket invoices cannot be printed. A customer-friendly approach will never fail. It is possible to complete the process in a timely manner and still allow fans the chance to visit the facility to sit in prospective seat locations. Many ticket offices actually create an open-house-type format to provide this service to fans. Such a service helps fans make difficult decisions that may actually help the seat relocation process run more efficiently.

SEASON TICKET TRANSFERS

Depending on the administrative policies of an organization, managing the impact of a priority system on a ticket office can be a challenging process. The area with perhaps the most potential to disrupt the integrity of a priority system is the ticket transfer process. Season ticket transfers are defined as the process by which either a portion or all seat locations in a season ticket account, also referred to as revocable seat licenses, are reassigned to others. Most organizations offer some sort of process for reassigning seats. Figure 4.2 illustrates a sample season ticket transfer form (Denver Broncos Ticket Office, 2005).

Some organizations utilize an open or unlimited transfer process. An open or unlimited process allows season ticket holders to reassign specified seats in an account, or all seats in a season ticket account, to anyone. The transfer process becomes more complicated if an organization allows groups of seat locations to be divided and reassigned to multiple new account holders. In contrast, a closed or limited transfer process restricts season ticket holders from reassigning seats at all or limits the reassignment of

DENVER BRONCOS
RESERVED SEAT SEASON TICKET ASSIGNMENT FORM
(Valid from September 15, 2005 until December 31, 2005)

PART I

TO BE COMPLETED BY THE CURRENT SEASON TICKET HOLDER OF RECORD
(OR ON BEHALF OF A DECEASED SEASON TICKET ACCOUNT HOLDER)

The undersigned does hereby assign and transfer to the party named in Part II the Broncos season ticket locations identified below, effective February 1, 2006.

Name/Company Name: ____________ Social Security #: ____________
Attention (If Company): ____________ E Mail Address: ____________
Address: ____________
City: ____________ State: ____________ Zip: ____________
Day Telephone Number: ( ) ____________ Evening Telephone Number: ( ) ____________
Season Ticket Account Number: ____________ Priority Number: ____________

Seat Locations to Be Transferred: Section: ________ Row: ________ Seats: ________
Section: ________ Row: ________ Seats: ________

Note: If the seats are simultaneously transferred to more than one person, one of the transferees must be designated to be assigned the priority number associated with this account. The other transferee(s) will receive a new priority number. If you transfer less than all of your seats to one or more persons, you will retain your current priority number and the transferee(s) will receive a new one.

PART II

TO BE COMPLETED BY THE PROPOSED SEASON TICKET HOLDER OF RECORD
MUST BE AN IMMEDIATE FAMILY MEMBER FOR AN ACCOUNT HELD BY AN INDIVIDUAL, OR AN AFFILIATE FOR ACCOUNTS HELD BY PARTNERSHIPS, CORPORATIONS OR LLCs.
(ALL AS MORE PARTICULARLY DESCRIBED ON THE REVERSE SIDE OF THIS ASSIGNMENT FORM)

By executing this agreement, the Proposed Season Ticket Account Holder of Record agrees to accept the conditions of purchase and use, and other terms, conditions and policies set forth and modified from time to time by the Denver Broncos Football Club, including without limitation the "Season Ticket Account Policies" set forth on the reverse side of this form.

Name/Company Name: ____________ Social Security #: ____________
Attention (If Company): ____________
Relation to current account holder: ____________
Address: ____________
City: ____________ State: ____________ Zip: ____________

Day Telephone Number: ( ) ____________ Evening telephone number: ( ) ____________
E-Mail Address: ____________

PART III

To Be Completed In The Presence Of And Acknowledged By A Notary Public.

BY EXECUTING THIS ASSIGNMENT FORM, WE REPRESENT AND WARRANT TO THE BRONCOS THAT THIS ASSIGNMENT COMPLIES WITH THE "LIMITED TRANSFER POLICY" PORTION OF THE "SEASON TICKET ACCOUNT POLICIES" SET FORTH ON THE REVERSE SIDE OF THIS FORM. WE HAVE PROVIDED TO THE BRONCOS INFORMATION OR DOCUMENTATION DEMONSTRATING THAT THE PROPOSED ACCOUNT HOLDER IS AN "IMMEDIATE FAMILY MEMBER" OR AN "AFFILIATE" OF THE CURRENT ACCOUNT HOLDER, AS DEFINED THEREIN. WE AGREE THAT THE BRONCOS MAY IMMEDIATELY REVOKE THE SEASON TICKET ACCOUNT ASSIGNED HEREIN IF IT DETERMINES, IN ITS SOLE DISCRETION, THAT WE HAVE NOT COMPLIED WITH THE "LIMITED TRANSFER POLICY."

Current Season Ticket Holder Of Record:	**Proposed Season Ticket Holder Of Record:**
Printed Name: ____________	Printed Name: ____________
Signature: ____________	Signature: ____________
The foregoing instrument was acknowledged before me this ______ day of ________, ____ (year).	The foregoing instrument was acknowledged before me this ______ day of ________, ____ (year).
My Commission expires: ____________	My Commission expires: ____________
Notary Public: ____________	Notary Public: ____________
Printed Name: ____________	Printed Name: ____________

(SEE REVERSE SIDE FOR ADDITIONAL INFORMATION)

FIGURE 4.2. Reserved Seat Season-Ticket Assignment Form, 2005

seat locations or accounts to immediate family members. Immediate family members typically include parents, grandparents, and siblings. Historically, organizations trying to build demand offer an open transfer process as an incentive to build a base of support. However, when demand is strong, an open transfer process can create a secondary market where fans sell the transfer of seats to the highest bidder, often for thousands of dollars per seat, sometimes directly to ticket brokers. An open transfer process may also disrupt a season ticket waiting list if one exists. For example, in the late 1990s, the Denver Broncos still utilized an open transfer process. Because the Broncos were consistently competitive and demand for tickets was greater than the supply, season ticket holders would routinely place ads in the classified sections of the *Denver Post* and *Rocky Mountain News* offering to transfer their season tickets for a set price or to the highest bidder. This allowed many prospective season ticket holders to completely bypass the season ticket wait list by receiving transferred seats from existing account holders. Subsequently, when demand reaches a certain level, many organizations convert to a closed transfer process to limit the reassignment of seats to immediate family, reduce activity in the secondary market, and reinstate integrity to the wait list process. The secondary market will be discussed in depth in Chapter Eight.

When seats or accounts are transferred, one of the most difficult tasks is determining what to do with the priority assigned to the account. Because priority must have the ability to be placed in a specific rank order for the purpose of assigning season ticket holder benefits, priority may only be assigned to one account. Therefore, only one new account holder may receive the priority of the original account. All other new accounts receiving tickets from the original account would receive new priority numbers. For example, if a season ticket holder has eight seats in an account and wishes to transfer two seats each to four different people, one of the new accounts would receive the original priority number, and the other three individuals would receive new priority numbers. Table 4.1 provides a more detailed illustration of this process. The season ticket holder transferring the tickets is typically allowed to determine who receives the original priority number.

Significant complications have been experienced by sport organizations when an open transfer process has been utilized. This is especially true in an environment with a strong demand for tickets. In summary, the issue relates to how the ticket accounts are marketed, advertised, and managed. Ideally, season ticket accounts and seats should be classified as revocable seat licenses, wherein the ownership of the seats always remains with the institution or sport organization. Within the industry, these rights have been argued and litigated considerably. Legal ramifications of the transfer process will be addressed in depth in Chapter 9, Legal Aspects of Ticket Operations.

TABLE 4.1 Application of Priority Number in the Ticket Transfer Process

	Original Account	New Account Holder #1	New Account Holder #2	New Account Holder #3	New Account Holder #4
Year Established	1960	2009	2009	2009	2009
Number of Seats	8	2	2	2	2
Priority Number*	346	346	22,001	22,002	22,003

*Out of an estimated 22,000 Season Ticket Accounts

FACILITY RELOCATION

According to many ticketing professionals, planning for and executing the relocation of season ticket holders from an existing building to a new facility is perhaps the most challenging task most administrators can face. This is especially true in sports with extremely large bases of season ticket holders. According to Derek Thomas, Manager of Corporate Partnerships with the Denver Broncos, relocating fans to similar seats in a new facility is difficult for numerous reasons. Just a few reasons include the process by which seats were relocated, the desire of fans to have exactly the same sight line/proximity as at the old facility, the difference in numbers of seats at different levels in the new facility, the less favorable proximity to amenities, the different atmosphere in the new seating area, and the increase in ticket pricing in the affected area.

As in the distribution of many ticket-related services, the fairest method for relocating season ticket holders to a new facility is by utilizing priority. In addition, most teams use a relocation questionnaire to gauge the wishes and desires of fans at the new facility. Regardless, a wealth of complications still rise to the surface during the relocation process, most of which deal with the location of seats as compared to locations at the old facility or that of other season ticket holders. Because no two facilities are completely alike, it is virtually impossible to relocate fans to exact seats in a new facility. Therefore, when creating relocation literature to distribute to fans, sport and entertainment organizations typically use language such as "reasonably comparable seats," "seats in a similar location," or "seats as close as possible" when referring to possible relocation areas in a new facility.

Season ticket holders with full season ticket packages are relocated first based on priority, and then season ticket holders with partial plans, if any exist, are relocated by priority in the order of the largest partial plans (New York Yankees, 2009). For example, in baseball, a number of partial plans may be sold to the public based on number of games (e.g., 41, 20, 15, 12, 11). For fans with existing partial ticket plans, sport organizations may offer a chance to secure better seats in a new facility as an enticement to upgrade to a full season plan. By upgrading to a season plan, fans with partial plans may be placed in the full season pool of fans during the initial phase of seat relocation. However, within each pool of fans, priority usually dictates the order in which fans have the opportunity to select seats. In some cases, organizations specifically state that assigned seat locations for partial plans will not likely be comparable to existing seat locations.

The ambiguous language associated with relocating seats to "similar" seats at a new facility, as well as the way seat relocation survey responses are interpreted, can sometimes create frustration for fans. Due to the differences in facility design, this language is used intentionally in literature to avoid making a commitment, or implying a commitment, to a specific seat location that the organization may not have the ability to provide (Reedy v. Cincinnati Bengals, 2001). Fans must always keep in mind that there are no property rights associated with tickets, unless specifically identified. This is true with some personal/permanent seat licenses. Non-premium tickets are generally considered revocable seat licenses. Therefore, season ticket holders, either full-season or partial plan, are legally classified as licensees. Some teams use language in all literature that refers to season ticket holders as licensees.

Other concerns to consider in regard to facility relocation include:

1. Sight line/proximity to the field; obstructed view. This can include fans walking up aisles in front of seats, and the distance between seats and the entertainment.
2. Less seating. Due to the addition of club seats, suites, etc., there may actually be less seating in certain levels of a new facility. If this occurs, it may be necessary to upgrade fans to new premium seat options or face the risk of not having enough seats for existing fans in certain levels of the stadium.
3. Proximity to amenities, such as concourses, shopping areas, restrooms, and concession stands.
4. Different atmosphere, including people around the seats and their language and behavior.
5. Ticket prices. Seat location may have to change based on the new price of tickets.

TICKET WAITING LISTS

In order to be fair to all customers, a priority system must also be used if demand is great enough to utilize a waiting list for tickets. As seats become available, there are several types of waiting lists that ticketing administrators may need to utilize. How season ticket waiting lists are managed is important, especially in locations with high demand where seat availability may take a generation. There are two primary wait lists used in ticket operations during the regular season, the season ticket wait list and the returned tickets wait list.

Season Ticket Waiting List

Existing season ticket holders may want to add additional seats to their existing account. There are several approaches to achieving this, depending on the philosophy of the organization, level of demand, and number of people on the waiting list. Some organizations offer additional seats to season ticket holders during the regular renewal process. With this approach, season tickets holders may add a limited number of seats (usually two) to their existing account, with access based on their priority number. These additional seats are typically less desirable and separate from the current seat locations. A second, stricter approach is to add season ticket holders to the end of the existing wait list. This philosophy is used in order to maintain the integrity of the wait list, especially if few seats are available.

The stricter approach maximizes the number of different people that have access to becoming a season ticket holder. The stricter approach is important for several reasons. First, organizations never want fans to perceive that it is impossible to secure tickets. If this happens, fans may become frustrated and stop trying to attend events. This is obviously counterproductive to what sport administrators are trying

Courtesy of Getty Images

to accomplish—exposing their sport product to as many fans and demographics as possible. This philosophy is supported by the Escalator Concept proposed by former sport industry executive Bernie Mullin. The philosophy states that sport organizations should invest more in nurturing existing customers than they should in trying to create new ones (Mullin, Hardy, & Sutton, 2007). To increase consumption, the sport organization must move fans up the escalator by getting them to attend more sporting events. Logically, diehard fans who do not have the ability to secure tickets to live events will discover alternative ways to consume the sport product. Unfortunately, this is where fans can fall off the escalator and become media consumers. An example of a media consumer is a fan who does not attend live events but watches at home, watches with friends, watches at sports bars, etc. Once fans change their behavior patterns, it may be extremely difficult to get them back to live events.

Another reason to make tickets accessible to as many fans as possible is to avoid creating an aging base of season ticket holders. In order to properly market a sports product, fans of all ages must be exposed. As with any consumer product, the earlier loyalty is created, the longer the relationship may be maintained throughout the fan's lifetime. Of course, tickets may be handed down from generation to generation through the aforementioned transfer process. However, in many cases, blue collar fans are the lifeblood of any organization, especially in sports. Corporate clients may purchase high-priced club seats and luxury suites, but the diehard fans who attend year-in and year-out create the atmosphere that routinely translates into a competitive advantage for sports teams.

Organizations must decide what to do with fans on the season ticket wait list that decline seats when offered. The policy will depend on the level of demand and how aggressive the team is in maintaining the wait list. One option is to move fans that decline seats to the end of the wait list. Another is to leave them in the current position on the list above others that may not have received an offer. Some fans prefer to stay on the list after declining seats because they do not like the available seat locations and believe that, if they stay on the list long enough, more attractive seats may become available. Although this approach is logical from the perspective of those fans, it may anger other fans lower on the list.

Returned Ticket Wait List

In many cases, administrators, athletes, talent, etc. will receive an allocation of tickets when they travel to out-of-town facilities. As mentioned earlier, ticket administrators use a house account to provide such tickets. Occasionally, tickets reserved for visitors go unsold. In an effort to maximize revenue, ticket administrators may make these unused tickets available to those within the organization, season ticket holders, or the public. In sports, season ticket holders may be placed on a wait list in priority number order to request unused tickets to away games. For example, if the Pittsburgh Steelers send 500 tickets to the New England Patriots for their upcoming game in Pittsburgh, the Patriots may only use 400 tickets to satisfy the needs of the administrators, players, coaches, and staff. The Patriots ticket office may then make the 100 remaining tickets available to Patriots season ticket holders requesting 50 tickets to travel to the game in Pittsburgh. The 50 remaining tickets are then returned by the Patriots to the Steelers with payment for 450 tickets. Subsequently, the Steelers may use the remaining 50 tickets from the Patriots in the same way, to satisfy any remaining ticket requests from Steelers administrators, players, coaches, staff, or season ticket holders. If any tickets still remain after all of those needs are satisfied, they may be put on sale to the general public on a first-come, first-served basis.

POST-SEASON

When sports teams participate in the post-season, additional invoices must be sent to season ticket holders. Traditionally, payments for season tickets only include payment for regular season contests. In the National Football League (NFL), near the end of the regular season, the league office authorizes teams with a viable chance to participate in the post-season to send post-season invoices to season ticket holders that includes possible home playoff games and dates. A sample of the document sent to season ticket holders is illustrated in Figure 4.3 (Denver Broncos Ticket Office, 1996). Because the maximum number of home playoff games for any team in the NFL playoffs is two, teams are authorized to invoice season ticket holders for two games. This is done because playoff games may be played on back-to-back weekends. If teams would only invoice season ticket holders for one game and the team moved on to play the next week, there would likely not be enough time to invoice fans for the second game. If fans are charged for two games and the team does not host a home game, loses the first game, or fails to make the post-season, teams traditionally allow fans to roll the payment forward to the subsequent season ticket invoice or receive a refund.

Based on availability and after the team has taken care of internal ticket needs, the purchase of a limited number of additional seats for the post-season may be offered to season ticket holders based on priority number. Remaining seats may be offered to the general public on a first-come, first-served basis.

1996 POST SEASON DATES

Saturday, December 28, 1996	AFC and NFC Wild Card Playoffs (ABC)
Sunday, December 29, 1996	AFC and NFC Wild Card Playoffs (NBC and FOX)
Saturday, January 4, 1997	AFC and NFC Divisional Playoffs (NBC and FOX)
Sunday, January 5, 1997	AFC and NFC Divisional Playoffs (NBC and FOX)
Sunday, January 12, 1997	AFC and NFC Championship Games (NBC and FOX)
Sunday, January 26, 1997	Super Bowl XXXI, Superdome, New Orleans (FOX)
Sunday, February 2, 1997	AFC/NFC Pro Bowl, Honolulu, Hawaii (ABC)

SUPER BOWL TICKETS IF THE BRONCOS ARE PARTICIPANTS

Should the Broncos participate in Super Bowl XXXI, the Broncos will conduct a random drawing in which season ticket account holders will have an opportunity to purchase Super Bowl tickets.

The random drawing will be conducted at a time deemed appropriate by the National Football League and invoices serving as notification will be sent to those randomly selected. All season account holders are automatically eligible for the drawing, notification is not required from interested season account holders.

Those season account holders randomly selected to purchase Super Bowl tickets will have an option to purchase a limited number of Super Bowl tickets, as indicated on the Super Bowl ticket notification invoice.

A limited time frame to pay for the tickets and instructions for ticket pick up will be included in the ticket notification invoice.

IMPORTANT ITEMS

- **Payment deadline is December 6, 1996**
- **To guarantee your season ticket locations for all home playoff games, full payment must be received at the Broncos Ticket Office prior to December 6, 1996**
- **No tickets will be refunded if the playoff game is played in Denver**
- **If the game is not played in Denver, you will automatically receive a playoff credit on your 1997 season ticket account**
- **Refund checks will be made payable only to the 1996 season ticket customer of record in accordance with the refund procedures outlined herein.**
- **If you elect not to exercise your post season option, it will not affect your 1997 renewal option in any manner.**
- **Dates for single game ticket sales to any Broncos home post season games will be announced at a later date by the National Football League and the Denver Broncos.**

NFL™ NATIONAL FOOTBALL LEAGUE

1996 DENVER BRONCOS POST SEASON CHECK LIST

FIGURE 4.3. **Post-season Checklist, 1996**

For post-season championship events, such as the Super Bowl, ticket distribution becomes more complicated. In most cases, because the governing body (e.g., NFL, NBA) controls the event and the distribution of tickets, there are a limited number of tickets available in relation to the entire base of season ticket holders. Therefore, only a portion of the account holder base will be offered tickets. Participating teams navigate this process by utilizing a lottery system weighted by the account holder priority discussed earlier in the chapter. The more seniority an account holder has, the higher the probability they will be selected in the lottery. Although those fans not selected will always be disappointed, such a system is the fairest way to distribute a limited number of tickets. Figure 4.4 illustrates a sample postcard that may be mailed to those season ticket holders not fortunate enough to be selected for the post-season lottery (Denver Broncos Ticket Office, 1997).

Thank you for your support of the Denver Broncos. In the event the Broncos are a participating team in Super Bowl XXXI, the Broncos have conducted a Super Bowl ticket lottery so that we may distribute tickets to season ticket account holders.

Since the Broncos last participated in a Super Bowl, two new teams have joined the NFL, which has significantly reduced the total number of Super Bowl tickets available to participating teams.

Unfortunately, your account has not been selected in the random drawing. With the large number of season ticket accounts to serve, the limited number of Super Bowl tickets does not afford the Broncos the opportunity to offer each season ticket account holder Super Bowl tickets. We regret not being able to offer your account Super Bowl XXXI tickets.

Thank you again for your continued support throughout this championship season.

FIGURE 4.4. Post-Season Lottery Postcard, 1997

CHAPTER SUMMARY

As this chapter indicates, priority associated with season tickets permeates numerous benefits and aspects of customer service. Sport administrators must create, implement, and manage fair and effective ways to reward fans for their support and patronage. It is the opinion of the author that, when benefits are based on the duration of the customer's account, rather than based on the amount of money spent, fans are more likely to support policies and procedures that govern the relationship. Sport staff must learn to provide superior customer service while protecting the best interests of the organization. When this is accomplished, fans have a positive experience and sport organizations profit.

LEARNING ACTIVITY

1. A professional sports team was successful in passing a public stadium referendum that will finance a new facility. The facility is currently under construction, and the ticket operations staff is attempting to relocate season ticket holders to the new facility. Unfortunately, there are many obstacles involved in completing the relocation to the satisfaction of fans, including an ineffective priority system, differences in facility design, and differences in new ticket prices. In order to provide the highest level of customer satisfaction, ticket operations staff must address each of these very difficult obstacles on a case-by-case basis and resolve them to the best of their ability.

   Due to differences in stadium design, you do not have any remaining similar seat locations for a group of eight long-time season ticket holders currently seated separately in pairs but in the same section of the stadium. Unfortunately, some season ticket holders with lower priority numbers, but fewer years as season ticket holders, were already assigned seats. Specifically, how did this scenario occur and how would you address and/or resolve the problem?

5

Ticket Pricing

Kevin Heisey and James T. Reese, Jr.

LEARNING OBJECTIVES

Upon completing this chapter, students will understand the various ticket pricing objectives, traditional methods for ticket pricing, and the inefficiencies that exist in the market for tickets. Students will understand how prices that perfectly meet demand for tickets are ideal in terms of ticket revenue generation. Finally, students will understand the principles driving new technologies, as well as ticket pricing methods that have emerged to address inefficiencies in the market.

KEY TERMS

demand-oriented pricing, dynamic pricing, price discrimination, price elasticity of demand, season tickets, variable pricing

INTRODUCTION

When *Sport Marketing Quarterly* (*SMQ*) assembled a panel of executives from the major professional sports leagues for its special issue on sales force management in sport, the panelists were asked "what keeps you up at night?" All three of the responses had to do with the challenges of pricing tickets in a rapidly changing environment ("Industry insider," 2011). The emergence of innovations such as formal secondary ticket exchanges, increased use of variable pricing, and dynamic pricing of tickets have all influenced and changed the way prices are set for tickets. Improvements in and increasing accessibility to new technology, as well as continued creativity and innovation among sport management professionals, make it likely that the recent changes seen in how tickets are priced will continue in the foreseeable future. Here we establish the fundamental principles behind ticket pricing and give examples of how those principles are reflected in practice.

Ideally, tickets are priced to perfectly meet demand; however, until relatively recently the technology necessary to do that was unavailable or unaffordable. Advances in technology have allowed sport managers to more efficiently set and adjust ticket prices through various forms of demand-based pricing. In this chapter, we examine the various objectives behind ticket pricing, then broadly describe traditional static ticket pricing practices as a foundation on which new practices have been built. Current trends can all be viewed as efforts by managers to address inefficiencies that exist in a market characterized by traditional ticket pricing. It is important to understand the nature of the inefficiencies, as well as the nature of how pricing practices can be modified to serve as solutions to inefficiencies in the market, leading to incremental increases in revenue. This dynamic is at the heart of the trends we have already seen in ticket pricing and will likely serve as the foundation for new developments yet to be seen on the market. Below, we describe these developments, specifically the movement toward demand-based pricing, the principle of price discrimination, and the practices of variable pricing and dynamic pricing.

A unique aspect of the ticket market is the dynamic between season ticket sales and prices and individual game tickets and prices. Season ticket sales provide financial certainty and stability to all sports franchises. The upfront, money-in-the-bank nature of season ticket sales ensures that they will remain a primary concern for sport managers far into the future. Both season tickets and game-day tickets must be priced with season ticket holders in mind. The season ticket holders are a franchise's most reliable, valuable, and prized customers. Prices for all tickets should be set so that season ticket holders feel valued by the organization and feel that they are getting the most value for their money (Reese & Mittelstaedt, 2001).

The treatment below holds to different degrees across different sport leagues and organizations. In the National Football League (NFL), teams play far fewer games, rely primarily on season ticket sales, normally draw capacity crowds, and play the vast majority of the games on Sunday afternoons. In the NFL market, there are fewer inefficiencies and less need for ticketing innovations. What is described as traditional pricing is seen to work well. In other leagues characterized by many more games scheduled on all days of the week, where filling the stadium or arena is a challenge, innovations in ticket pricing play a prominent role.

PRICING OBJECTIVES

Setting a price for tickets for a sport property or club can be driven by a number of objectives. Regardless, the pricing of tickets is a delicate balance. As summarized by Reese and Mittelstaedt (2001), "If tickets are priced too high, customers may seek alternative forms of entertainment. If prices are set too low, valuable ticket and supplemental revenues may be squandered, never to be recaptured by the organization" (p. 225). A club might use pricing to enhance its brand image, establish itself as a caring community partner, position its product as an upscale luxury item, position itself among competitors, or discourage competition. These objectives are not mutually exclusive. For example, a club will often simultaneously offer low-priced bleacher seats and expensive luxury seating to establish itself both as a caring community partner and a destination for high-end, luxury entertainment experiences.

A property could also set prices to maximize its profits. There are several unique characteristics of profit maximization in the sports environment. The admission ticket is not a standalone product. For example, clubs charge fans a price for parking and sell concessions and merchandise. Clubs also sell to sponsors and advertisers who are trying to reach fans. The advertising and sponsorships are more valuable when the crowds coming to the events are larger. Finally, clubs and leagues earn significant money selling broadcast rights to media outlets that are hoping to draw viewers and listeners. Television broadcasts are more attractive to the viewers at home when the crowds at the event are large and enthusiastic. Because of these factors, setting profit-maximizing ticket prices is not straightforward in most real-world contexts. In a given circumstance, higher ticket prices that might lead to an increase in ticket revenue could also lead to an increase in empty seats. If the reduction in non-ticket game-day revenue is of a greater magnitude than the increase in ticket revenue, then the price increase is clearly not a profit-maximizing strategy. The empty seats could also reduce the perceived value of future sponsorships and broadcast contracts, hurting profits over the long term. Thus, profit-maximizing ticket prices are related to the property's other key revenue streams.

If maximizing profits from ticket sales is looked at in a vacuum, one has to consider the marginal cost of selling an additional ticket. It is generally thought to be very low or essentially zero. The facility represents a fixed capital cost and the game-day staffing is also essentially fixed for each game (meaning that it is the same whether the stadium is full or not), so that selling an extra ticket and filling an empty seat adds little beyond the cost of printing a ticket. If one assumes that the marginal cost of selling an additional ticket and accommodating an additional fan is zero, then the profit-maximizing price is the same as the revenue-maximizing price. To establish foundational concepts below, we examine the pricing of tickets in a vacuum and assume that the main pricing objective is to maximize profits through maximizing revenue.

TRADITIONAL PRICING

While pricing to meet demand is theoretically the revenue-maximizing choice, much of traditional ticket pricing, where fixed prices are established in the offseason, is driven by other concerns and objectives. The major concerns of clubs are twofold. First, they are concerned about fans' possible perception that the clubs are setting prices too high or increasing them too much from the previously established prices. A major objective is to avoid the perception of price gouging for fear of alienating fan bases. Empirical studies consistently show that teams set prices that seem too low (Winfree & Rosentraub, 2012). A possible explanation is that they are extremely cautious about avoiding the perception of price gouging. A second, competing concern is that low prices might decrease the perception of value in the customer's mind. The fear is that if the team is weak and attendance is low, discounted or free tickets might draw fans, but those fans will balk at paying higher prices in the future, as the perception of the monetary value of a ticket will be set in their minds by the established low prices.

Traditional pricing is based on a low-technology model that involves establishing fixed prices for tickets, differentiated by location and service levels, prior to the season. From those prices, a baseline is formed from which to price and sell season ticket packages, which are a key component in a club's year-to-year revenue. Season ticket sales give clubs upfront cash and protect them from the uncertainties of the season as it plays out. Season ticket packages are priced at a discount from the fixed, single-game ticket price base, which reflects both the club's preference for receiving payment up front and an inducement for fans to buy the packages. In this scenario, a price for a single-game ticket is set, followed by season ticket prices that reflect a per-game discount off of the established, single-game base price. This is normally done in the offseason, months before the season begins. Conjoint analysis and willingness-to-pay surveys are formal methods used a) to determine ticket prices that align with fans' perceived value, and b) to set optimal prices. Conjoint analysis is a survey-based analysis of the product attributes that contribute to perceived value. Extensive data mining and analytics are also increasingly being employed in understanding fan profiles and pricing tickets accordingly.

One of the earliest attempts to retain a traditional pricing structure while still trying to maximize revenue was with the use of fan loyalty programs (Reese, 2007). Just as a retailer such as Exxon, Shell, etc. may offer a few cents off a gallon of gasoline for repeat customers with a rewards card, sport organizations may reward fans with sponsored prizes and discounts on tickets, merchandise, food, and beverages. Not only are these loyalty programs popular with fans, but they are also very effective in increasing attendance while maintaining the integrity of the original ticket price (Johnson & Reese, 2011).

Another effective strategy is changing how tickets and other amenities are combined into one package. Repackaging also allows the integrity of the original ticket price to be maintained, while adding other amenities such as parking, food, and beverages in one convenient price for fans (Johnson & Reese, 2011). An example of repackaging would be creating one price for admission to a game in a specific location; a priority parking pass; and a wristband for unlimited hot dogs, chips, popcorn, and non-alcoholic beverages throughout the game.

MOVE TOWARD DEMAND-BASED PRICING

Recent developments in ticket-pricing practices indicate a significant move toward setting prices to meet demand, which meets the objective of pricing to optimize revenue. Demand for tickets is a function of several variables. Team performance, market size, average household income within the market, quality of the opponent, championship implications of the game, weather, time of the year, and day of the week are all factors in the demand for tickets. For a given demand and assuming, for the sake of demonstrating a principle, a club has established one fixed, face-value ticket price prior to the season, the challenge is to set a price that comes as close as possible to perfectly meeting demand. Failing to price efficiently results in losses in potential revenue. A price that is set too high results in lower attendance and less ticket and other game-day revenue associated with empty seats. A price that is set too low results in a full stadium, but revenue is left on the table because many attendees are willing to pay more. With prices that are too low, it is possible to increase the price, still fill the stadium, and thus increase ticket revenue. It is impossible to efficiently price to meet demand when one static price (or a static set of prices) is set for all games months before they occur. Many of the developments in ticket pricing in recent years can be understood in the context of more efficiently pricing to meet demand.

A good way to think about the market dynamic of pricing to meet demand is through the responsiveness of demand to changes in price; this is known formally as the price elasticity of demand. Price elasticity of demand refers to the percentage change in the quantity demanded in the market brought about by a percentage change in price. When pricing tickets, clubs ideally set a price where the price elasticity of demand is equal to one. Price elasticity is measured by the formula $-(\%\Delta Q/\%\Delta P)$ where Δ is the symbol for change, Q represents quantity demanded, and P represents price. If the percentage change in quantity of tickets demanded is greater than the percentage change in price (implying that $-(\%\Delta Q/\%\Delta P) > 1$) it means any gains in revenue that result from a price increase are more than offset by the reduction in the number of fans buying tickets. In that case, price elasticity of demand is considered "elastic," and reducing the price increases revenue. Here, the reduction in price results in an increase in the quantity of ticket sales, and the additional revenue from those tickets is of a magnitude that outweighs the reduction in revenue per ticket.

If price elasticity of demand is "inelastic," meaning the percentage change in quantity of tickets demanded is less than the percentage change in price, implying that $-(\%\Delta Q/\%\Delta P) < 1$, then any additional revenue gained by increased ticket sales is more than offset by the reduction in price. In that case, increasing the price increases revenue. Here the team sells the same amount or fewer tickets, but the extra revenue per ticket is enough to outweigh any loss in the quantity of tickets sold. Ideally, clubs aiming to maximize ticket revenue set a price where the price elasticity of demand, $-(\%\Delta Q/\%\Delta P)$, is equal to 1 or commonly called unit elastic. This means that the monetary value of any increase (or decrease) in price will be exactly offset by the decrease (or increase) in the number of tickets sold. Any movement from that price, whether higher or lower, results in decreases in revenue.

Empirical studies consistently show that in practice, professional sports ticket prices are set in the inelastic range, implying that increased ticket prices would increase revenue (Winfree & Rosentraub, 2012). Possible reasons why the quantity of tickets demanded at the established prices is not responsive to increases in price could be lack of substitute products, the reality that the ticket price represents only a fraction of the overall price of attending a game, or it may be the case that prices generally are set lower than the revenue-maximizing level, possibly to meet some of the alternative objectives mentioned above.

Using a single, fixed ticket price established at the beginning of the season as described in the above demonstration scenario leads to two glaring inefficiencies. The first is that for each individual game the price could be closer to the market clearing price if it could be adjusted either prior to the season while setting prices based on previously known characteristics affecting that game, or at a time closer to the game after previously unknown elements that affect demand become known. This inefficiency, which results in a lively informal (and often illegal) market for tickets in the parking lots before games, can be addressed by employing variable pricing methods.

The second inefficiency is that not all fans place the same value on the tickets and have an equal willingness to pay. Thus, a single price will cause fans with a lower willingness to pay to be "priced out" of attending the game, while leaving revenue on the table by selling tickets to other fans at a rate lower than what they are willing to pay. This inefficiency can be addressed by employing methods of price discrimination as described in the next section.

PRICE DISCRIMINATION

Price discrimination is a microeconomic concept that plays a significant role in ticket pricing and the development of pricing innovations over the years. Technically, price discrimination is a practice by which a single seller of a unique good or service charges different prices to different buyers (Frank, 2002). As mentioned above, assuming a single ticket price for all buyers, there will be many who were willing to pay more for the ticket, but only had to pay the face value price. In this case the customer enjoys consumer surplus, which is defined as the difference between what a consumer is willing to pay and what he or she actually pays. For example, if the customer is willing to pay $65 but only has to pay $35, he/she would enjoy $30 of consumer surplus. For an established price, each actual customer is willing to pay at least the face value of the ticket (or they wouldn't be in attendance) so as a group they could enjoy substantial consumer surplus. However, for any established price, there are also consumers who would be willing to buy tickets, but only at a lower price and thus do not purchase tickets or attend the game.

If the objective of the sport property is to set a price that maximizes revenue, defined as the ticket price multiplied by the number of tickets sold, they can use price discrimination to sell more tickets and increase revenue. Summarizing from above, with higher prices, they realize more revenue per ticket sold, but also sell fewer tickets. If the increased revenue that results from the higher price is greater than the amount lost as a result of selling fewer tickets, it is beneficial for the organization to increase the price, and the price elasticity of demand is less than one, or inelastic. Conversely, if prices are lower, they will sell more tickets but receive a lower amount for each ticket. If the additional revenue resulting from an increase in the number of tickets sold at the lower price is greater than the amount lost as a result of selling the tickets at a lower price, it is beneficial for the organization to decrease the price, and the price elasticity of demand is greater than one, or elastic. In a context where a single price is charged to all buyers, the pricing decision is to set the single price that maximizes revenue or at the level that has a unitary price elasticity of demand, which is neither elastic nor inelastic. From a unit elastic price, an increase in price will result in reduced sales that outweigh the benefits of the higher price, and a decrease in price won't generate enough in new sales to outweigh the reduction in price.

However, if the sport organization can divide the market into segments consisting of those who are willing to pay more for tickets and those who are willing to pay less and charge separate prices to each group, they can realize the best of both worlds and increase total revenue. They can serve both the customers who are willing to pay more while charging them a higher price, but without losing those who are willing to pay less, who are charged a lower price. The ability to segment a market of customers into two groups and charge each group a separate price is known as second-degree price discrimination, and it results in an increase in revenue for the sport property compared to what can be realized with a single price. There are a number of mechanisms, often described as hurdles, that can be seen throughout the economy that allow customers to identify their willingness to pay. Some examples are customers being willing to wait in line or being willing to buy higher quantities to get lower prices. The sport spectator environment provides several natural methods for dividing customers and charging different prices. Charging customers who are willing to pay more a higher price and allowing them to sit in seats in more desirable locations that have a better view of the action is a simple example.

Segmenting customers into two groups and charging each group a separate price that aligns with how much they value the product results in an incremental increase in revenue for the organization, but it does not stop there. For each step the organization can take it further, in terms of increased segmentation of customers into more groups with a greater array of prices, it realizes incremental increases in revenue. The theoretical ideal that ultimately maximizes revenue is the ability to perfectly price discriminate, which means providing each customer with a completely unique experience and charging them the price that exactly matches their willingness to pay for the experience. While the theoretical ideal is impossible to achieve in reality, each movement toward it represents an incremental increase in revenue. Much of what has evolved in the market for tickets over the last few decades can be understood in terms of an increase in market segmentation across several dimensions (seat preferences, preferences for amenities, preference for certain opponents, certain days of the week, group size, etc.), resulting in incremental increases in revenue. For a given ticket demand, innovations that further segment markets and allow clubs to charge more for the customers who are willing to pay more while offering lower-priced options to those who are not, will necessarily lead to realizations of revenue amounts that become progressively closer to the theoretical optimum.

VARIABLE PRICING

If the objective of ticket pricing is to optimize revenue, prices should be set to match demand as accurately as possible. The demand for tickets varies for the events throughout the schedule as some games are clearly more attractive to fans than others. Clubs move toward achieving optimal revenue by varying their ticket prices to reflect the variable demand across the schedule.

For example, the Major League Baseball (MLB) season runs from April until October with most games occurring at night. One could easily discern that there might be less demand for early and late-season weeknight games because of school children's need to wake up early for school the next day. Games on weekends and holidays should attract a higher demand as more fans have free time to attend. A series against a popular opponent or a nearby rival should attract higher demand. Weekend games in September when many teams might be out of contention, and baseball is competing with college and professional football for the sports fan's attention, should attract lower demand. Clubs can vary prices to reflect the variation in demand, which should lead to an overall increase in both attendance and revenue.

Ideally, the higher prices for the high-demand games shouldn't be so high as to reduce attendance. In that case, the club should see an increase in ticket revenue with little else changing in terms of other game-day revenues, assuming fans' purchases of concessions and merchandise are not affected by the higher ticket prices. Lower prices for the lower-demand games should result in more tickets being sold, a higher attendance, and an increase in other game-day revenues such as parking, merchandise, and concession sales due to the larger crowd.

In addition to increased revenues, other benefits of variable pricing include addressing the concerns regarding price gouging (in the case of higher prices) or decreasing the perception of a ticket's value (in the case of lower prices). As long as fans perceive that a holiday weekend series against a marquee opponent represents a different, better product than an April weeknight game against a non-descript opponent, they should not perceive the higher-priced games as price gouging or the lower-priced games as establishing a low value for all games. Additionally, the variable prices for different quality games serve as a form of price discrimination, with unattractive games being a form of hurdle mechanism for budget-conscious fans who may want to take their family to a few games throughout the season, but are not willing to pay the normal price. The lower prices for the low-demand games allow the budget-conscious fans to have access to the live game experience at a lower cost, and the higher prices for the high-demand games extract some of the consumer surplus from those who are willing to pay the high prices to attend the most attractive, in-demand games.

Variable ticket prices can be set prior to the season based on clear factors that affect demand. For example, in 2004, nine MLB clubs used some form of variable ticket pricing. The levels of distinction ranged from the San Francisco Giants and the Atlanta Braves with two, to the Colorado Rockies and New York Mets, who employed four distinct pricing levels. The Giants had separate weekend and weekday prices; the Braves' prices were called "regular" and "premium." The Rockies used the terms "marquee," "classic," "premium," and "value," while the Mets used "gold," "silver," "bronze," and "value" (Rascher, McEvoy, Nagel, & Brown, 2007). A study by Rascher et al. concluded that ticket revenue for the 1996 MLB season would have increased by an average of 2.8% per team if all teams would have employed this type of variable ticket pricing (Rascher et al., 2007).

In recent years, variable ticket pricing has become more sophisticated as teams such as the Atlanta Braves and Cleveland Cavaliers have employed computer modeling that inputs demand-related variables and projects attendance for each game (Fisher, 2010). Originally this was done prior to the season, but it is now done in season as well. Considering factors that affect demand and are known prior to the season has moved clubs toward optimizing ticket revenue. However, inefficiencies remain if the club is unable to adjust prices in season to reflect factors that become known during the season.

DYNAMIC PRICING

The success of both variable pricing and the emergence of a formal secondary ticket market has led some teams to adopt a dynamic pricing system. With tickets already being exchanged in secondary markets characterized by fluctuating prices that often result in fans willingly paying far more than face value for tickets, clubs have sought ways to capture that extra ticket revenue for their organizations. Dynamic pricing, a demand-based system similar to what is used in the hotel and airline industries, appears to offer a solution.

Clubs using dynamic pricing update prices as often as once per day in response to changing conditions based on demand and sales forecasts from sophisticated mathematical programs offered by firms such as Qcue and Digonex Technologies Incorporated (Fisher, 2010). This addresses the market inefficiencies noted above and results in the club's ticket revenues being closer to the ideal optimum. It also results in an additional sales pitch for ticket sellers: "buy today and lock in your price."

The most prominent team in the pioneering of dynamic pricing is the San Francisco Giants, who first experimented on a section of seats in 2009 and adopted it for all non-season tickets in 2010. The Giants estimate that dynamic pricing resulted in an incremental increase in ticket revenue of 7% that season (Overby, 2011). Other clubs using dynamic ticket pricing are MLB's Houston Astros and St. Louis Cardinals, the National Basketball Association's Cleveland Cavaliers, and the National Hockey League's Dallas Stars and Florida Panthers (Muret, 2011).

A challenge in using dynamic ticket pricing is the potential conflict with season ticket holders, a team's most committed and loyal customers. If demand falls in season, prices could fall to lower than, or close to, the price paid by the season ticket holder. This could lead to season ticket holders feeling that they may have been better off not buying season tickets and instead purchasing tickets on a game-by-game basis. The season ticket holders, and the certain, up-front revenue they account for, are seen as the core customers of the sports business. Clubs are wise to avoid anything that detracts from the value of their season tickets and to act quickly in addressing concerns of the season ticket holders.

The primary solution to the problem described above is to adopt a ticket price floor that is higher than the per-game price that season ticket holders pay. An additional or alternative solution is to print variable ticket prices on the season ticketholder's individual tickets (Fisher, 2010). If the price printed on the season ticket holder's game ticket for a predicted low demand game is lower, then the price one pays for a single ticket can be lower without the perception that the individual ticket buyer is getting a better deal than the season ticket holder. Additionally, in the event the ticketholders cannot use or sell their tickets to a low-demand game, the perceived "loss" would not be as much. Conversely, if they were to sell their tickets to a high-demand game, they could charge a higher price without the perception that they are gouging or taking a profit.

FUTURE TRENDS

Brent Stehlik, Senior Vice President of Ballpark Operations for the San Diego Padres and an executive on the *SMQ* panel cited at the beginning of this chapter, stated that "tickets have become a commodity like wheat or copper" ("Industry insider," 2011). Like commodity prices, ticket prices are becoming increasingly variable due to efforts by sport managers to become increasingly able to meet fluctuating demand. Lower costs and more accessible technology should lead to continuation of the trend of tickets being priced similarly to other assets and commodities traded in the market. Technology that allows bar codes to be instantly sent to mobile devices will allow ticket exchange and pricing to become even more efficient.

A final example of the trend of ticket pricing behaving like pricing of other assets and commodities is the adoption of using the sale of futures options as a pricing strategy for selling post-season tickets. With futures options, fans pay a fee to guarantee access to face value priced tickets for a specific post-season game if the team of their choice makes it to that point in the post-season. If the team makes it, the purchaser gets to buy a ticket at the preset price. If they fail to advance that far, the option becomes worthless. MLB officially sells futures options on playoff tickets, and futures options for Super Bowl tickets are sold on the secondary ticket market (Winfree & Rosentraub, 2012).

CHAPTER SUMMARY

This chapter provided insight into a variety of traditional and cutting edge ticket pricing options. These options range from traditional static pricing methods to revenue generated from online ticket exchanges, as well as variable and dynamic pricing strategies. The benefits and limitations of each are discussed in an effort to help determine the best environment to maximize the effectiveness of each strategy. Finally, the chapter explains how ticket prices that meet consumer demand are ideal in terms of generating ticket revenue for a sport organization.

LEARNING ACTIVITY

1. You are the director of ticket operations at a small college that participates in Division III athletics. The school is a perennial contender for the NCAA Director's Cup, which identifies the most successful (in terms of winning) Division III athletic departments across the nation. Your institution has extremely successful football and women's basketball programs and attracts a moderate following of fans in the local community. However, the culture across campus among students is not to attend athletic events, even though there is no cost of admission for students due to a mandatory athletic fee added to the cost of attendance. Your task as the director of ticket operations is to come up with a plan to increase overall attendance and ticket revenue. The athletic department will provide limited funds to implement your new program.

6

The Ticket Sales Process

Mark Washo

LEARNING OBJECTIVES

Upon completion of this chapter, students will have gained an understanding of how customer service, client relationship management (CRM), and outsourcing supports a team's overall ticket sales efforts. In this chapter, we will take a closer look at all aspects of professional sports ticket sales. Starting with the basic fundaments of the sales process, we will look at how sports teams train their staffs and how they go about proactively selling the various ticket sales products that teams offer.

KEY TERMS

account executives, closing, CRM, customer service, group sales, needs analysis, outsourcing, presenting, prospecting, referrals, retention, role playing, sales training, season tickets, single game sales

INTRODUCTION

Before further discussions about sports ticket sales can occur, it is important to understand the overall ticket sales process. The sales process in professional ticket sales is the same as any other professional sales will be in any industry. The most successful sales professionals, whether in sports or not, learn how to excel with the following basic aspects of the sales process: prospecting, fact finding/needs analysis, presenting, closing, and referrals.

Professional sports ticket sales executives (account executives) must become proficient at all aspects of the sales process. Most professional sports teams will provide sales training on all key steps of the sales process.

PROSPECTING

Prospecting involves mastering many techniques for identifying potential clients for your respective team. The most common form of prospecting includes utilizing the phone to connect with potential ticket buyers. Most teams have established lists of single game buyers, online buyers, or buyers whose names they have captured at grassroots marketing events in the community. Account executives prospect lists by simple "warm calling" techniques of contacting individual buyers to learn of their buying habits and future plans to attend games. Mastering telephone prospecting is a critical skill for account executives.

It is becoming more and more challenging to connect with potential clients via telephone due to the caller ID capabilities of most phones. Therefore, ticket sales account executives must also learn how to leave effective voicemails. Account executives are typically trained to leave voicemails with the intent of educating the perspective customers as to why they should investigate a direct, one-on-one relationship with the team.

Many teams will provide qualified lists, which account executives will use to target potential ticket buyers. However, the very best ticket sales professionals learn how to prospect on their own. There are many ways to identify potential ticket buyers for a sports team, and teams are typically encouraged to brainstorm ways to identify potential ticket buyers and how to connect with them.

Another important part of the prospecting process is learning how to use email as a prospecting tool. Many teams will use email to mass market special ticket offers or promotions. However, account executives also use personalized email outreach to complement direct telephone sales efforts. Email marketing is becoming a more effective tool because account executives can attach ticket sales information, stadium maps, seating diagrams, pictures of actual seat locations, and even video messaging to the email.

Along with phone and email, there are other proven prospecting techniques. These techniques include attending networking events, grassroots marketing events, conventions, conferences, and specific business industry events to connect with people in search of new business leads. Other ideas include hosting team events such as meet-the-team cocktail hours, prospecting breakfasts, client lunches, and entertaining at games.

Additional useful prospecting tools can be found online using websites and social media applications. Many online, subscription-based prospecting tools exist, such as Hoovers. Other great prospecting resources can be found using Facebook, LinkedIn, and Twitter. More businesses, youth sports organizations, and nonprofits are using social media to further promote themselves, and these social media websites can be sources of prospecting.

Although professional ticket sales account executives rely heavily on utilizing phone and email, as well as networking, to sell tickets, teams still need to develop sales professionals that can get out into the market and connect with potential clients face to face. These in-person sales are necessary to sell tickets to corporations, youth groups, affinity groups, and nonprofit groups. In order to have success in face-to-face sales, account executives must learn the next step of the sales process, which is called fact finding or conducting a needs analysis.

FACT FINDING/THE NEEDS ANALYSIS

Fact finding includes conducting a needs analysis, wherein account executives try to learn the needs of their prospective clients. Identifying "hot buttons" and areas of opportunity is a critical part of successful ticket sales.

Sports tickets can be utilized by companies and organizations for many reasons. Retaining existing clients, finding new business, improving employee morale, and hosting staff social events are main motivators for companies to invest in sports tickets. Raising money or building awareness for a cause or organization is a key motivating factor for many youth organizations and nonprofits. Providing a fun social entertainment outlet for members, employees, donors, or volunteers can be a main motivator for other organizations and groups that are potential ticket buyers.

Many argue that fact finding is the most important step of the sales process because, during a needs analysis, reps will uncover everything they need to know to make sales. If the needs analysis is properly done with an individual ticket buyer, a rep will learn important facts such as budget, seat preferences, knowledge level about team, number of games the fan plans on attending, and general demographic information. If fact finding is conducted with a company or organization, a rep can learn about marketing strategies, customer targets, advertising plans, awareness campaigns, membership information, brand building, retention of existing customers, and how they find new sales or customers.

In an effective fact finding session, an account executive can learn answers to important questions such as: Is the perspective buyer looking for the cheapest seats or the most expensive seats? Is the buyer planning on attending many games or only a few games? Does a company need more clients? Do they need to retain their existing clients? Are they interested in supporting community programs? Do they need to build awareness? Do they need to raise funds? Are they looking for social activities for their members to gather and bond?

The very best ticket sales account executives learn how to sell benefits (referred to as benefit selling), as opposed to feature selling (all the "bells and whistles of your team's ticket packages"). Benefit selling means that ticket sales account executives focus on the benefits that the individual, company, or organization will receive if they invest in a ticket sales plan with the team.

PRESENTING

Once account executives learn as much as they can about a prospective client during the fact finding stage, they should be ready for the next important step: proposal development in order to present a recommendation to the potential buyer. With increased efforts to attract new ticket buyers, teams are now getting more creative by creating unique and targeted ticket packages. Teams are creating ticket sales packages that not only include tickets but also other team "assets." These assets can include unique VIP experiences, merchandise, food and beverages, and low-level marketing exposure. Many ticket sales packages are becoming "mini sponsorship" packages.

Therefore, teams are enabling account executives to have more flexibility in creating sales packages. Even if VIP experiences or other team assets are not involved in a package, a proposal that includes season tickets, group tickets, or a fundraising opportunity can still be positioned as creatively as possible.

The most effective sales presentations are those that demonstrate that the team truly has the best interests of the client in mind, based on what was learned during the fact finding phase. A few individual examples of this would be creating a family four-pack for those looking to go to games with their families, or a VIP on-field seat experience for those looking for the best seats up close to the action. A creative youth soccer package could include a volunteer appreciation ticket program or a sportsmanship award package. A few corporate packages include an employee morale program or a client retention program. Tailoring and naming each package to suit the needs of the prospect will help teams to have more success.

CLOSING

This leads to the final step of the sales process and what many feel is the most "fun" part of selling. This is the close or, as many sales trainers will refer to it, the "opening of the relationship." There are many, many sales trainers and books that discuss the "art of the sales close." You will hear about the hard close, the suggestive close, the feel, felt, found close, the ask for the deposit close, and other catchy closing phrases or techniques.

However, the very best ticket sales professionals typically do not have to rely on any sales closing techniques other than simply asking for the sale.

REFERRALS

Most ticket sales account executives learn about the importance of getting referrals early in their careers. They will also typically have positive experiences getting referrals that turn into new business. Yet, although they will hear about the importance of referrals in sales training and will learn that they work from personal experience, most will not ask for referrals enough. Much like an exercise program, one must make asking for referrals a habitual part of the sales process. Because this is challenging and takes time, the power of referrals must be emphasized to inexperienced account executives.

All sales trainers will teach and coach referral techniques, and there are many that are effective. However, much like any sport, practice makes perfect, and the more account executives practice referrals, the better they become

SALES TRAINING AND RESOURCES

Most sports teams now invest in sales training for ticket sales account executives and understand the importance of investing in sales training. Ticket sales training money is now a core budget item within teams' operating budgets. This includes sales training for ticket sales account executives and sales managers. Many teams also invest in sales training for all front office staff in order to build a sales-wide "sales culture."

Teams execute an array of tactics to train their sales teams. Teams that have a strong sales culture typically make sure they train new ticket sales hires; they will create a "sales boot camp" training program for these new hires. Sales boot camps can be anywhere from one- to four-week sales programs. Training includes all aspects of the sales process: product knowledge training and overall training on the team or organization.

Teams also rely on both internal and external methods to train their sales teams. The best sales directors institute regular and ongoing sales training. This includes training segments during weekly sales meetings, weekly role play sessions, and consistent stand-alone training. Although the sales director conducts most of these internal structured sales training sessions, other directors from within the organization can also be invited to assist with the training sessions. Team executives with ticket sales backgrounds are often asked to participate in internal sales training.

Good internal sales training typically includes role play sessions. Role play training, much like daily practice that a sports team conducts with players, includes practice sales sessions. Role play training is effective with any aspect of the sales process, including cold calling, prospecting, fact finding, closing, and referrals. Sales directors often turn role play sessions into games or rep-to-rep competitions, adding more fun to the role play.

Teams also rely on external sales training expertise. This includes both bringing outside sales trainers into the organization and sending sales team members to sales conferences and seminars. There are many professional sales trainers who offer sales training services to teams. Teams also occasionally work with each other, where Team A invites the sales director from Team B to help train Team A's sales staff. Sales training sessions vary in length and duration. They can be small, one-hour sessions or week-long sales seminars.

There are several companies, as well as individuals, that provide sales training services. A few companies offer a boot camp-like environment where people physically go to a location for two to three days and receive real-time, on-the-job sales training. Other companies are now offering online sales or job placement training. However, most of the companies and reputable sales trainers will make visits to teams and typically spend one or two full days providing full sales team training, followed by individual training. Many sales trainers have built a solid reputation, and reputable ticket sales trainers' names are circulated within the industry. Most team sales directors know sports-specific sales trainers, and many work off of a referral basis only. Teams will typically share information with other teams if they have a positive experience with a ticket sales trainer, and they often recommend trainers to each other.

Teams that provide the best sales training utilize a blend of methods to train their sales teams. This includes regular sales training, internal trainers, external trainers, and the fostering of an overall sales training culture.

SEASON TICKET SALES

Season ticket sales are considered by many to be the lifeblood of any sports team organization. Season tickets make up the majority of NFL and NBA teams' overall ticket base, and other sports teams will claim that they do not have enough of them. Season ticket holders typically have the majority of prime ticket locations in a stadium, arena, or ballpark.

Many sports sales organizations have dedicated account executives who focus solely on season ticket sales. Season ticket holders are primary stakeholders of the team and feel a sense of ownership toward the seats they "own" for a team's entire season. Teams can structure proactive ticket sales efforts in many ways, and there are many philosophies on the best way to structure sales teams. Some teams believe in a "full menu marketing" sales approach, meaning all reps can sell all packages and products, while other teams believe in focused sales efforts separating season ticket account executives from group sales account executives.

Regardless of how a team structures its sales department, season ticket sales is one of the most critical sales efforts for a team. There are many potential ticket buyers for season tickets. The two biggest target audiences for season tickets are individual fans and corporations. Fans invest in season tickets because they are fans of the team and are emotionally connected to their favorite team enough to financially invest in them. They give up both their time and money in order to support their team. They are also typically motivated by having access to the best seats. Many individuals feel not only a sense of ownership, but also social status and even pride in owning season tickets for their favorite team. You will hear many fans brag about their 50-yard-line seats, seats off the dugout, courtside seats, or right off the glass seats.

Teams will prospect for new individual ticket sales by attempting to reach individual ticket buyers with direct sales tactics. Account executives will call past single-game ticket buyers or names collected at team events in order to try to sell ticket packages. Inside sales teams also typically focus more heavily on individual ticket buyers.

Corporations also invest in season tickets for many reasons. Companies are in the best position to invest in premium seating. Premium seats include suites, club seats, and field level seats. They are also typically the best seat locations, as well as the most expensive, so the average individual fan cannot afford these types of seats.

Corporations invest in sports tickets to entertain and maintain their key clients. They also have a certain sense of social status when offering their field level seats, suite tickets, or club seats to their existing clients. Company A might have an advantage over its competitor, Company B, if Company A has access to dugout seats at Yankee Stadium, sky suites at the Cowboys Stadium, or floor seats at Madison Square Garden.

Companies also use sports tickets to reward employees for performance, service to the organization, and hitting benchmarks, sales goals, or quotas. They also use tickets to help develop new business. Companies will typically develop an internal "pecking order" for corporate-owned seats. Priority is given to business development or retention. This means prospective clients are first on the list, current or existing clients second, and employees last.

Teams will attempt to sell tickets to companies using direct ticket sales efforts. The most effective way to sell corporate ticket packages is via face-to-face meetings. However, teams have had success selling ticket to corporations through phone calls, emails, faxes, or snail mail.

Season ticket sales can be challenging for many reasons. The two primary obstacles that keep individuals or companies from investing in season tickets are time commitment and money.

If an individual invests in season tickets for a team, he or she is making an investment of time and money. Following a favorite MLB, NBA, NHL, or MLS teams requires a 20- to 72-night commitment stretched over six to nine months. The NFL, which has the shortest season of all, is still a 10-game, five-month commitment. Though teams now provide a variety of flexible payment options, a commitment to season tickets for any team is significant. Depending on location and amenities, the financial commitment may range from hundreds to millions of dollars per year.

Companies face the same challenges when deciding to invest in season tickets. Budgets are always an obstacle. Especially in a down economy, sports tickets are perceived as a luxury item, something a company may want but does not need. When looking for cost-cutting measures, it is easy to cut sports tickets from the budget.

The other challenge that companies face is time commitment. Even for large companies that have 450 employees, using game tickets can be a problem. A company must appoint someone within the organization to be the tickets' administrator. There must be a process in place to allocate tickets and then properly track the usage. Many companies drop season tickets because they deem the tickets too burdensome to administer. Many times, tickets go unused and are deemed a waste for the company.

The sale of a season ticket can be a short or long process. Many individuals or companies can decide during the first meeting or phone call whether or not they want to invest in season tickets. Therefore, the sale can happen on the first contact. However, due to the investment of both time and money, a season ticket sale can also take several weeks or months.

GROUP SALES

Group sales represent the most significant source of ticket sales for most professional sports teams. Teams with the least amount of season ticket holders and more ticket sales inventory due to having a large stadium or lengthy season have the highest dependence on group sales. Major League Baseball and minor league baseball teams, for example, have a high reliance on group sales. So do the majority of Major League Soccer teams, due to the fact that less than 30% of MLS teams' stadiums are occupied by season ticket holders.

This is exciting news because group sales can be the most creative ticket sales for any account executive. Any group or organization that has at least 10 to 15 members can become a group sales candidate for a sports team. Groups have many motivations for organizing a group outing.

There are literally hundreds of potential groups to target for group sales. A short list of group sales targets includes companies, nonprofits, faith-based organizations, hobby groups, and social cause groups, and there is actually a very large group target market. Virtually all groups, including gun clubs, fishing clubs, Boy Scouts, Girl Scouts, PTAs, Kiwanis clubs, music clubs, youth sports teams, member associations, alumni groups, birthday parties, bachelor parties, engagement parties, retirement parties, and companies, can organize as a group for ticket sales. Many groups are simply looking for a social gathering opportunity to further connect their members with each other. A sporting event is the perfect environment in which groups can connect.

As with season ticket sales, teams might have organized and dedicated account executives focusing on group sales. While season ticket prospects are typically a more finite audience of potential buyers, group sales prospects are a much larger target audience and require more creativity. Group sales require more of a relationship-based sale. The account executive must identify the group leader within each group; the leader will organize, promote, and motivate the rest of the group members to attend the sports team function.

The sales process can take longer for a group sale than a season ticket sale. Although smaller organizations can quickly and easily invest in a small group of 15 or 20 tickets, larger group sales of 50 to 350 tickets can take longer to cultivate, promote, and sell. Group sales are as dependent on the needs analysis process as any other ticket sales product. During the fact finding session, account executives must learn why a group wants to explore a group outing. Key facts must be learned, such as how many members the group has, whether they are trying to raise money or awareness, whether they want the cheapest or best seats, and what dates and times work for the group. All of these key questions must be answered before a successful group outing can be planned.

There are typically three primary target markets for group sales. They are corporate groups, youth groups, and affinity/nonprofit groups. When selling group tickets to companies, there are three main sales options. The first option is that a company pays for all the tickets and underwrites the cost for the entire group, thus providing

Courtesy of Gary Lake

a free event for employees or clients. The second option is for a company to pay for half of the group tickets and pass along a heavily discounted opportunity for clients or employees. Providing an opportunity for 50% of the typical costs, with possible food options, is still a very attractive employee or client benefit.

The final way companies can still work with a team is to simply provide a group discount opportunity to their employees or clients but not pay for any of the tickets. This option is actually an extreme advantage to sports teams because it does not require any out-of-pocket costs for the company; therefore, overcoming the objection about costs is easy to handle. All the company has to do in this model is forward along an email or order form notice to all employees or post information in employee or client areas on the company website. Essentially, the company simply has to help promote the group outing and encourage participation. All sports teams have to do is provide the best possible seats and the best possible price, which further entices the company to promote the group outing as a true benefit for having an affiliation with the company. This is the most common method of promoting a group event with a corporation.

There are basic steps that account executives typically follow when trying to organize a group outing. The first component of a successful group outing is to first and foremost identify the group leader; the most successful groups will always be those that have the most passionate and dedicated group leaders. Group leaders can be driven and motivated by many factors. It may be that they are huge fans of the team and simply want to plan a group outing because they enjoy attending games themselves and think that it would be great fun to attend the game with a group. Or they might be motivated by the opportunity to raise money or awareness for their group. If the group is a nonprofit organization, its members can be very motivated to raise money and awareness for their cause. The group leader could also be motivated by putting on a great event for their group members because successful social outings help further connect group members with the company or organization. Regardless of the motivation of the group leader, identifying the go-to person in the organization is critical for a successful group ticket sale. This group leader will be involved in many aspects of organizing the group, including group planning, promoting, collecting money, making payments, and being on hand to organize game-day events.

The next and most obvious step in the building of a successful group outing is to pick the game date for the group. Although this sounds basic, picking an attractive date that fits well into an organization's schedule is a critical step toward a successful group outing. It has to be a date that the organization is excited about, which will also hopefully match group promotional or giveaway nights. Once a date is identified, the group leader and account executive must then select the price or promotion to offer the group members. Picking a price that is too high might scare away participants, while picking a price that is too low with horrible seat locations might also jeopardize group participation. Through a needs analysis meeting and based on the needs of the group and the group attendee make up, the best possible price should be determined. Once the ticket price is determined, the next step is to decide if the group outing is a fundraiser promotion or simply a group event.

The next step typically involves asking for the money and picking out the seat location. If a group is paying for all or a portion of the tickets, then most teams will require some type of up-front deposit. Depending on the team, this deposit can be as little as 20% to as much as a 75% deposit toward the total number of tickets the group is planning on selling. The deposit shows a good faith commitment to the sports team and typically gives teams the assurance they need to hold the seats. If the organization is not paying any money toward the tickets, teams still may ask a group leader to make a good faith deposit, typically in situations where the group leader is asking the team to hold seat locations.

If the group is not paying for the tickets but facilitating a group discount for its members, teams might be open to holding some seat locations without a deposit. This would be a team-by-team decision or policy. However, if a group leader can promote a specific section or row of seats to potential group attendees, this will typically encourage people to join the group. At the very least, based on price decision, the team should be able to identify potential sections of the facility to promote to group attendees.

The final step in the group process is for the group leader and team to decide upon a mutually agreeable deadline for final payments. Typically, teams like to get final payment for group sales one week to 10 days prior to the game day. This provides the group leader with time to distribute the tickets to the group attendees. The final order date also gives the group leader a date to promote to group attendees, which may help them commit to attending the outing.

No matter how firm group deadlines are, groups will always have last-minute buyers. Different teams will have different policies on how to handle these add-on orders. Some teams will be flexible about allowing group attendees to order group tickets up until game day. Others will have stricter policies and not offer any group discounts or additional group tickets as early as 72, 48, or 24 hours before a game. This decision is also typically driven by ticket operations managers, whose job is to regulate ticket sales inventory. They also have to hold seats, release seats, and put unsold tickets back in the system. Therefore, ticket sales directors, account executives, and ticket operations managers must all work together to develop consistent policies for group sales.

These policies include deadlines, holding seats, returning seats, and even consignment ticket practices. Consignment tickets are another group sales tactic where a team will give a block of unpaid tickets to a group leader in exchange for a promise to pay. Therefore, the group leader takes on a group of tickets and attempts to sell them to the group. The group leader then pays the team for the tickets sold and returns the unsold tickets back to the team for resale. Different teams will have different consignment policies, and some teams will not offer any type of consignment group ticket program. Consignment policies typically correlate with the number of available tickets, as well as the team's difficulty in selling tickets. Teams with a lot of tickets to sell with little demand will typically have flexible consignment policies, while teams with limited tickets to sell and high demand for their tickets might not offer consignment tickets at all.

Group sales provide an important revenue stream for many sports teams. More and more sports teams are becoming reliant on group sales to fill their respective stadiums. Although companies, youth sports leagues, and affinity groups make up the majority of teams' group sales efforts, group sales has endless possibilities and allows account executives to be extremely creative. In the end, any organization or gathering of 10 or more people could qualify as a group. The following is a random listing of groups to which sports teams have sold tickets in the past: community nights, ethnic nights, birthday parties, bachelor parties, bar nights, camp days, fan club nights, adult social clubs, career fairs, church groups, faith groups, alumni associations, parks and recreation, DARE, PTA, Rotary clubs, Kiwanis clubs, YMCA, Special Olympics, conventions, high schools, colleges, Boy Scouts, Girl Scouts, Boys and Girls Clubs, retirement communities, social clubs, chambers of commerce, credit unions, wine tasting groups, cooking groups, military nights, VIP experiences (pregame events, tailgate parties, player meet-and-greets, high-five lines, team tunnels, player escorts, National Anthem), and team vendors.

SINGLE-GAME TICKET SALES

Most sports teams have some type of availability for individual tickets. Teams with high ticket demand, such as most NFL teams or high-profile teams like the Cubs, Yankees, Red Sox, or Lakers normally have limited individual ticket inventory. Fans usually have to seek the secondary ticket market such as StubHub or RazorGator for access to these tickets. Teams with limited individual ticket inventory typically do very little with the available seats.

Single-game ticket sales is often the category that is neglected by teams and should probably receive more attention. Most sports teams' ticket sales departments focus on season tickets, group tickets, and multi-game package sales. Teams' professional ticket sales departments usually do not spend much time or many resources on individual ticket sales.

Other teams such as MLS, MLB, and most minor leagues have a lot of individual ticket inventory. These teams will have a stronger season ticket and group sales effort. Teams will bundle individual tickets into smaller packages or mini-plans that the account executives can sell. They will look to team corporate partners, media partners, third-party vendors such as Ticketmaster, and their own internal marketing departments to help sell individual tickets.

Most teams rely on the marketing and sponsorship fulfillment departments to develop individual ticket offers and help promote individual ticket sales. Teams also rely on third-party ticket vendors to assist with individual ticket sales. Ticketmaster is probably the largest vendor servicing sports teams' individual ticket sales efforts. Ticketmaster executives will often work with team executives to develop special online individual ticket offers. Ticketmaster will support these offers and campaigns via email promotions or online special offers. VIP experience packages and upgrade premium seat packages are the types of deals Ticketmaster typically likes to offer its fan base. Ticketmaster offers can be very powerful and have a lot of impact because they have such an extensive database. Also, many sports fans will search Ticketmaster if they are looking to purchase sports or entertainment tickets.

The marketing department's efforts can be twofold. First, the marketing department will often work with media partners to offer special individual ticket offers. Radio stations typically like offering special individual ticket offers to their listeners. They will support these special ticket offers both on air and online. Many radio stations have frequent listener programs or email newsletter subscribers and like making special offers to this audience, which is extremely targeted and typically effective. Successful radio ticket promotions include using the call letters of the station (i.e., Hot 101.1 offering $10.11 tickets for a game) or offering a special ticket deal for a specific section (join the 97.5 station listeners section). They also like to offer unique VIP experiences to their listener base, such as pregame tailgate parties, player meet-and-greets, or other unique experiences like guest press box visits or an event broadcast on their station.

Radio stations also like doing remote game-day broadcasts, which also typically include some type of individual ticket offer. An example is a broadcast at a grassroots marketing event like "come visit the FM 99.9 booth at the Chili Cook-Off for $15 DC United Tickets all day long."

These same individual ticket offers also work with other media outlets such as newspapers, the Internet, and television. Print partners have the luxury of newspaper space, and although many newspapers' readership is decreasing, newspapers still like to offer sports ticket deals, and "clip and save" order forms still work for some sports teams. Newspapers also have online components to support any print advertising, as well as frequent reader or subscriber programs, and they are always looking for special ticket offers to show value added for members in these programs.

Sports television stations also are able to make special individual ticket offers. Most are supported by the teams' broadcast partners, who have in-game inventory at their disposal to make special individual ticket offers. During a live play-by-play broadcast, a local television channel can support special ticket offers by reading announcements or scrolling printed text across the bottom of the screen during pregame, halftime, or postgame. An example of a television promotion could be as simple as "fans enjoy the Comcast Sports Net 4-pack, which includes four tickets, four hot dogs, and four sodas. Visit www.Yourfavoriteteam.com, and click on the Comcast Sports Net special offer button to purchase this discounted package." The on-air broadcasters have numerous opportunities to promote this package during the game.

There is another higher-risk, but high-reward, potential partnership between teams and media outlets. This idea is called a revenue share promotion and involves including a team's media partner as a true "risk partner." The media outlet agrees to either very minimal or no upfront advertising investment from the team. However, the team and the media partner agree to a revenue share once ticket revenue greater than the team's average is achieved. The media outlet agrees to use all open and available advertising inventory to help promote ticket sales to a team. This includes ad spots, on-air mentions, heavy online promotion, PR content or athlete in-studio appearances, and possibly on-site or remote presence during a game. Basically, the media outlet takes as much inventory as it can for a two- to three-week run-up to the game to promote the game as much as possible. Once the game is completed, ticket sales revenue is calculated, and if the baseline ticket revenues are exceeded, the media outlet gets whatever revenue split they agreed upon with the team.

This promotional idea involves a lot of trust and true partnership between the sports team and the media outlet. The team has to be willing to share confidential ticket sales and ticket revenue numbers with the outlet in order to properly share revenue. The upside is that if the partnership is truly successful in selling tickets to the game, the revenue share can be significant for the media partner. It is revenue that the teams do not mind sharing because they greatly exceeded their average ticket sales. Often times the advertising partner uses unsold advertising inventory, which many do not mind doing.

Courtesy of Getty Images

The downside for the media partner is the possibility that the promotion fails and all of their incremental adverting and PR efforts do not result in incremental ticket sales for the team. Then they do not receive any upside advertising dollars and have used a lot of unsold inventory on the team instead of potentially adding value to other advertising clients. A team and media partner revenue share does involve a certain amount of risk, but if successful, it has reward for both the team and media outlet.

The final effort made by teams to drive incremental individual ticket sales typically comes out of a partnership between team sponsors. Sponsors of a team typically have a great opportunity to help support and drive individual ticket sales. Many teams will run special ticket offers or promotions with individual tickets with sponsors, in particular with retail partners. Large companies like Pepsi, Budweiser, Best Buy, McDonalds, Dunkin Donuts, and local grocery store chains will run cross-promotions with teams promoting individual tickets. Buy one get one free offers, 50% discounts, and coupon promotions will be negotiated between sponsor and team to help promote individual ticket sales.

UPGRADING FANS

Many teams believe that they must focus on getting fans on the "conveyor belt" of ticket buying. Once they get a fan on the conveyor belt, they can focus on tactics for upgrading those fans. They can upgrade fans two ways. One way would be getting them to attend more games, thus investing in more tickets in their respective ticket plan. The other is to get them to invest more money by upgrading seats or VIP experiences. Therefore, the fan may only come to one or two games per year, but instead of having them invest in a $99 holiday package in the upper deck, they can successfully upgrade them to $150 per ticket, per game field seats.

The "get the fan on the conveyor belt" philosophy works like a conveyor belt in an assembly line. The ticket salesperson convinces a fan to invest in the smallest possible ticket package, then takes them to a multi-game package, and then ultimately converts them into a season ticket holder.

One can also cross sell fans under the same upgrade philosophy. Cross selling involves developing strong relationships with group leaders via their group experiences in hopes of converting them into season ticket holders; it can also entail getting to know season ticket holders better, identifying the season ticket holders who are also members of groups, and turning them into group leaders.

CUSTOMER SERVICE AND RETENTION

Although the majority of this chapter focuses on ticket sales, a critical aspect of any team's ticket sales efforts is customer service and retention. Teams are starting to put a lot more focus and emphasis on client retention in particular. It is very difficult to acquire new clients, and it is equally as challenging to replace lost clients, especially season ticket holders. Many sports teams realize that, if they have a 10,000 season ticket holder base and renew only 70% of those ticket holders, they have lost 3,000 season tickets. They would therefore have to sell 3,000 tickets just to get them back to what they lost. Teams have quickly realized that losing 20-30% of their season ticket base is not the way to grow their business.

Therefore, more and more teams are adding a dedicated customer service support function to their overall ticket sales efforts. The customer service department is charged with providing the highest quality customer service and care for the team's season ticket holders. They are also on the front lines of the renewal process and handle all of the day-to-day needs of a ticket account. These can include payments and account change information such as credit card changes and address changes. They are also available to handle any customer service issues of the ticket holders, which include poor game-day experiences or general complaints.

There are many differing philosophical views on how a customer service and ticket sales department is structured and areas of focus it should have. Some teams have the ticket sales department focus on generating all the new sales, and once a new season ticket account is brought to the organization, the account is handed over to the customer service department for account management. The sales rep that sold the new account does not have any further interaction with that client, nor do they share in the ticket sales renewal commission.

Other teams structure the relationship between ticket sales and customer service as a mutual collaboration, with the ticket sales representative maintaining a relationship with the client and working side-by-side with customer service.

CONTACT RELATIONSHIP MANAGEMENT (CRM)

A very critical element of a team's ticket sales effort, and a discipline that can be overlooked, is CRM or database management. CRM is referred to by a variety of different names, such as contact relationship management, customer relationship management, and client relationship management. Teams will use many methods to manage their data and the relationships with their season ticket base. Some teams will have a dedicated database manager, while others will rely on the box office to provide database management support. Some teams will rely on the marketing department to provide this support.

There are also many computer software programs available to teams to help them manage their data. Ticketmaster offers a database management system through a program called Archtics. Archtics has many CRM features, including tools to email various segments of the database. Other new companies are emerging, such as Glitnir and Ticket Leap, that help teams manage their ticket databases and provide CRM support as well, including mass-emailing capabilities.

There is also general business database management software that might not be compatible with ticket operations functions, such as printing or processing ticket orders, but do provide great tools to manage data. A program called Goldmine has been in existence for many years and is used by many teams. Goldmine provides advantages over other ticket operations software and enables teams to build multiple fields, keep many pieces of information on each client, and has sales forecasting and prospecting tools. Other new web-based companies are also starting to offer comparable services to Goldmine, such as Salesforce.com or Constant Contact. Constant Contact allows teams to manage their email database.

Regardless of which system or software a team uses, or which department or person is tasked with managing data, database management is a critical functionality of a team. Teams are trying to build better databases that allow them to offer more targeted ticket sales messages, and to build better communication paths for their ticket holders. Teams have created many subsets of their database with which to communicate. This includes season ticket holder e-newsletters, premium ticket holder newsletters, emails from sales group leaders, and ways for fans to connect such as kids' clubs, fan clubs, or coaches' clubs.

Teams also can manipulate data to send stronger direct mail or email campaigns to target segments of their database. For example, a team can host a coaches' night promo. Therefore, having the ability to send an email or postcard to all coaches within a database is extremely important. Alternatively, a team might be offering a group leader night; therefore, being able to target all group leaders in a database is extremely important.

OUTSOURCING OF TICKET SALES

Outsourcing ticket sales is a new trend that will likely become more prevalent in the sport industry. Outsourcing of sponsor sales has been commonplace within the sport business landscape with both professional teams and Division I colleges and universities. However, full outsourcing of ticket sales has not caught on as it has with sponsorship sales. With the success of outsourced sponsor sales, as well as the increase in the number of agencies looking to become an outsourced sales resource, professional sport business will begin to see more outsourcing of ticket sales inventory.

Many professional sports teams have used outside agencies to help them sell large sponsorship packages. Typically, teams will outsource larger sponsorship opportunities such as stadium naming rights, founding partners of stadiums, season presenting sponsorships, and front-of-jersey sponsorship. However, they will typically keep most of their sponsorship inventory in-house and have both sponsorship sales and sponsor servicing resources within their team.

If teams could, they would retain 100% of their sponsorship inventory, which means they would retain 100% of the revenue. However, many teams still look to outside agencies to help them sell larger sponsors' inventory items and will gladly pay 10-20% commission to agencies that help them land larger deals.

In the college and university market, full outsourcing of sponsorship sales is more prevalent than in professional sports. Professional sports teams will typically outsource only a small percentage of their sponsorship inventory, whereas universities may outsource their entire sponsorship inventory.

Companies such as ISP Sports, Learfield Sports, CBS, and Nellegan have been successfully handling outsourced sponsorship sales for colleges for close to 20 years. The university will take a guaranteed buy from one of the outsourcing companies and turn over the entire sponsorship inventory to them. The outsourcing company will then share a percentage of the overall sponsorship revenue once a pre-negotiated minimum sponsorship revenue target has been attained. Many colleges and universities feel that guaranteed money and potential share of additional revenue once a revenue plateau is attained is a better model for them than having to take sponsorship sales in-house.

Since the sponsorship outsourced model has been so successful with both professional teams and colleges, there is no question that this trend will filter into professional ticket sales development. There are currently a few companies that have started to offer outsourced ticket sales services, and a few others that have provided phone call center services.

There are four primary ways a team can receive outsourced ticket sales assistance from an outside agency:

1) Outsourcing ticket sales inventory to a third-party ticket sales call center.
2) Special project or event ticket sales for a contracted period of time.
3) Professional ticket sales development consulting or special project.
4) Fully outsourcing ticket sales.

Outsourced Sales to a Call Center

In this model, a team turns over lead lists to an outside firm, in an effort for this firm to sell tickets on the team's behalf. There are a handful of companies that have offered these services in the past and continue to offer them today. A team typically has to pay an initial small retainer or set-up fee, plus negotiate a commission that it will pay to the outsourced ticket sales call center (typically 10%-20%).

The team typically turns over sales leads that its current ticket sales account executives do not have time to prospect. Many sports teams have focused efforts on growing their respective databases, but they typically do not have enough ticket sales account executives to contact all the leads they have acquired. Even if a team has an inside ticket sales staff, many times it still cannot contact all of the stockpiled leads.

An outsourced ticket sales team will not be as familiar with the team's ticket sales packages, products, and stadium. Therefore, the team must meet with the outsourced agency ticket sales reps and attempt to train this staff as much as possible. Ticket sales training will include product knowledge, as well as the team's overall sales philosophy. The advantages of working with an outsourced ticket sales call center are that teams will realize additional ticket sales and ticket sales revenue, and will also be sure that as many leads as possible are contacted.

The challenge of working with an outsourced call center is that a team can lose quality control. Having an outside entity represent a sports team means that the team must trust that the outside sales staff will be able to represent the team and brand as well as the team's own employees would. The fact that teams are concerned with quality control, as well as the consensus that they can do their own ticket sales better than anyone else, means that teams do not traditionally explore this opportunity.

Special Project for Contracted Period of Time

Another outsourced ticket sales engagement involves having an outside agency come in for a contracted period of time in order to work side by side with an existing ticket sales team. This option is typically utilized for a special project or event, such as an all-star game or championship game, or during a specific sales period, such as season ticket or group ticket season.

There are a handful of agencies that offer these services, and they could be a growing trend. Many sports leagues are also developing team or club services departments within the league office to assist teams with ticket sales development. The NBA was one of the first professional sports leagues to develop such a department, the Team Marketing and Business Operations (TeamBo) division. Other leagues, such as Major League Soccer, have followed the NBA's lead.

If a sports league does have a team or club service department, this department is usually tasked with supporting each team in the league in the way of best practices, sales training, and sales training events. However, for larger league-wide events, league staff can be contracted out for a three- or four-month period of time to help sell tickets in a market. Both the MLS and NBA have used club services team staff to help sell tickets for all-star games and championship games.

The positives of bringing in an outside agency to work side by side with an existing ticket sales team are increased ticket sales and revenue. Having additional ticket sales resources will typically result in additional ticket sales. One challenge of bringing in an outside agency to help sell tickets is concerns about quality control. As with outsourcing to a call center, the outside agency will not be as educated about the team or team's ticket sales products as full-time employees would be. The other challenge is that, at times, an outside ticket sales agency can become a distraction for an existing sales team. Although having more ticket sales resources will typically lead to more sales, having more people in a sales office could be distracting if not properly managed. Another concern is making sure that leads are properly distributed and prospect lists properly assigned. Having additional ticket sales reps could lead to territory and sales disputes, which could jeopardize the overall sales culture.

Professional Ticket Sales Development Consulting

Another way a team can utilize outside sales support is to contract with a company to help it improve its existing ticket sales practices or help it create a professional ticket sales team. Most professional sports teams do have a proactive outside ticket sales force, but surprisingly, not all teams do. However, most Division I colleges and universities do not have a proactive ticket sales force, and most should.

This engagement would simply involve having an outside agency come into a team's front office and work with it to develop a ticket sales team. This would include pricing analytics, stadium mapping, and development of a ticket sales plan, as well as recruiting and training a new ticket sales staff and hiring a capable ticket sales director to manage and run the newly created department. This is a newer model but sure to be a growing trend, and several companies have already started to work in this space.

Full Outsourcing of Ticket Sales

The final way a team can utilize outsourced ticket sales is to fully outsource all of its ticket sales to a third party. As indicated earlier in the chapter, this is prevalent in sponsorship sales but will most likely be a growing trend with colleges and universities, as well as with some professional sports teams.

Similar to the model already prevalent with sponsorship sales, an outside agency would offer to pay a guaranteed fee to a sport organization to acquire the entire ticket sales inventory. The agency would then recruit, hire, and train the ticket sales staff and sell the tickets as if they were employees of the sports team. They would then offer a split on revenue once mutually negotiated minimum ticket sales revenue targets were achieved.

One positive of this type of engagement is that the sport organization would be guaranteed ticket sales revenue and would also share in additional revenue if minimum sales targets were achieved. It would also alleviate a team or entity from having to take on the payroll, insurance, and administrative expenses of hiring its own in-house ticket sales team. The challenge of outsourcing ticket sales is that revenue opportunities can be forfeited because a percentage of ticket sales would be given to the outside agency. There are also ticket inventory issues to be negotiated. Many colleges and universities use the best ticket sales inventory for large donors. Professional sports teams use the best ticket sales locations for their highest paying sponsors or investors. Giving up full ticket sales inventory would be a challenge that would have to be negotiated between parties.

Although there is a potential growing trend for fully outsourced ticket sales, as of this book's publication, it still is a new concept and idea. Time will tell whether or not entrepreneurs and sports entities alike will be able to embrace this new opportunity in ticket sales.

CHAPTER SUMMARY

This chapter provided information that can help the reader to achieve a better understanding of professional ticket sales, including the steps of the sales process and the various methods teams use to train account executives. This chapter also provided information about how teams sell season tickets, group tickets, and individual tickets. Additionally, it covered the various ways other departments can support a team's ticket sales efforts, as well as the importance of database building and management. Finally, it should be apparent that outsourced ticket sales are a growing opportunity for professional sports job seekers. There will be an increase in opportunities for those that can master the art of professional ticket sales development.

CASE STUDY

In 2009, the Washington Freedom, a women's soccer team, began playing in the newly formed Women's Professional Soccer League (WPS). WPS is the second attempt to establish a professional soccer league for women. The previous league, the WUSA, went defunct in 2003 after three playing seasons.

All of the teams playing in the inaugural season of WPS followed a basic business template in regard to front office staffing. However, as the first season grew near, teams began to realize that perhaps the original staffing plan was not properly built to fully support and maximize ticket sales. The original staffing plan for each WPS team only called for two ticket sales account executives and no sales manager or director. Some of the teams in WPS realized early on that only having two full-time ticket sales account executives was not going to be enough to be able to sell the desired number of tickets. They increased their ticket sales staff above the required two full-time account executives

The Washington Freedom finished in the bottom third of season ticket sales and group sales. Both season ticket sales and group sales are a direct result of proactive ticket sales efforts, as well as a measurement of how good a team's ticket sales effort are. Although the Freedom finished in the bottom of the league in season ticket sales and group sales, the organization did lead the league in other ticket sales categories such as box office advance and walk-up sales.

The team, with ownership support, decided to restructure the front office in July of 2009, too late to have a dramatic impact for 2009 ticket sales, but in time to maximize ticket sales for 2010. They hired a full-time ticket sales manager, five account executives, and a full-time customer service rep. The previous ticket sales staff had employed only two ticket sales account executives and no sales manager or customer service resource. The Freedom also hired an experienced director of ticket sales to help lead the new sales team effort. This director had previous professional sports ticket sales and sales management experience.

The first project assigned was to evaluate all of the 2009 ticket sales and, via sales analytics, determine a new sales pricing model for the Maryland Soccer Plex Stadium. The second project was to recruit, hire, and train a new ticket sales team. Most of the reps hired into the sales department had previous ticket sales experience. The new sales manager believed in creating a positive ticket sales culture, with ongoing and continued sales training. The new sales department had new compensation plans and incentive programs, which reward ticket sales performance. The Freedom also added other resources in the organization to help support and drive ticket sales, such as a ticket operations manager, a grassroots marketing manager, a social media/PR manager, and dedicated sponsor sales and service resources.

Within five months of having the new ticket sales team in place, 2009 season ticket units had already been eclipsed. Also, due to the new pricing model, ticket sales units doubled and season ticket revenue tripled. This is an impressive turn-around in less than six to eight months.

This case study clearly demonstrates that adding a well-trained and proactive ticket sales team will lead to increased ticket sales performance. Basic sales analysis and the adoption of a reprising strategy, along with increased ticket sales efforts, can have a quick and significant impact on ticket sales growth. This example is one of many that exist in professional sports and reinforces the importance of the effort that teams must put toward professional ticket sales development.

7

Ticket Distribution

Shelley Binegar

LEARNING OBJECTIVES

Upon completion of this chapter, students will have an understanding of the most efficient and effective ways to distribute tickets. Students will also gain an appreciation for the multiple constituencies involved in ticket sales and understand that each must be addressed individually.

KEY TERMS

hard tickets, will call, pass list

INTRODUCTION

Ticket distribution may appear on the surface to be a simple process: take an order, print a ticket, and mail the ticket. However, once a person looks more closely, it becomes clear that it is anything but simple. The actual, physical process of distributing tickets, whether hard tickets or through a pass list, can be complicated. If attention is not paid at every step and a thought-out procedure is not in place, mistakes can easily be made. If fans do not receive their tickets or have problems picking up their tickets, it can result in bad publicity and, in some circumstances, loss of revenue. As the old saying goes, a happy customer tells one person, and an unhappy customer tells 10. There is no customer unhappier than one who does not receive his/her ticket.

After the purchase of the ticket, receipt of the ticket is the next most important step to a fan. Unfortunately, one policy cannot be applied to all constituencies. Each group has unique needs. To go further, one policy will not apply in all circumstances, even to the same group. Therefore, each group and circumstance needs to be addressed prior to its actually happening so that everyone can be prepared and things can run smoothly.

In this chapter, the main constituencies involved in ticket sales will be discussed, and basic policies and procedures for distribution during the regular season and during post-season will be outlined. Each facility, team, or event will have its own individual needs and groups that it will need to address. As with all policies, it is vital to remain flexible. After each major event, the distribution process should be reviewed to see if improvements can be made for future events. The landscape of sporting events is ever changing and so should be the procedures and policies associated with them.

STAFF AND COACHES

Most organizations give their employees complimentary tickets or, at the very least, the opportunity to purchase tickets prior to their going on sale to the public. Whatever an organization's policy is on staff tickets, a ticket director must find a way to distribute these tickets in the most effective and efficient manner possible. Numerous factors should be considered when determining the best distribution method: demand for the tickets, size of the staff, Internal Revenue Service (IRS) regulations, and past usage.

Staff tickets may be handled differently for events that have a high demand than they are for events with low demand. In a high-demand situation, it may be easier and more efficient for a ticket office to print hard tickets and distribute them prior to the event so as to limit lines and staffing needs on the day of the event. In a lower-demand situation, printing hard tickets for everyone could be considered a waste of resources, both time and money, when using a pass list at the gates could be as effective. A pass list can be a simple typed list or one constructed with a complex software program such as playerguest.com or passlists.com. Both methods result in a printed list with the names of those who are to receive a ticket and a line for their signatures.

Along with demand for tickets, the size of the staff receiving the tickets should be considered. For instance, a college athletic program that sells tickets to six sporting events—football, volleyball, men's basketball, women's basketball, gymnastics, and wrestling—with a staff of 200 employees who each receive four tickets per sport, could end up printing 4,800 tickets. Double the size of the staff and the numbers can quickly multiply. This also ties into the efficiency of printing paper tickets versus using a pass list. As previously mentioned, there is a real cost associated with printing paper tickets, as well as a soft cost of the time involved. Printing hard tickets that go unused can be seen as wasteful.

If it is determined that paper tickets are the best distribution method, additional questions need to be asked. Are staff tickets solely for the use of staff members, or can those staff members give their tickets to a neighbor, friend, or family member if they cannot attend? Can they sell these tickets? Can they give them to their mechanic for a discount on car repairs? The National Collegiate Athletic Association (NCAA) does not regulate tickets for staff like it does for players; however, most organizations have internal policies prohibiting such situations.

© Stock.XCHNG/duduhp

In 2004, a contractor in Lexington, Kentucky, told reporters that he was "paid" with complimentary tickets for work done at the University of Kentucky's offensive coordinator's house, a clear violation of the university's complimentary ticket policy ("UK president," 2004). This certainly is not the only incident, but it is one of the more public ones. A particularly public scandal occurred in 1991 when the then-head men's basketball coach of UNLV, Jerry Tarkanian, known to many as "Tark the Shark," was investigated for leaving complimentary tickets for Richard "Richie the Fixer" Perry, a person with known ties to sports gambling. Perry was later convicted of fixing harness races and charged with conspiracy to commit sports bribery in connection to a Boston College point-shaving incident (Dwyer, 1991). Because of these issues and many more, some organizations now require staff members to sign a statement outlining what is allowed and, more importantly, what is not in order to be clear and avoid any public embarrassments.

Besides adhering to the specific policies of the organization, the regulations and rules of the IRS must be considered. There is much debate in the ticketing industry with regard to whether an employee must claim complimentary tickets as taxable fringe benefits. The IRS has numerous categories in the "Taxable Fringe Benefit Guide." In which category complimentary tickets falls is up for interpretation. Some organizations do not consider complimentary athletic tickets as a taxable fringe benefit because the event is not sold out; therefore, the organizations do not assign a value to the tickets because they would have otherwise gone unused. On the other hand, the IRS states that "the value of the benefit is determined by the frequency it is provided to each individual employee..." ("Taxable Fringe," 2010). In this situation, the value of the ticket is not the determining factor, but rather the frequency with which the tickets are distributed. Following this theory, some athletics departments do not issue season tickets to employees but instead have the employees pick up tickets on a game-by-game basis.

The best advice on how to handle the IRS regulations is to consult your organization's legal counsel. Allow them to determine whether the tickets are taxable income or not. As with any interpretation, get the decision in writing. If it is determined that the tickets should be considered as additional taxable income, follow all IRS rules and regulations, including completing all federal forms.

Lastly, when determining which is the best distribution method for staff, information is power. With the use of bar coding, a ticket office can tell who is and is not using their tickets. If less than half of the staff is regularly attending events, it would seem to make sense to stop issuing hard tickets and begin using a pass list. This is an area that can be evaluated yearly and can vary event to event.

PLAYERS

It is important to remember that players have lots of friends and family who want to support them. Setting policies for how many tickets players can receive will be discussed in Chapter 10; however, the process for distribution will be discussed here.

The process will differ depending on the level of competition and type of event being discussed. The most rigid would be at the collegiate level. The NCAA has numerous policies that guide a ticket director on what can and cannot be done, which are detailed and addressed in NCAA Bylaw 16 ("NCAA Division I Manual," 2009).

Player Guests Pass List		
Name of Player	**Guest Name**	**Signature**
Johnny Smith		
Guest 1	Johnny's Dad	
Guest 2	Johnny's Mom	
Guest 3	Johnny's Brother	
Guest 4	Johnny's Friend	
Name of Player	**Guest Name**	**Signature**
Guest 1		
Guest 2		
Guest 3		
Guest 4		
Name of Player	**Guest Name**	**Signature**
Guest 1		
Guest 2		
Guest 3		
Guest 4		
Name of Player	**Guest Name**	**Signature**
Guest 1		
Guest 2		
Guest 3		
Guest 4		

SAMPLE

FIGURE 7.1. Sample Pass List

For instance, each player is allowed to receive only four complimentary tickets to each regular season event and six complimentary tickets for a championship or bowl game. The NCAA is very specific with regard to not issuing hard tickets. All player guest tickets must be issued through a pass list, and once the guest shows photo identification and signs the list, he/she must immediately enter the stadium, thereby eliminating the chance of a guest selling the complimentary ticket and creating a NCAA violation for the player ("NCAA Division I Manual," 2009). A sample player pass list is provided in Figure 7.1 ("Player Pass List," 2005). The important requirements are the signature line and which player's tickets are being used.

As strict as the distribution rules are for NCAA student-athletes, the opposite is true for professional tickets. Most professional players are not required to leave names but are simply allowed to distribute hard tickets to friends and family. This is also true for championships. For instance, each professional football player in the National Football League (NFL) is issued two tickets to the Super Bowl. They are given the paper tickets and allowed to do what they want with the tickets, as long as they do not scalp them. If they choose to sell their tickets for face value, they may do so. If caught scalping tickets to the Super Bowl, players, coaches, and team officials are subject to fines by the league. In 2005, Minnesota Vikings head coach Mike Tice was fined $100,000 for scalping his tickets, and two of his assistant coaches were fined $10,000 each ("Super Bowl," 2009).

In order to know the best way to distribute tickets for players, make sure to consult all governing body rules and regulations, the organization's policies, and when all else fails, ask the players what they prefer.

MEDIA

People often forget to include the media when discussing the distribution of tickets. Although the media may not be issued hard tickets, they are always issued a credential, which should be considered a complimentary ticket as it does get them into the event for free. Credentials are often overlooked by many but can cause many problems. The media should request the necessary working credentials through an organization's media department. However, these credentials need to be monitored and tracked. There are two main ways to distribute credentials to the media—through a pass list where the credential is picked up on the day of the event, or through issuing a credential prior to the event. The technique may differ depending on whether a working media credential for the season or a credential for a single event is being issued.

If an organization chooses to use a pass list, a separate entrance should also be used to avoid lines and waiting. The media typically arrives to an event before regular fans, and media personnel often have large bags/equipment with them that can take longer to search and clear security. A photo ID, as well as a signature, should be required to pick up any and all credentials. This way, should there be any debate as to who is using a credential or whether a credential was picked up, a record can be consulted.

Specifically when issuing credentials for a season, many organizations will issue a season credential prior to the first event through the mail or personal delivery. When using this method, it is extremely important to number each credential or have a name printed on the credential for security purposes. The concern is that someone other than the intended could gain access to the event by using the credential. Using certified mail is another way to help ensure delivery to the correct person.

During an event, a ticket director must be able to verify who should be using the credential if questioned and how the credential was distributed. For example, if on game day a photographer is continually out of the designated media area, security personnel should be able to look at a credential and either see a name and ask the user for a verifying ID; or check the number, call the ticket office, and be told to whom the credential was issued and then verify with an ID.

FANS

The fans are clearly the most important constituency with regard to practically every facet of an event, and ticket distribution is no different. There are many aspects to consider when determining the best method of distribution, including timing, security, and alternative methods.

Timing is important because if a fan orders tickets too close to the event, mailing may no longer be an option. If tickets are mailed too close to the event and not received, it will require issuing duplicate tickets, as well as causing increased lines and problems on game day. There is no science as to how close is too close to mail. As a guide, two weeks is considered the threshold at which to stop mailing and begin requiring pick up, either prior to the event at the ticket office or at a Will Call window on the day of the event. The only exception would be if using a priority mail system. Although this may seem like a good idea on the surface, a ticket director needs to consider the cost versus the benefit. Priority mail can be expensive as compared to the cost of additional staffing at the Will Call lines on the day of the event.

Courtesy of Getty Images

Going hand in hand with timing is security. When mailing tickets, there needs to be some sort of procedure in place to help ensure that the correct person is receiving the tickets. This applies to mailing and

Will Call. The first step is to always verify the mailing address. This cannot be done enough. The ticket office is one of the last places a person thinks to alert when changing addresses. Each time a ticket office staff member has a person on the phone, the mailing address should be verified. In addition to the address, the day the tickets are mailed should be noted. An easy way to accomplish this is to put in place a standard policy that states that tickets are mailed the same day they are printed. All computerized ticketing systems automatically record the date the tickets are printed. Should a fan call and claim to never have received the ticket, a staff person could pull up the record and at least know when the tickets were dropped in the mail. This is a starting point for tracking the tickets.

If within the two-week window, tickets should be left under the ticket purchaser's name, unless arrangements are made by the purchaser for someone else to pick up the tickets, at the ticket office or at a Will Call window. Photo identification and signature should be required to pick up the tickets.

Another way to track and increase the security measures on distribution is to use a priority mail system such as FedEx or UPS. Although costly, a ticket director should consider the value of the tickets versus the cost of using a priority mail system. If the value of the tickets is $100 per ticket, spending $3 or o$4 on mailing does not seem unreasonable. Conversely, if the value of the tickets is only $5 or $10, spending more than 50% of the value of the ticket on the mailing cost may be excessive.

Most people believe that these are the only two methods of distribution for fans; however, ticket directors need to continue to look for ways to decrease costs and increase customer service. Alternative ticket distribution methods are one way to do this. One alternative method is to hold a ticket pick-up day. This can be held in conjunction with another event, such as a scrimmage or fan day. Fans who attend the event can pick up their tickets, which saves the mailing cost, increases security by checking photo IDs, and increases customer service since questions can be answered and problems corrected on the spot.

Another alternative method would be hand delivery of the tickets. For instance, if fans live locally, a ticket office should consider partnering with an organization's development or fundraising office. Oftentimes a development officer is looking for an excuse to visit a donor. This provides a perfect reason and helps eliminate costs and increase security for the ticket office. Ticket directors should engage other departments in brainstorming new ways to distribute tickets that may benefit everyone.

CONSIGNMENT

With the advancement of technology and ease of purchasing tickets online, the use of consignment tickets has decreased but is still an accepted distribution method. Consignment tickets are hard tickets given to a person or organization for resale. For instance, an athletics department may print one hundred $10 tickets for a home football game and give them to a local Boy Scout troop to sell. No payment is necessary at the time of distribution by the ticket office to the Boy Scout troop. On a predetermined, mutually agreed-upon date, the Boy Scout troop will need to return any unsold tickets

Ohio Athletics Ticket Office
Complimentary and Consignment Form

TO:

DATE:
SPORT:

Complimentary Tickets

Ticket Type	Section	Row	Seats	Total # Issued

Consignment Tickets

Ticket Type	Price	Section	Row	Seats	Total # Issued

DATE RECEIVED TICKETS AS LISTED.

RECEIVED BY

ISSUED BY

Please sign and return one copy to: Ohio Athetics Ticket Office
PO Box 689
Athens, OH 45701

FIGURE 7.2. **Sample Consignment Form**

and full payment for any sold tickets. If the troop sells 80 of the 100 tickets, it would need to return 20 tickets and a payment of $800. The date on which the tickets are returned should be far enough in advance of the event day that the returned tickets can be voided and returned to the computerized ticketing system as open seats and sold to other fans. A sample consignment form is presented in Figure 7.2 ("Complimentary and Consignment Form," 2002).

This method is more commonly used for Olympic sports or with events that have a lower demand. The theory behind consignment tickets is that by using individuals or groups in the community to sell tickets, more people can be reached, which will hopefully result in a higher attendance.

Another common use of consignment tickets is for visiting teams. It is standard for the home ticket office to consign tickets to the visiting team's ticket office. This accomplishes two things: 1) It alleviates volume from the home team's ticket office by directing visiting team fans to its own ticket office, and 2) it allows the visiting team's ticket office to support its own fans by providing a customer service function. In extreme situations, if the home team did not give consignment tickets to the visiting team, it would be nearly impossible for visiting team fans to get tickets because the home team would sell out to its own fans. For instance, if Ohio State did not give consignment tickets to Michigan, there would be little chance for Michigan fans to attend a Michigan at Ohio State football game. Ohio State would simply sell the tickets to its own fans. However, if it did this, Michigan would be sure to return the favor the next year. Therefore, some conference offices have regulated how many consignment tickets a home team is required to make available for a visiting team. For non-conference games, consignment tickets—including the number available and date on which they must be returned—are typically outlined in the official game contract. It is extremely important for a ticket director to know these numbers. Missing a return date could end up costing thousands of dollars.

AWAY GAMES

The majority of the scenarios in this chapter apply to home game tickets. Away game tickets are often handled and distributed differently. When a ticket office is selling tickets for an away game, the procedure for distribution must change. The primary reason is that the ticket office did not print the tickets and therefore cannot rely on the automatic recording of seat locations and print dates. The tickets were printed by a different office, so the ticket office must manually record locations and mailing dates. For instance, if Fan A purchases tickets from School A's ticket office for a game being played at School B, and later Fan A loses said tickets, School A's ticket office must be able to call School B and inform them of the exact seat locations and name of the person who is in need of duplicate tickets. Without the location, Fan A is simply out of luck and would need to purchase another set of tickets. The same theory applies for recording the mailing date. As mentioned previously, when tickets are printed in house, the computerized ticketing system records the date the tickets were printed. If the tickets are mailed the same day, then the print date can also be used as the mailing date. However, because away game tickets are not printed in house, the mailing date must be manually recorded in order to track the tickets in case a fan claims to have never received them. Record keeping is a vital part of being a ticket director.

POST-SEASON

Ticket distribution policies for a post-season contest—whether it is a conference tournament, a national championship, or a playoff game—are typically different than regular season policies and certainly more strict. One of the main reasons for this is the elevated cost of post-season tickets. There is a direct correlation between the price of the ticket and the security level of the ticket distribution. Spending the money on certified mailings would be out of line if the price of the ticket was only $20. However, if the price of a single ticket was $728.00 (the cost of a ticket to the 2010 Final Four) paying for overnight delivery or certified mail would be more than warranted ("NCAA Final Four," 2010). If for some reason a person did not receive the tickets in the mail and it became necessary to create duplicates, it is much more difficult to do so for a championship event. A team's ticket director does not have the ability to create duplicates but must go through the venue instead. This creates complications for both the ticket office and, more importantly, the fan. The chance of this happening can be significantly reduced by either mailing tickets in a secure fashion or by requiring each fan to pick up the tickets at Will Call. More and more ticket offices are requiring fans to pick up their tickets at the event, eliminating the cost of mailing and reducing the chance of mistakes. Why then is this not considered a standard operating procedure? It is because there are negatives, particularly in regard to customer service. Most fans do not want to wait in a line at the event, especially if they are meeting people who are not arriving at the same time.

Not only is the cost of the ticket higher for post-season events, the demand for the ticket is also typically higher. With increased demand comes an increased risk that tickets will be stolen. A ticket director needs to be cognizant of this situation and adjust policies accordingly.

POLITICS OF DISTRIBUTION

There is rarely a situation that is exempt from the influence of politics. Ticket distribution is no different. When deciding on the best method to distribute tickets, ticket directors must take into consideration who will be affected, what their response will be to the method chosen, and how they would respond or defend the decision if questioned by their superiors.

One of the biggest issues to consider is to whom the tickets are being distributed. For instance, if the tickets are for a large donor, exceptions to the standard policy for distribution to fans may be made. If the tickets are for the head coach of the team competing, exceptions may be made for his family. Asking a supervisor for his/her opinion is always recommended in order to not be on an island should a complaint occur. Although there will be standard policies set for distribution, a separate set of policies should also be discussed for VIPs, head coaches, dignitaries, etc.

CHAPTER SUMMARY

Deciding on the best method of distribution for tickets is dependent on numerous factors including, but not limited to, the constituency targeted, the event, the price, the demand, and the venue. One method will not be applicable for all groups or situations. A ticket director needs to realize this; evaluate the situation, costs, customer service level, and security, and then make the best decision possible. As with anything, there are no absolutes. Methods should be periodically evaluated and analyzed to see if a better way can be developed. The biggest mistake a ticket director can make in regard to distribution is to rush a decision, not communicate the method clearly, and think that one method fits all groups and situations. Take your time, evaluate, be creative, and always communicate.

LEARNING ACTIVITY

1. Develop a ticket distribution policy for a men's home basketball game for a staff of 250, in which each employee receives four complimentary tickets and the average usage of complimentary tickets is only 25%. Would the policy change if the usage was 75%? Would it change if, instead of a home men's basketball game, it was the Final Four?

8

Secondary Ticket Market

Joris Drayer

LEARNING OBJECTIVES

Upon completion of this chapter, students should have an understanding of the role of the secondary ticket market, as well as the positive and negative aspects of the practice of ticket resale. Additionally, students should understand how the primary and secondary markets interact and influence each other.

KEY TERMS

brokers, demand-based pricing, real-time pricing, scalpers, secondary ticketing sponsorship, secondary ticketing websites, supply and demand

INTRODUCTION

The secondary ticket market includes all tickets that are resold after they were initially distributed by the sport property in the primary market. The secondary market has existed for decades in one form or another; however, it has only recently been thrust into the center of the ticketing landscape. The growth of this market correlates most strongly to the growth of the Internet. Indeed, the Internet has given ticket buyers and sellers access to willing partners all over the world instead of being restricted to local markets. Subsequently, some sources say that the secondary ticketing industry is, by itself, a $10-$25 billion industry (Belson, 2011; Fisher, 2005; Stecklow, 2006).

Although improved technology has only recently facilitated the exchange of tickets and allowed for the growth of the secondary market, this industry has been a fixture in the sport landscape for much longer. This aftermarket exists for a variety of reasons, many of which stem from strategies implemented by sport properties in the primary market. First, tickets must remain transferable. Sport properties often put tickets for events on sale months in advance and season ticket holders commit to their tickets months before the season starts. Although many fans certainly do all that they can to plan their lives around their favorite sporting events, sometimes they cannot prevent other obligations from interfering with their daily lives. Subsequently, sport properties have acknowledged that their tickets must remain transferable. Some properties, most notably the World Cup (soccer), have tried to tie tickets to passport numbers, credit cards, or other forms of identification. However, these systems have had little success, especially when considering the complaints of fans with extenuating circumstances and a need to resell their tickets.

Besides the fundamental need to keep tickets transferable, the other main reason that a secondary market exists is the traditionally conservative pricing strategies in the primary market. Pricing in the primary market is often kept low to attract fans of all income levels and is often based on revenue needs of the organization and rarely based on consumer demand for that event (Reese & Mittelstaedt, 2001). Therefore, when there is an event with extremely low demand, prices may be considered too high, and the event may end up with unsold tickets. In the secondary market, fans may look for bargains when sellers are left with the possibility of not being able to sell their tickets at all, given the large number of tickets available. On the other hand, when there is a high demand event, sport properties end up with a sold-out event and many unfulfilled fans (Boyd & Boyd, 1998). Subsequently, those fans are left to find other ways to acquire tickets and are frequently willing to compensate existing ticketholders very well for giving up their tickets.

The secondary market has traditionally consisted of two key constituents: street scalpers and brokers. The forthcoming sections outline the unique aspects of each group and their importance in the secondary ticket market and is followed by a section on the changing shape of secondary market, largely resulting from the ability of the Internet to facilitate secondary market transactions.

STREET SCALPERS

At virtually every event in the sport and entertainment industries, street scalpers will position themselves strategically outside of the venue and offer to buy and sell tickets in the hours leading up to the event (and oftentimes after the event has actually started). Street scalpers provide a service to those individuals who decide that they would like to attend an event at the last minute. However, very few street scalpers will buy tickets directly from the primary market. Most street scalpers are looking to quickly buy and sell unwanted tickets that have already been purchased from the primary market. Subsequently, many street scalpers carry signs that state "I Need Tickets." With this in mind, street scalpers also provide a convenient outlet for people with extra tickets to recoup some of their initial expense.

Street scalpers provide a key service to many fans under the aforementioned circumstances. However, they also provide a key service for teams and event promoters. By facilitating last-minute transactions, street scalpers actually help to reduce the number of unused tickets. Ticket revenue is critically important to sport organizations, but the total impact of a sold ticket is limited when the ticketholder does not actually attend the event. Indeed, revenue from ancillary services (concessions, parking, and merchandise) can be up to $15 per person for each event. Even though the sport property is not making any money directly from the redistribution of tickets, they do profit from the presence of scalpers through an increase in this ancillary revenue.

Besides buying unwanted tickets, some street scalpers gain access to tickets by developing relationships with local ticket brokers who are unable to sell tickets in the months, weeks, and days leading up to an event. These relationships help protect brokers from the risk of unsold tickets while providing street scalpers with access to tickets without having to pay for the tickets up front. Of course, with this relationship, all profits are shared between the two parties.

Courtesy of Getty Images

It is important to note that, with the exception of a few premium seats and a few premium events, ticket scalping in the hours before an event is not a highly lucrative business, with the vast majority of transactions occurring at a price well below the face value of the ticket, which is another benefit for last-minute ticket buyers. So if you have a segment of the industry that is not highly profitable and provides substantial benefits to fans, brokers, and teams, why do street scalpers have such a negative reputation?

In many ways, street scalping operates just like a regular business. The "company" provides a product and a service to fans and brokers alike and gets compensated for its work. However, they are different in a few key areas. Street scalpers do not have a physical store location, a website, or even a listing in the phone book. They operate almost completely anonymously. As such, when there is an issue with their product, they have little, if any, accountability. Unfortunately, some street scalpers take advantage of this anonymity and create fake tickets, fashion duplicated tickets, or misrepresent the quality of the ticket. Again, street scalping is not a lucrative business and depends heavily on the street scalper's ability to get the best tickets, so there is a substantial reward associated with having more high quality tickets (even if they are fake or duplicated) with relatively little risk. With no way to identify the scalper who sold the fraudulent ticket (there are no written contracts and rarely even an exchange of names), fans are left to complain to the event box office or ticketing department and expect a resolution to their problem. This places a heavy burden on team and event personnel who are trying to create the best possible experience for their fans.

Also detracting from the fan experience is the fact that scalpers can often be pushy, impatient, and rude. Of course, time is a critical component of the street scalper's business, so there is relatively little time for casual conversation. Most street scalpers would prefer to have each exchange occur as quickly as possible so that they can maximize their profitability in the hours before an event. However, from the team or event promoter perspective, they would prefer that their fans be able to walk around free from the harassment of some of these individuals.

In the end, most organizations tend to accept the negative aspects of this industry in exchange for a substantial boost in ancillary revenue from the resale of unwanted tickets that would otherwise go unused (Drayer, Stotlar, & Irwin, 2008). In fact, many organizations will place tickets aside to deal with issues of fraudulent tickets just to ensure a positive experience is had by all fans. However, most organizations will also enforce policies to ensure that the resale of tickets occurs off of venue property so that fans do not associate the operations of the street scalpers with the operations of the team or event.

BROKERS

Unlike street scalpers, ticket brokers do tend to operate as legitimate businesses. They typically have a physical store location, a website, and a listing in the phone book. In order to run the business effectively and efficiently, tickets brokers usually have a small staff to assist with store management, ticket acquisition, relationship building, and other administrative tasks associated with running any small business. Many brokers are licensed (more on licensing later), and most have a specific set of policies and procedures designed to provide security to consumers regarding the quality and authenticity of each ticket, as well as aid in dispute resolution.

A ticket broker's profitability can vary substantially from year to year. Factors such as the state of the economy, an underperforming team, or an injured or suspended star player can significantly affect the value of a ticket. Based on this unpredictability, many ticket brokers are not at all profitable, with many tickets going unsold or selling well below face value (Drayer et al., 2008). Brokers undertake substantial risk in acquiring tickets to events, and with so much underperforming inventory, they are often forced to overprice some of their premium inventory. Indeed, one of the primary criticisms of ticket brokers is that they charge prices that are too high for the average fan. The counterargument is that they have to charge these prices for premium events in order to offset losses from their low-demand inventory.

In either case, the primary determinant of the profitability of brokers is access to premium tickets, just as it is with street scalpers. However, due to the accountability associated with running an official business, most ticket brokers do not duplicate, recreate, or misrepresent tickets. The potential damage to their business and their consumer base would likely be irreparable. However, because competition for premium tickets to premium events is so fierce, ticket brokers are left to find different ways to acquire tickets. Given that traditional consumers have access to fewer tickets as a result of these strategies, these ticket acquisition practices have been heavily criticized by consumers and the media (Drayer & Martin, 2010; Drayer, 2011). For example, in team sports, many ticket brokers will become season ticket holders in order to gain access to the best seats for every game. Using this strategy, brokers are guaranteed tickets to every game and although many of these tickets may sell at or below face value, a few high demand games can offset the considerable expense associated with becoming a season ticket holder.

Given the high cost and high risk associated with purchasing season tickets, some brokers are unwilling to take such strong positions on tickets. These individuals instead focus their ticket acquisition efforts on individual high-demand events. This strategy often involves less of a financial commitment and more of a time commitment. With the majority of single-game or single-event tickets now sold online, ticket brokers and their staff will spend their time flooding the Internet when tickets for single games or events go on sale in order to have the best chance of gaining access to the greatest number of premium seats to premium games. Although the website may limit the number of tickets each individual can purchase in a single transaction, with several people online simultaneously, brokers can input several names and several addresses to circumvent this restriction. Some electronically savvy ticket brokers may take this strategy a step further by utilizing computer programs designed to ensure that they have access to tickets before humans do. Both of these strategies frustrate fans that feel shut out of the primary market and are forced to pay premiums in the secondary market. Further, many teams utilize pricing and distribution strategies that are designed to keep tickets affordable and accessible for all fans (Courty, 2003; Drayer et al., 2008; Reese & Mittelstaedt, 2001). With hundreds and perhaps thousands of brokers and their computers interfering with this process, many teams and event promoters are also frustrated by increased presence of ticket brokers.

LEGALITY OF TICKET RESALE

Of central importance to both the street scalper and ticket broker business is the legality of reselling tickets. There is currently no federal law that governs the resale of tickets. The federal government has let each state determine its laws around this practice. In order to protect fans from the occasionally unethical and illegal practices of street scalpers, many states have implemented statutes that restrict ticket resale to some degree. Of course, the form of these statutes varies considerably from state to state (a summary of each state's laws is available in Table 8.1), and their effectiveness is widely debated. Most statutes either prohibit the resale of tickets at any price above face value or restrict the maximum amount above face value for which a ticket can be resold. It

TABLE 8.1. State by State Summary of Anti-Scalping Laws as of 2010

Current state of anti-scalping laws	States
No laws or restrictions on ticket resale	Alaska, Colorado, Idaho, Iowa, Kansas, Maine, Minnesota, Missouri, Montana, Nebraska, Nevada, New Hampshire, North Dakota, Ohio, South Dakota, Tennessee, Texas, Utah, Vermont, Virginia, Washington, West Virginia, Wyoming
Some restrictions on ticket resale	Alabama, Arizona, Arkansas, California, Connecticut, Delaware, Florida, Georgia, Hawaii, Illinois, Indiana, Maryland, Massachusetts, Mississippi, New Jersey, New Mexico, New York, North Carolina, Oklahoma, Oregon, Pennsylvania, Wisconsin
Ticket resale above face value is prohibited by law	Kentucky, Louisiana, Michigan, Rhode Island, South Carolina

is important to note that the resale of tickets at or below face value is legal in all 50 states. Ticket brokers and other advocates for ticket resale claim that these laws violate their right to free enterprise. However, state courts, as well as the Supreme Court of the United States, have consistently held that these restrictions of free enterprise are not unconstitutional because the laws were created in the interest of public welfare (Elfenbein, 2006; Glantz, 2005).

THE CHANGING SHAPE OF THE SECONDARY MARKET

The introduction and growth of the Internet has made ticket resale easier than ever. Subsequently, this industry has grown exponentially in the last 10 to 15 years. What was once an industry dominated by street scalpers and local ticket broker businesses is now worldwide enterprise conducted by thousands of entrepreneurs. Indeed, now anyone with a computer can easily buy and resell tickets to a willing consumer anywhere in the world. Often, websites such as StubHub.com, RazorGator.com, and TicketsNow.com facilitate these transactions and charge a percentage of the final sell price to both the buyer and seller for the website's service. Improved technology has made the practice of exchanging tickets much more commonplace and much more legitimate. As a result of the growth of this market, many states have either changed or eliminated their ticket resale statutes in recent years. These states are either making it legal to resell tickets at any price or are trying to narrowly tailor the language of their statutes so that they apply specifically to unruly street scalpers instead of more legitimate ticket brokers.

The increased ease of exchanging tickets, along with the slow shift toward government deregulation of the market, has led to tremendous growth of the secondary market. However, not only are more individuals getting involved in ticket resale, but teams and event promoters are getting involved, too. Indeed, in 2001, StubHub agreed to partner with the Phoenix Coyotes of the NHL in the first-ever sponsorship in the secondary ticketing category. Teams in other sports leagues would follow soon after, beginning with the Seattle Mariners in MLB (2001), the Los Angeles Clippers in the NBA (2001), and the New York Jets in the NFL (2002).

In the initial deals, teams would actually get a percentage from each secondary market transaction. The more recent deals closely resemble sponsorship deals in other product categories where the team gets an annual payment (often worth $1,000,000 or more per year) and the secondary ticketing company gains the right to be called "the official secondary ticketing company" and the right to place signs on team websites and within the stadium or arena. In fact, not only has virtually every team signed a deal of this nature with a secondary ticketing company, each of the major American sport leagues has a league-wide sponsorship with one of the major secondary ticketing companies. The major secondary market companies are StubHub, RazorGator, and TicketExchange (the secondary ticketing arm of primary market giant Ticketmaster). Major concerts, events, and other entertainment entities have entered into deals with these companies as well. See Table 8.2 for a sample of key secondary market deals.

TABLE 8.2. **Summary of Key Secondary Market Deals**

Sport Property	Secondary Ticket Provider
University of Southern California	StubHub
Arizona State University	StubHub
Washington Wizards	StubHub
Major League Baseball	StubHub
Ultimate Fighting Championship	StubHub
Daytona Int'l Speedway	StubHub
Michigan Int'l Speedway	StubHub
National Basketball Association	TicketExchange by Ticketmaster
National Football League	TicketExchange by Ticketmaster
National Hockey League	TicketExchange by Ticketmaster
Denver Broncos	TicketExchange by Ticketmaster
NCAA College World Series	TicketExchange by Ticketmaster
Legg Mason Tennis Classic	TicketExchange by Ticketmaster
Los Angeles Galaxy	TicketExchange by Ticketmaster
British Columbia Lions (CFL)	TicketExchange by Ticketmaster
Boston Red Sox	Ace Ticket
Rose Bowl Game	RazorGator

From the perspective of the sport property, entering into a secondary ticketing partnership presents a number of substantial benefits in addition to the direct sponsorship revenue from these deals. Initially, the ability to resell tickets on a team-endorsed website was reserved for full and partial season ticket holders. Prior to these deals, season ticket holders that were not able to attend an event would either have to give their tickets away, go through considerable trouble to find a willing buyer, or simply let the tickets go unused. As a result of the increased ease of selling unused tickets, season ticket holder retention has generally increased for teams entering into secondary ticketing partnerships (Berman, 2005). Although these arrangements are increasingly allowing all fans to resell on this platform, the benefit to season ticket holders has been the most significant.

Allowing fans the opportunity to resell is not only a benefit to the ticket holder but also a direct benefit to the team. By reducing the number of unused tickets, teams are able to regain revenue from ancillary services such as concessions, parking, and merchandise sales. Assuming each fan spends at least some money on these ancillary services, even a small boost in attendance can mean substantial revenue increases over the course of a season.

Given the negative view of scalpers by many sport properties, the opportunity to decrease the presence of scalpers is a welcome one. Indeed, by facilitating the resale of tickets in the days, hours, and even minutes before the game, these secondary market partnerships can serve the same purpose that scalpers do now, only in a more secure environment. Although the initial secondary market partnerships required the physical exchange of tickets (usually via overnight mail), as tickets become increasingly electronic (paperless), the ability to instantly exchange tickets could rid the industry of the presence of street scalpers altogether.

Finally, as prices in the secondary market are typically demand based, teams, leagues, and other sport properties can learn valuable information about the value of their tickets (Drayer & Shapiro, 2009). By monitoring ticket prices in the secondary market, teams can learn which events have higher values placed on them by patrons. This can help to enhance pricing strategies in the primary market in order to optimally price tickets. For example, teams may learn that they do not have enough price points for their seats, that a fireworks show increases the value of a ticket by a certain dollar amount, or that a bad weather forecast decreases the perceived value of a ticket by a certain dollar amount. All of this information can be used to enhance a general pricing strategy, a variable pricing strategy, or even a real-time pricing strategy.

ORGANIZATIONAL RESISTANCE TO THE SECONDARY MARKET

Despite the aforementioned benefits to participation in the secondary market, sport properties have been considerably hesitant to fully embrace the secondary market. By embracing the sponsorship model and not integrating the secondary market operation into its own primary ticket market operation, sport properties have effectively distanced themselves from the practice of reselling their own tickets. Although each organization is ultimately free to take its own stance on the secondary market, regardless of their reasons, there appear to be a few key reasons that some organizations in the primary market have reservations about the secondary market.

The most obvious reason for this resistance is the anti-scalping laws, which remain present in certain markets. Naturally, if ticket resale above face value is illegal, then no sport property is going to engage in or even facilitate those transactions. Of course, as these barriers continue to be relaxed across the country, this reason is likely to become less prevalent. In addition to the state laws mentioned earlier in this chapter, some counties have laws that may differ from the state laws. For example, in the State of Colorado, it is legal to resell tickets to anything (with the exception of ski lift tickets) at any price, regardless of the face value. However, within the city and county of Denver, there is an ordinance that forbids the resell of tickets at a price above face value. Violation of this ordinance is a misdemeanor and is punishable by at least a $100 fine or up to 180 days in jail. Subsequently, the Denver Broncos have placed a face value cap on the resale of tickets posted on their official secondary ticketing website (run by Ticketmaster's secondary ticket arm, TicketExchange). However, despite the legal risk associated with facilitating the resale of tickets in violation of the city ordinance, the anonymity provided by the Internet makes enforcement almost impossible. Indeed, a web-based violation of the city ordinance would have to occur between a willing buyer and seller, both of whom are physically located within Denver's limits. If only one party is located within the city limits, then the ordinance has not been violated. Further, many secondary market websites do not require that the buyer and seller post their names or even an exact seat location (often only section number and row number are provided). As such, it is extremely difficult for law enforcement officials to specifically identify those sellers that are in violation of this relatively minor city ordinance.

Many of the other reasons for organizational resistance to the secondary market are motivated by the threat of negative public relations. Again, some of the traditional views of the secondary market are based on impressions of street scalpers illegally reselling and harassing patrons while they attend an event. This unpleasant view held by some consumers is reason enough for some sport properties to refuse to partake in the practice of reselling tickets. However, the aforementioned benefits of participating in the secondary market often supersede the risk of negative public perception.

The risk of negative consumer perception does not end with the downbeat historical views of street scalpers. Some consumers grow frustrated by other aspects of ticket resale as well. Teams often intentionally keep their prices as low as possible so that more fans can afford to attend games. The premiums that are charged in the secondary market defeat this purpose and make attending a sporting event unaffordable for many fans and their families. The frustration felt by these consumers may negatively impact their otherwise positive views of the team or event. Further, no sport property wants its consumers to feel like it is engaging in price gouging, regardless of whether those prices are set in the primary market or in the secondary market. Although most, if not all, sport properties do not resell their own tickets or price tickets in the secondary market (they only facilitate the transactions between buyers and sellers), creating an association between the team and high ticket prices could negatively impact consumer opinion of sport properties. Additionally, teams profit from selling their tickets in the primary market. By reselling their tickets or even just facilitating the resale of tickets, teams are profiting from the same ticket multiple times. Although this is not exactly an example of price gouging, it is an example of teams asking for even more money from their loyal consumers.

POSSIBILITIES FOR THE FUTURE OF THE SECONDARY MARKET

Currently, the secondary market is in a state of transition. Individual philosophies vary regarding the future of this industry. Although almost everyone agrees that tickets have always and will always need to remain transferable, there is currently a great deal of discussion regarding how these transfers will take place. In particular, members of the primary market are considering a variety of strategies for eliminating, controlling, embracing, or participating in the secondary market. The implementation of any of these strategies has a tremendous impact on the secondary market.

The first school of thought is that the secondary market capitalizes primarily on fluctuations in demand. If tickets were priced more efficiently in the primary market, then the secondary market would not profit from the resale of tickets and would likely be significantly minimized. The ability to transfer tickets would remain since people's plans may change in the weeks, days, and hours before an event. However, the price of tickets in these transfers would likely be at or below face value. Supporters of this pricing strategy believe that fans will understand that demand changes and that some games may be priced higher or lower based on a variety of factors. One potential strategy for people holding this philosophy is to enhance their organization's variable pricing structure in the primary market. Instead of only two or three different price points, an enhanced variable pricing strategy could potentially have different price points for virtually every game. By attempting to accurately predict the games with particularly high or low demand, sport properties could potentially reduce the profitability of ticket resellers. Simple longitudinal research can be conducted to determine which games tend to draw bigger crowds. Not only could this strategy enhance ticket revenue for high-demand games and increase attendance for lower-priced, low-demand games (likely resulting in higher ancillary revenue), but it could also reduce many of the negative aspects of the secondary market (pushy street scalpers and price gouging).

However, there are a few potential pitfalls with this strategy. Some individuals feel that sport properties are sending the wrong message about the value of their product by allowing the price to fluctuate (Lefton & Lombardo, 2003). Suggesting that there is such a thing as a "premium" game also suggests that the rest of the games are less than premium. This is a difficult message for some organizations to send to their potential consumers. Additionally, sport properties that use a variable pricing strategy typically set their prices well before the season starts. Although research can be used to predict demand for many games, there is a risk that demand estimates may change throughout the season. For example, suppose that a home game against LeBron James and the Miami Heat is considered to be among the top drawing games all year and is therefore priced among the highest priced games of the year. However, imagine that LeBron James hurts his knee early in the season and is unable to play, so the Heat are no longer a contending team and no longer have their star player playing. Would this still be considered a "premium" game? By setting prices before the season starts, organizations are unable to account for many of the situational factors (e.g., team performance, injuries, weather) that may influence demand either positively or negatively. This particular scenario and others like it could lead to an abundance of unsold seats.

Realizing this inefficiency, some have suggested that the best way to truly price tickets as accurately as possible is to implement a real-time or dynamic pricing strategy, where ticket prices would in many ways resemble prices on the stock market, fluctuating day by day or even hour by hour to reflect market demand for each ticket. This strategy would allow prices to accurately reflect the demand conditions at each moment, which, again, would reduce the profitability of the secondary market to the point that it may no longer be a viable business. The benefits of this strategy are similar to those of the enhanced variable pricing strategy. Prices for lower-demand games would be lower, which may encourage more fans to attend, therefore enhancing ancillary revenue. Prices for higher-demand games would be higher, therefore enhancing ticket revenue without negatively influencing attendance.

Although this strategy would seem to eliminate the profitability of the secondary market, it may not. Again, much like the stock market where individuals make predictions about the future value of stocks and buy stocks that they believe will increase in value in the future, a real-time pricing strategy in the primary ticket market would lead brokers to speculate about the future value of tickets and try to capitalize on moments of inefficiency. So although this strategy may not eliminate the presence of the secondary market, it would certainly enhance the profitability of sport properties in the primary market. In addition to not wanting to send mixed messages about the value of the product, the uncertain receptivity of fans to fluctuating prices remains the primary reason for organizational resistance to this strategy. However, in 2009, the San Francisco Giants implemented this strategy with selected sections within the stadium and expanded this approach in 2010 to include all other seat locations. Since then, several teams in MLB and other leagues have adopted a similar strategy.

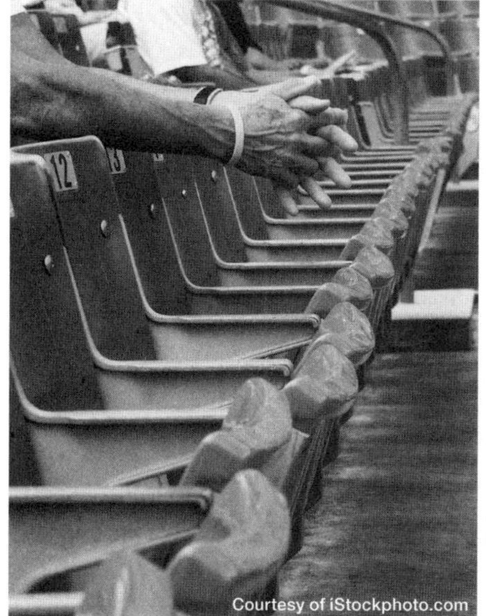
Courtesy of iStockphoto.com

Variable or dynamic pricing is designed to minimize the presence of the secondary market while enhancing profitability in the primary market. However, there is one remaining strategy that enhances profitability while embracing, possibly even encouraging, the secondary market. Sport properties have the opportunity to integrate their primary and secondary markets into a one-stop ticketing operation. In this scenario, fans are free to buy and resell tickets on the same platform as the team's primary operation. Whenever fans need to sell tickets, they can simply come back to the team's website and post their tickets for sale.

Because the team controls the transfer of tickets, it can ensure the authenticity of each ticket while earning additional revenue from transfer fees. Teams would also maintain the same benefits as the current secondary market sponsorship deals (e.g., season ticket holder retention, reduction of no-shows) and should be able to minimize the presence of the street scalper segment of the secondary market because they would be able to facilitate legitimate transactions in the hours and minutes before each game. Further, with full information about the value of their tickets, teams can efficiently price their tickets to maximize attendance and ticket revenue, and fans will also be more informed as to the actual value of their tickets. Additionally, with this information, along with an increase in the availability of tickets, the actual price of tickets should remain relatively low. Teams would likely have to set a price floor to ensure that tickets did not fall below a certain value for their low-demand games. In addition to the concerns associated with real time pricing strategies, opponents of this model worry about the public response to profiting from the sale and resale of tickets (potentially multiple resales) and the potential pitfalls from encouraging ticket holders to resell tickets.

CHAPTER SUMMARY

In the end, members of the secondary market will be forced to adapt to the organizational policies presented in the primary market. Given the need to transfer tickets for all events, the secondary market will never cease to exist. It may, however, change shape several times as sport properties in the primary market determine the best way to satisfy the needs of fans while earning the revenue necessary for their continued success. Successful ticket resellers will need to find a way to provide a service necessary to fans while understanding the complexity of price and demand fluctuations.

LEARNING ACTIVITIES

1. Why are tickets viewed differently than other products? A person can resell anything, make a profit and be considered a successful businessperson (e.g., eBay). However, when it comes to tickets, resellers are often perceived in a negative light. Why?
2. What are a sport property's options for participating in the secondary market? Which one would you choose? Why?
3. If the price of a ticket is $50 and it is resold for $100, what is the value of that ticket? What does the face value of the ticket represent? If you were representing a team, would you try to keep your prices low to attract lower income patrons, even if that meant pricing tickets below the true value of those tickets?
4. Is there a problem with a team or other sport property encouraging fans to resell their tickets? Why or why not?

9

Legal Aspects of Ticket Operations

Mark A. Dodds, Kristi Schoepfer Bochicchio, and Peter Han

LEARNING OBJECTIVES

Upon completion of this chapter, students will have an understanding of the many legal aspects of ticket operations, the use of tickets as a liability waiver, and the legal view of not accepting the expectation of future season tickets as a property right against numerous scenarios. This chapter also creates a vehicle to connect ticketing to marketing, advertising, facility management, player personnel, and finance departments.

KEY TERMS

facility relocations, liability, negligence, property right, season ticket expectation, transfers, waivers

INTRODUCTION

There are numerous legal issues affecting ticket operations evolving from statutory, contractual, constitutional, and common law; legal issues related to ticket sales are plentiful. First, the ticket back often contains a waiver that the sport organization uses to absolve itself of liability. The sport organizations try to use the waiver language as a defense against negligence claims. Second, a ticket seller must be cognizant of resale laws within a respective jurisdiction because they may impact the ticket seller and the ticket buyer. Lastly, many plaintiffs have attempted to use season ticket expectations to succeed in lawsuits against sport organizations. Although courts have traditionally held that a ticket is a revocable license, (Reese et. al, 2004) many ticket holders believe there is a property interest inherent with the purchase and possession of the ticket (In *Re: Platt v. Boston Red Sox Baseball Club,* 2003). This leads to conflict in many different areas within the ticket operations department. For instance, the marketing department might send out collateral material that implies an expectation of future ownership, or in contrast, the sales department might secure multi-year agreements. It is important that these types of business initiatives be approved by legal counsel prior to putting the organization in a poor legal position. Ticketing personnel should always remember the emotional connection that their customers (season ticket holders) have to their product (team). Employees in ticket operations need to be aware of the many legal restrictions impacting ticket operations.

WAIVERS OF LIABILITY FROM PERSONAL INJURY NEGLIGENCE

A ticket to a sporting event is a revocable license with significant legal implications. In addition, many sport organizations choose to print exculpatory language, in the form of a waiver or disclaimer, on the backs of the physical tickets. Although this practice cannot harm the sport organization, very rarely will a ticket back waiver successfully function as a release of legal liability (Tryboski, 2005).

As discussed by Appenzeller (2005), a waiver is defined as a contract in which a service user agrees to waive the right to pursue legal action against the service provider for claims of ordinary negligence resulting from harms incurred (p. 63). As contracts, waivers must conform to the basic contract law requirements of offer, acceptance, and consideration (p. 63). Further, waivers (as contracts) must conform with the public policy requirement that they not be overbroad or against the best interests of society (p. 63). Additionally, waivers are typically found as standalone documents or placed within a broader contract, such as a membership agreement (p. 63). However, when located on a ticket back, a waiver is more commonly referred to as a disclaimer.

The majority of sport leagues and teams place a disclaimer on the back of each ticket. For example, the Chicago Cubs' ticket backs read:

> Holder assumes all risk accidental to the game of baseball, whether occurring prior to, during or after the game, including (but not exclusively) the danger of being injured by or in connection with any thrown bat or thrown or batted ball. Holder agrees Major League Baseball, the National League, the teams, their agents and players are not liable for any resulting injury.

Although the intent of the language is to prevent legal liability for any harm suffered by a spectator at Wrigley Field, the language and format used prove ineffective to the achieving of the desired outcome.

Specifically, when commonly used tests of waiver validity are applied to ticket back language (such as that used by the Cubs), the ineffectiveness becomes clear. Although tests for waiver validity vary greatly among jurisdictions, all waivers deemed valid must adhere to the aforementioned requirements of contract law (Appenzeller, 2005). Using the Chicago Cubs' language above, it is easy to see why ticket back disclaimers for spectator events are rarely upheld as valid: there is no signatory requirement or evidence that the ticket holder agreed to the language, the language tends to be overly broad in violation of public policy, and most ticket back disclaimers are inconspicuous.

Case law substantiates the ineffectiveness of ticket back disclaimers. In *Yates v. Chicago National League Baseball Club* (1992), the Chicago Cubs were sued after a spectator was struck in the face with a foul ball. The Cubs refuted the claim with the disclaimer language on the back of the ticket. Relying on the Second Restatement of Torts, §496B, the court held that, because the disclaimer on the back of the ticket was printed in type set so small that a reproduced copy was illegible, the disclaimer was not effective. Also in 1992, the Chicago White Sox were sued by a spectator injured by a foul ball. After the team asserted that the ticket back disclaimer was a bar to liability, the court found that the disclaimer presented a question of fact as to whether the plaintiff received adequate warning, but was not a bar to the claim (*Coronel v. Chicago White Sox,* 1992).

There are several other cases in which a sport organization, most commonly a baseball or hockey team, asserted a disclaimer in an attempt to bar litigation. For example, in *Costa v. Boston Red Sox Baseball Club* (2003), the Boston Red Sox were sued after a patron received serious facial injuries from a foul ball. The Red Sox had disclaimer language printed on the back of the ticket; however, the disclaimer was not the reason for the Red Sox's legal victory. Similarly, the Milwaukee Admirals hockey team was sued when a 30-year-old fan was struck by a hockey puck, even though she was seated behind a Plexiglass screen. In granting the Admirals' motion for summary judgment, the court noted that the ticket back waiver was one of many acts by the Admirals to warn fans of the potential danger, but the disclaimer alone was not the basis of the outcome (*Moulas v. PBC Productions Incorporated,* 1997). In neither of these cases, nor similar ones, was the exculpatory language on the ticket back the sole reason for dismissal of a claim; rather, dismissal was predicated on other legal theories such as assumption of risk, open and obvious danger, and the "baseball rule," a common and statutory law that prohibits a finding of liability against baseball teams in fly ball and bat cases. As such, a ticket back waiver or disclaimer alone is an insufficient method of liability prevention.

Although the case law clearly substantiates the likely ineffectiveness of a ticket back disclaimer, sport organizations still follow this practice. In the 2009 season, the University of Connecticut used a hybrid form of a ticket back waiver to protect against liability resulting from increased security pat-down procedures (Fitzgerald, 2009). Specifically, the University gave all ticket holders entering the stadium a white card with information regarding the new security procedures, as well as the following language: "By tendering your ticket…, you consent to such procedures and waive any related claims against the State of Connecticut, Northland AEG LLC, University of Connecticut, USA Security Services, or their respective agents" (Fitzgerald, 2009, para. 2). This waiver was likely in response to right of privacy cases filed against the San Francisco 49ers and Tampa Bay Buccaneers for similar security procedures (Fitzgerald, 2009). Further, waivers or disclaimers on ticket backs may be required as part of facility lease agreements. While negotiating a new lease, the city of Wisconsin Rapids required the Northwoods League, a baseball organization, to provide disclaimer language on the back of every ticket ("Lease Agreement," n.d.).

Additionally, an important distinction must be noted. Although disclaimers on ticket backs rarely serve as a bar to litigation in spectator sports, participant activities can render a different result. Specifically, the snow skiing industry has successfully used waiver language on the back of tickets. In *Silva v. Mt. Bachelor* (2008), a district court in Oregon held that the exculpatory language on the back of a lift ticket was sufficient to bar litigation. In an attempt to defeat the waiver, the plaintiff argued that (1) it was not enforceable because it was not negotiated; (2) he did not sign the waiver; and (3) the waiver was overly broad. In granting the defendant's motion for summary judgment, the court ruled that the waiver was not an unequally bargained adhesion contract because there was no evidence of imbalance; that the plaintiff was made aware of the waiver by numerous highly conspicuous signs at the ticket window instructing patrons to read the waiver; and that the release did not violate public policy and, thus, was not overly broad. Although the ski industry is certainly the exception to the well-supported rule that ticket back exculpatory language is mostly ineffective, this trend in participant activity waivers may continue to develop.

TICKET RESALE

Ticket scalping, or the resale of event tickets for above face value, is a trend that has significantly increased in recent years (Reese & Snyder, 2005). The secondary market for tickets has become quite lucrative. Once originally reserved only for scalpers patrolling the outside of the stadium or arena and then for a few ticket brokers, the resale market has created a commodity market for event tickets. Although in-person resale and private party transactions occur for almost every sporting event, the largest measurable increase has come in the online market. In 2006, websites such as eBay, StubHub, and RazorGator estimated annual ticket sales of approximately $3 billion; 2012 projections show an increase to $4.5 billion (Kirkman, 2008–09). Due in large part to the emergence of Internet technologies, the increase in ticket scalping, specifically online ticket scalping, has created a number of legal questions.

Legal issues related to ticket resale can be categorized in two ways. First, legal questions regarding the regulation of ticket resale, whether in person or online, are plentiful. This regulation is currently controlled by the state legislatures; however, little consistency exists among the states with regulatory statutes (Duffy, 2006). Second, legal questions regarding the resale rights of sport organizations and third-party brokers, as well as issues involving computer software developers, have emerged in recent years.

State Regulations

As detailed in Table 9.1, there is little consistency among the state laws that regulate ticket resale. Some states only regulate ticket resale when it is conducted within a certain distance of the event (which would have no impact on Internet transactions); some states prescribe specific requirements for resale over the Internet; some states prohibit any form of resale; and some states have no prohibitions at all. Most important to note is the fluidity of these statutes. The summaries below, listed by and applying within specific jurisdictions, are current through 2009; however, as will be discussed, the current trend at the state level is modification of existing law and, in some states, deregulation.

Regardless of the jurisdiction or statute involved, state level regulation presents many challenges. First, a significant number of ticket resale transactions take place over the

TABLE 9.1. Ticket Resale Regulations by State

State	Regulation
Alabama	Requires resellers to pay a $100 license tax, unless resale happens via the Internet (Ala. Code §40-12-167, 2009; Public Act 2009-568)
Arizona	Allows ticket resale if the transaction occurs more than 200 feet from an event (Ariz. Rev. Stat. §13–3718, 2009)
Arkansas	Prohibits ticket resale to collegiate or high school sporting events or any charitable event; Prohibits ticket resale to musical events, but allows resellers to impose a reasonable service charge for handling or credit card use (Ark. Stat. §5-63-201, 2009); Prohibits speculative selling of event tickets over the Internet to live entertainment, theatre, or musical performances; this prohibition does not apply to sporting or athletic events (Ark. ALS 573, 2009)
California	Prohibits ticket resale for above face value on the grounds of an event, except with permission (Cal. Penal Code §346, 2009)
Colorado	Prohibits resale of any ticket for any skiing service or skiing facility (C.R.S. 18-4-416, 2009); Other ticket types allowed for resale, except in the city of Denver. Resale of tickets in the city of Denver is prohibited, unless conducted via the Internet (Denver Revised Municipal Code Ord. No. 7-293 and No. 7-294); Prohibits restriction of resale ability as a term or condition of a season ticket package contract (C.R.S. 6-1-718, 2009)
Connecticut	Prohibits ticket resale for above face value within 1,500 feet of an event, except with permission (Conn. Gen. Stat. § 53-289c)(2008)
Delaware	Allows resale generally, but prohibits resale for over face value on the day preceding and the day of events held at the Bob Carpenter Center of the University of Delaware, NASCAR races held at Dover Downs, or on any state or federal highway artery (11 Del. C. §918, 2009)
Florida	Allows resale without price limits through an Internet website that meets the following criteria: (1) website must be authorized by original seller; (2) website must guarantee full refund if the event is cancelled, the purchaser is denied admission through no fault of his own, or the ticket is not delivered in the way the purchaser requests and this results in an inability to attend the event; and (3) website must disclose its guarantees and that it is not the original issuer, seller, or reseller and does not control the pricing; Allows ticket resale for only $1 more than face value to: multi-day or multi-event tickets to a park or entertainment company, a University of Florida student reselling a ticket to a University event, or other ticket sold through an Internet website that does not meet above criteria; A person who uses or sells software to circumvent an Internet ticket seller's security measures or access control system is liable for a civil penalty equal to damages treble the amount for which the ticket sold (Fla. Stat. §817.36, 2009)

Table 9.1. Ticket Resale Regulations by State

Georgia	Prohibits anyone other than a registered ticket broker from selling a ticket for more than face value plus a $3 service charge, unless the event sponsor authorizes a higher resale amount (Ga. Code Ann. §§43-4B-25, 2009); Prohibits resale within 1,500 feet of venues that seat less than 15,000; within 2,700 feet of venues that seat 15,000 or more (Ga. Code Ann. §§43-4B-28-30, 2009); Prohibits acquisition of more than 1% of the tickets to any event (Ga. Code Ann. §§43-4B-28, 2009)
Hawaii	Prohibits resale of tickets to boxing matches (Haw. Rev. Stat. §440-17, 2009)
Illinois	Allows resale by registered ticket brokers and via the Internet (720 ILCS §§375/1.5, 2009)
Indiana	Prohibits resale of tickets to boxing matches (Ind. Code §25-9-1-26, 2009)
Kansas	No state statute; however, the City of Topeka prohibits resale within the city and at Heartland Park Topeka (Topeka City Codebook §54-7, 2009)
Kentucky	Prohibits resale of any ticket above face value absent permission from issuer (Ky. Rev. Stat. §518.070, 2009)
Louisiana	Prohibits in-person ticket resale for above face value; Allows ticket resale at any price via the Internet, assuming the resale website meets the following criteria: (1) website must be authorized by original seller and event operator; (2) website must guarantee full refund for event cancellation, if the purchaser is denied admission without fault; or (3) if the ticket is not delivered as promised resulting in an inability to attend the event; An exception to the above Internet policy exists when (1) the ticket is to a university sporting event and allocated to a Louisiana legislator or (2) a student ticket issued by a Louisiana university (La. Rev. Stat. §4:1, 2009)
Maryland	Prohibits resale of tickets for more than the admission price by any boxing, wrestling, or kickboxing promoters (Md. Code §4–318, 2009)
Massachusetts	Prohibits resale for more than $2 above face value; prohibits resale closer than 20 feet from a venue (520 MA ADC 8.01; M.G.L.A. 140 §185D, 2009)
Michigan	Prohibits resale (Mich. Comp. Laws §750. 465; 2009)
Minnesota	Allows resale generally, but prohibits use of software to circumvent a ticket security or access control measure (Minn. Stat. 245 §609.806, 2009)
Mississippi	Prohibits resale to any event held on state property and collegiate athletic events (Miss. Code Ann. §97-23-97, 2009)
Missouri	Specifically indicates no regulation of a city, county, or other political subdivision shall prohibit the sale or resale of an admission ticket at any price (§67.306 R.S. Mo., 2009)
Nevada	No state statute; however, the city of Las Vegas prohibits resale for above face value (Las Vegas Municipal Code 10.52.030)

New Jersey	No person other than a registered ticket broker can resell a ticket for more than 20% above face value, or $3 above face value, whichever is greater; registered brokers can only resell at a price not to exceed 50% above the face value. These provisions do not apply to resale via the Internet (N.J.S.A. 56:8-33, 2009); Restricts registered brokers from reselling within the vicinity of an event, defined as any street, highway, driveway, sidewalk, common area, parking area, or areas adjacent to these spaces (N.J.S.A. 56:8-34, 2009)
New Mexico	Prohibits resale to collegiate sporting events, but allows resale to other events. Also, resellers are allowed to impose a service charge (N. M. Stat. Ann. §30-46-1, 2009)
New York	Allows resale by registered resellers without percentage over face value restrictions, but prohibits resale on the street within 1,500 feet of a venue with a seating capacity of more than 5,000 (N.Y. Arts & Cult. Aff. §25.08 and §25.13, 2009)
North Carolina	Allows resale for greater than face value, but reseller must guarantee full refund if (1) the event is cancelled, (2) the purchaser is denied admission through no fault of his own, or (3) the ticket is not delivered in the described manner; Venues can file a notice of prohibition with the Secretary of State to prohibit resale to specified events at the venue. Prohibition information must be conspicuous; Allows resellers to impose a service charge up to $3 (N. C. Gen. Stat. §14–344, 2009)
North Dakota	Authorizes municipalities to regulate resale (N.D. Cent. Code 40-05-01.26; 2009)
Ohio	Authorizes townships and municipalities to regulate via resolution (ORC Ann. 505.95, 2009; Ohio Rev. Code §715.48, 2009)
Oklahoma	No state statute; prohibits resale in excess of face value in Oklahoma City (Oklahoma City Ordinance §7-132, 2009)
Oregon	City of Portland prohibits resale in excess of face value (Code of the City of Portland §14A.50.060); Prohibits the sale or use of software to circumvent, thwart, interfere with, or evade a security control measure or access control system that a ticket seller uses to ensure equitable distribution (ORS 646.608, 2010)
Pennsylvania	Allows resale via the Internet, without reseller registration, if the website meets specific criteria (4 P.S. §202, 2009); Allows resale for $5 or 25% over the face value, whichever is greater (4 P.S. §211, 2009); The city of Pittsburgh prohibits the resale of tickets to any event at PNC Park or Heinz Field, unless the reseller is licensed and selling within the "reselling zone" (City of Pittsburgh Ordinance 726.01)
Rhode Island	Prohibits resale over face value, except for a service charge up to $3 or 10% over its face value (R. I. Gen Law §5-22-26, 2009)

TABLE 9.1. Ticket Resale Regulations by State

South Carolina	Prohibits resale over face value for events sponsored by higher education institutions, except for a service charge of up to $1; Allows resale of tickets to an open market event through a website or permitted physical location when the reseller guarantees a full refund if (1) the event is cancelled, (2) the purchaser is denied admission through no fault of his own, or (3) the ticket is not delivered in the way the purchaser requests and this results in an inability to attend the event (S.C. Code Ann. §16-17-710, 2009)
South Dakota	Allows municipalities to regulate resale (S.D. Codified Laws 7-18-29, 2009)
Tennessee	Prohibits the sale or use of software to circumvent, thwart, interfere with, or evade a security control measure or access control system that a ticket seller uses to ensure equitable distribution (Tenn. Code Ann. §39-17-1105, 2009)
Virginia	Authorizes localities to prohibit resale, except when resale is via the Internet; Prohibits intentional use of software to circumvent the equitable ticket buying process (Va. Code Ann. §15. 2-969, 2009)
Wisconsin	Prohibits resale of tickets to the state fair (Wis. Stat. §42.07, 2009); City of Green Bay requires resellers to register in order to resell tickets for NFL games or any other event at Lambeau Field (Green Bay Municipal Code 6.12, 2009)

Internet, and often across state lines; thus, personal jurisdiction and choice of law concerns arise (Kirkman, 2008–09). Second, enforcement of a statute in cyberspace is virtually impossible. For example, if a reseller in Rhode Island were to use Craigslist.com to post tickets for sale at 25% above face value, accept payment online via PayPal, and ship the buyer the tickets, there is no reasonable method to enforce the statute (Kirkman, 2008-2009). For this reason, several states, such as Virginia, have recently modified prior prohibitive legislation and currently allow Internet transactions.

Modification of state regulations has become the trend; the state statutes are by no means stagnant. For example, in 2008, North Carolina enacted deregulatory statutes on a trial basis that expired on June 30, 2009. The state legislature opted to not continue the trial provisions beyond the expiration date, but during the trial period, resale for any amount was allowed on websites meeting statutory requirements. In fact, in the past several years, many states have made statutes more lenient, consistent with a free market approach. Other states that have in some way deregulated resale include Alabama and New York. In contrast, some sport teams are asking their state legislatures to increase stringency in the statutes. The Milwaukee Brewers are lobbying the Wisconsin legislation to modify the existing statute, which only prohibits resale of state fair tickets, to include provisions that give municipalities authority to enforce regulations regarding resale on the grounds of Miller Park (Foley, 2010). Many states, such as Virginia, Tennessee, and Oregon, have recently passed legislation that makes the use or sale of software that circumvents or interferes with the promoters' online ticket sale process illegal.

With so many inconsistencies in both statutes and enforcement, regulation of ticket resale, particularly over the Internet, is nearly impossible. Although resale websites such as eBay and StubHub provide the state laws to users and encourage users not to violate these laws, these transactions are seldom policed. Similarly, in-person transactions continue to flourish. Under the current legal framework, ticket resale will be a persistent part of the event ticket landscape.

Beyond the state regulatory issues lies the body of case law that impacts sport organizations, third-party resellers, and software developers. The expansion of the secondary ticket market has generated new legal issues related to ticket resale. In *Cavoto v. Chicago National Baseball Club* (1993), the Chicago Cubs were sued by a class action group of fans after the team's parent company established its own ticket-brokering firm, Wrigley Field Premium Ticket Services. The Cubs sold choice seat locations at face value to Premium, who then sold them at above face value to fans. This allowed the Cubs to capitalize on revenues generated by the secondary market, as well as control part of the Cubs' secondary market. The fans alleged that this practice violated the Illinois anti-scalping law. The trial court ruled that the Cubs had not violated the statute because the statute did not prohibit the Cubs' parent company from establishing a ticket brokerage entity. On appeal, this decision was affirmed.

Also wanting to gain control in the secondary market, the New England Patriots sued StubHub in 2006, seeking access to the names, addresses, and phone numbers of season ticket holders who resold their tickets on StubHub's website (*New England Patriots, L.P. v. Stubhub, Inc.*, 2007). The Patriots alleged that StubHub was encouraging resale in violation of both team policy and Massachusetts's anti-scalping laws. StubHub countered the claim with allegations that the Patriots were trying to monopolize control of the secondary market for Patriot games. The Superior Court of Massachusetts held that StubHub needed to release the names to the Patriots, who were given broad permissions to use those names and other identifying information to enforce organization policies (*New England Patriots, L.P. v. Stubhub, Inc.*).

Although the Patriots sought to control resale of their tickets by legally challenging StubHub, other professional sport teams and leagues have chosen to collaborate with online resellers. For example, in 2007, Major League Baseball (MLB) signed a five-year deal with StubHub, making the website the official online reseller for the league's member clubs and allowing StubHub space on team websites to facilitate "fan-to-fan" resale (Lee & Mohl, 2007). Similarly, the National Football League (NFL) has a resale arrangement with Ticketmaster (Branch, 2007) and National Basketball Association (NBA) teams, such as the Phoenix Suns, facilitate a resale marketplace where fans can resell tickets at any price (Ticketmaster, 2007).

Although online resellers have successfully collaborated with sport and entertainment organizations to facilitate resale, there have been instances in which the reseller has sought to control the secondary market without permission from the organization or entertainer. As discussed by Kreps (2009), Bruce Springsteen scheduled shows at the Izod Center in New Jersey in 2009. Based on previous Springsteen concerts in the state, these shows were expected to sell out very quickly. On the on-sale date of February 6th, Ticketmaster began to sell tickets to the show at the arena, at ticket outlets, over the telephone, and via the Internet. However, when using the Ticketmaster website, some customers were immediately directed to TicketsNow, a ticketing resale company owned by Ticketmaster. This resale site offers tickets at a substantial price premium over the face value. The affected customers and Mr. Springsteen were extremely angry at this practice because tickets were still available at face value on the Ticketmaster site. The New Jersey Attorney General investigated the matter and reached a settlement with Ticketmaster/TicketsNow. The company had to pay $350,000 to cover costs associated with the investigation; pay attorney and administrative fees; create a wall between the two divisions for a year so that customers would not be directed to the TicketsNow site, even after a show sold out; refrain from paid Internet search advertising to lead customers searching for Ticketmaster to reach TicketsNow; and not begin sales for the resale tickets on TicketsNow until the primary sale began on Ticketmaster. Further, a random drawing was held for Springsteen fans that were affected by the mishap for tickets to the shows.

Manipulation of ticket availability is a trend that has spawned both common and statutory law. In *Ticketmaster, LLC v. RMG Technologies, Inc.* (2007), Ticketmaster filed a complaint against RMG Technologies and other individual brokers alleging that RMG produced and sold software that allowed users to circumvent Ticketmaster security and quantity access measures, resulting in ticket purchases in excess of allowable quantities. RMG was accused of interacting directly with clients to aid in mass ticket procurement. RMG argued that its practices were not in violation of social policy and that Ticketmaster received full payment for all tickets purchased. However, the court ruled in favor of Ticketmaster on the grounds of copyright infringement and the Digital Millennium Copyright Act, awarding Ticketmaster over $18 million. Perhaps resulting from this case, in some jurisdictions, such as Oregon and Florida, ticket resale statutes specifically prohibit use of these software applications.

Ticket resale presents a myriad of legal issues that may impact sport organizations, third-party brokers, software developers, and ticket purchasers. Because these laws have experienced significant revisions in the last five years, practitioners should be diligent and remain current on statutory and common law impacting the secondary market.

TICKET SALE ISSUES

Most legal issues with ticket sales are based in contract law. A legal contract requires an offer, acceptance, and consideration. Contracts that involve a transfer of goods for a cost create a property interest in those goods. The buyer owns the property. Although many season ticket holders argue that they have a property right to their tickets (a belief that they own rights to the seats in perpetuity), the courts have consistently rejected these claims. Instead, the courts have held that the season ticket holder's interest in renewable rights to the season tickets is separate and distinct from the game tickets themselves. Therefore, the ticket sales transaction is not a contract for future tickets.

The buyer owns the tickets for that year but should have no legal expectation of owning the tickets in the future. Each season ticket is a revocable license wherein the team reserves the right to review the account prior to offering those tickets the following year. The team retains the property rights to those tickets and can decide not to sell the tickets the following year. The ticket holders have nothing more than a license to purchase tickets, which the team can revoke at any time. As the following situations detail, the mere expectation of purchasing the season tickets on a yearly basis does not change that legal holding.

Donations to Athletic Departments

Many professional teams and college athletic departments require additional donations in order to purchase season tickets. These donations are separate from the ticket price and sometimes offer tax incentives for the purchaser. However, civil lawsuits have resulted from these donations to athletic departments. For example, many long-time season ticket holders brought a claim against the University of Pittsburgh (*Schultz v. Pitt,* 2005) athletic department after a change in donation policy. In preparation for the 2002-03 basketball season, Pittsburgh guaranteed season ticket holders their existing season ticket locations as long as they donated a minimum amount to the Panther Club (*Schultz*). Prior to that season, ticket location was not based on a threshold financial donation; rather, location was dictated by the price of the tickets themselves. The lawsuit was settled out of court but ultimately required the ticket holders to donate to the Panther Club. In this case, the marketing department had earlier communication with season ticket holders guaranteeing their tickets as long as they continued to purchase them but later changed its policy. Ticket administrators must recognize that all ticket marketing materials, including (but not limited to) brochures, information on websites, advertisements, press releases, and ticket renewal forms may be considered part of the contractual relationship with season ticket holders. The marketing materials could create a contract between the team and the ticket holder, and any change from the claims in the marketing materials might result in a breach of contract claim against the athletic department.

Overcharging

In *Heidrick v. PDB Sports, Ltd* (2002), two Denver Broncos season ticket holders brought breach of contract and unjust enrichment claims against the Broncos. These claims were based on a 1967 city ordinance stating that the Broncos' ticket prices "shall not exceed similar charges in comparable facilities...without written permission of the mayor." This was reinforced in a 1977 user agreement for a bond issued to raise funds for stadium renovations (*Heidrick,* 2002). The plaintiffs contended that between 1984 and 1999 the ticket prices were higher than those found at comparably sized NFL venues and that the team did not have the mayor's permission. The court found that the plaintiffs were not parties to the original agreement, nor beneficiaries to the 1977 user agreement, so the breach of contract and the unjust enrichment claims failed (*Heidrick,* 2002).

Pre-Season Ticket Purchase Requirement

Season ticket holders are often required to purchase pre-season game tickets or additional tickets in their ticket packages. In 2000, a judge threw out a lawsuit from a New Orleans Saints season ticket holder who contended that he was unfairly required to buy an extra ticket to the first home game. He claimed that he would not be able to use that ticket and further asserted that the only reason to require this additional ticket sale would be to sell the game out for local broadcast revenue. His legal argument was rooted in contract law, asserting that the requirement was an adhesion contract and, thus, unenforceable. The court held that the plaintiff knew or should have known about the extra ticket from the marketing materials and that the provision was not burdensome or harsh; therefore, the claim failed. Because the court ruled in favor of the Saints, many teams now require the purchase of tickets to less attractive games in order to purchase tickets to the marquee games on the schedule. The ticket holders always have the option of not purchasing the tickets or buying single game tickets.

Right to Renew

Many season ticket holders argue that their season tickets create a property interest for future purchase. In other words, the season ticket holders claim that they should be guaranteed a contract offer for the tickets the following year because they bought tickets the previous year. For example, in *Rayle v. Bowling Green State University,* (1981), a season ticket holder claimed a property interest in the two season tickets purchased from Bowling Green State University. This initial purchase required a payment of $1,000. The plaintiff was required to purchase the tickets and pay a yearly service fee, ranging from $50 to $75 per seat. In 1998, the school raised the cost for the ticket and service fee to $1,000 per year for five years. The school offered to "buy back" the seat for the initial $1,000 payment. The plaintiff refused and brought a lawsuit against the school. The court refused to acknowledge the property rights claim and held that the original contract did not limit the amount that could be charged as a service fee or define the purpose of such a fee.

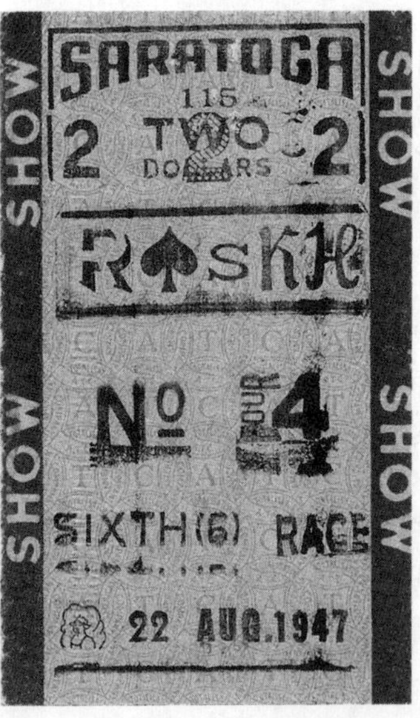

Season ticket holders commonly split season tickets—two or more persons contribute money and share the tickets. In *Tauber v. Jacobson* (1972), one person bought four Washington Redskins season tickets annually, and then collected money from three friends for the remaining three tickets. After the arrangement had lasted eight years, Tauber told the others that he would not sell them the tickets because he had committed to selling them to a banking client instead. The appellate court ruled that Tauber was the purchaser on record, thus bound by the contractual relationship, and that mere expectance of a continued course of conduct was not enough to create a property interest, even in situations where the disappointment of expectations results in heavy financial loss.

Although a court might dismiss his claim, Tauber would be the only person to claim an interest in the tickets, not the others who were not listed on the order form. In other words, the plaintiffs did not have a claim against the purchaser or the team selling the tickets because they were not on record as purchasers.

Misplaced/Lost Tickets

Typically, ticket backs have language to protect the team in the case of misplaced or lost tickets. In *Ganey v. New York Jets Football Club,* (1990), the New York Jets printed "Tickets cannot be replaced if lost, stolen or destroyed" on the back of the tickets. A season ticket holder lost his tickets and was required to purchase replacement tickets. He sued the team for the double billing. The Jets implemented this policy to prevent improper entry into the stadium by persons who obtained free duplicate tickets from the false claims of lost or misplaced tickets by season ticket holders. The court agreed with the team and strengthened the team's policy of refunding unused tickets if the originals are found. This type of ticket policy is common among teams and helps to ensure the general safety and welfare of attendants by limiting the number of missing tickets. The court agreed that without this type of policy, there would be an increase in the number of "missing" tickets that could lead to fraudulent ticket scalping. Also, this policy offers protection to the other ticket holders and event staff from fans who gain improper entry into the stadium. The increased number of persons trying to gain entry might require additional security, thereby raising costs.

In an effort to reduce rising costs while addressing issues such as lost or stolen tickets, event promoters and ticket vendors utilize available technology in ticket sales. For example, a ticket purchased on a website can be printed as a traditional ticket or a corresponding bar code can be sent to a ticker buyer's mobile phone. The bar code can easily be forwarded to another mobile phone if the ticket buyer wishes to transfer the ticket to someone else for any reason. In this case, it would help to decrease the number of unused tickets for an event (Weiner, 2009). Another applied technology, paperless ticketing, requires a buyer to use a credit card and valid photo identification, such as a driver's license, to verify the sale of a ticket at a gate or an entrance instead of bringing a paper ticket (Bayton & Edwards, 2011; Show, 2009). Paperless ticket technology is considered an effective tool for event promoters to prevent scalpers from making profits on event tickets (Burbach, 2009). Because the ticket information is contained within the event promoter, any ticket transfer would require the event promoter to change the information on its computer system. In effect, this transaction eliminates the ticket scalper because there is no paper ticket to transfer to a new person. Instead, the fan looking to purchase the ticket would need to use a mobile device and buy the ticket through the team's computer system. It not only protects a ticket buyer from paying an unreasonably higher price than face value of a ticket, but it also increases potential revenue for an event promoter to run the secondary ticket market.

Although paperless technology may be able to protect the interests of event promoters and ticket buyers, some experts have addressed concerns and potential problems regarding the use of paperless tickets. First, paperless tickets may cause delay at the entrances and gates as ticket takers verify and print out the seat location information (Branch, 2009). Second, paperless tickets may not be a convenient option because they requires that a cardholder be present at the gate (Burbach, 2009). For example, it would be very inconvenient for parents who need to buy concert tickets for their children unless they definitely plan to escort their children to the gates. As another example, if a cardholder purchased tickets for friends, the cardholder must wait for them in order for them to enter as a single group. In short, the use of paperless ticket technology has advantages and disadvantages. An event promoter should have a clear understanding of all the aspects of an event before deciding whether or not to implement paperless ticketing.

Account Transfers

Account transfer (giving season ticket holders the ability to give their tickets and future offers for tickets to someone else) is a practice that many sport organizations do not allow (Reese et. al., 2004). The season ticket holder wants this privilege in order to receive revenue for the right to tickets. The ticket holder would be able to sell the rights to the future tickets to the highest bidder. Unless the team has sold personal seat licenses (PSL), sport organizations want to ban this activity because it puts other season ticket holders at a disadvantage. Most teams allow ticket holders to move their seats to better locations based on availability. By allowing account transfers, these better locations might never be available. Recently, some teams have begun to allow limited account transfers based on certain criteria. Unless it is monitored, this change in policy might result in future litigation.

In *Brinkhaus, et al. v. PDB Sports* (1996), the Denver Broncos revised the club's season ticket account transfer policy. The original policy allowed season ticket holders to sell the rights for the tickets to anyone on the open market. The new purchaser would then be allowed to buy those tickets from the Broncos in the future. The revision limited the transfer of tickets to immediate family members for individual tickets and to "successor" companies for corporate-owned tickets. The Broncos said the reason for this change was that the open ticket selling prevented fans from upgrading their seats to better locations via a priority system and increased frustration and loss of fans' loyalty to the club. However, in 1997, the team was sued by fans who claimed that the tickets should be considered an investment and the new policy was an infringement on their right to increase the value of the investment. In the settlement of the lawsuit, the team reinstated the original policy.

Another case details an account transfer between two individuals. In *Kully v. Goldman* (1981), William Goldman reached an oral agreement with Robert Kully whereby Goldman would purchase four University of Nebraska football season tickets for himself and four season tickets for Kully. Kully brought a claim against Goldman when, 17 years later, Goldman did not purchase tickets for Kully. The court rejected arguments by Kully that the arrangement created a contract between the parties and that a trust was established whereby Goldman was compelled to purchase the tickets in the future. The court reasoned that the university was not required to sell Goldman the tickets in the first place and could reject his application at any time. Because Goldman had no legal claims to the tickets, Kully did not either.

Further, a plaintiff would have difficulty proving ownership of season tickets if the tickets were purchased through a corporation. In *Re: Platt v. Boston Red Sox Baseball Club* (2003) the case involved a trustee for a Boston Red Sox season ticket holder who was not allowed to sell the right to purchase the season tickets because the trustee failed to establish the crucial proof that an individual person owned the tickets. Because the tickets were in a corporate account, a single individual could not claim ownership of them. However, the court was inclined to accept the argument that the Red Sox automatically renewed season tickets and had an arbitrary manner of accepting transfers, and that this undefined policy "would give rise to a reasonable expectation that season tickets are automatically renewable by their previous year's holders" (*Platt,* 17). In the future, a court may create a property interest in the tickets, although no court has done so yet.

Due to the high construction costs of many new sport arenas, personal seat licenses (PSL) have become a very common instrument to raise money. As discussed by Reese et. al (2004), A PSL transfers the ownership of the seat location to the purchaser of the PSL. This person can purchase the season tickets in that location for as long as he/she wishes. The person can also transfer this PSL on the open market but might be subject to minor selling restrictions imposed by the team.

Bankruptcy and Estate Issues

Similarly to account transfer, some season ticket holders have tried to sell the rights to their tickets in order to settle debts or pass their tickets via their will. Because no property rights exist with season tickets, a person does not have permission to sell his "renewal rights" to satisfy other debts (In *Re: Warren Liebman,* 1997). The rights to the future tickets remain with the team. This is because season ticket holders are generally awarded the opportunity to renew, but this action is not guaranteed by the team. In other words, the season ticket holder would be powerless to stop the team from declining to sell the tickets (In *Re: William Harrell v. Phoenix Suns Limited Partnership,* 1995).

Many teams include estate transfer language as part of their season ticket account information. For example, the San Diego Padres only allow transfers if the customer of record meets one of three situations. First, in a divorce where the account was held jointly, the Padres may award the seats to the ex-spouse who is awarded the seats in the divorce settlement. The Padres are not obligated to the ex-spouse who does not retain the seats. Next, in the case of the death of a spouse where the account was held jointly, the account will be changed to the name of the surviving spouse. Finally, in the case of a death where the account was not held jointly, the Padres will name the surviving spouse as the customer of record (San Diego Padres Season Ticket Account Title Policy, 2011).

TICKET ISSUES RELATED TO PLAYERS OR TEAM ACTIONS

There have been a number of lawsuits against teams based on actions of players and the teams themselves. Many fans claim a team's competitiveness is a part of the contractual agreement for the tickets and base their purchase decisions on the team's ability to win games. However, real economic constraints often necessitate trading highly productive and popular players. Many different lawsuits have resulted from a team's personnel actions going against a fan's perception of needed roster moves to increase the chances of winning.

Competitive Team

In *Sports of The Times: Striking Back at the Marlins* (Araton, 1998), a fire sale of a competitive but expensive team was analyzed. In late October 1997, the Florida Marlins became the youngest team to win a World Series. During the following offseason, the Marlins got rid of 12 players from their World Series roster to lower its payroll from $53 million to $24 million. Two season ticket holders brought a lawsuit against the Marlins because they felt betrayed by the dismantling of the team. The lawsuit contended that the pre-season sales collateral sent to prospective season ticket holders featured many of the players who were traded to other teams. In their place were less experienced and lower-priced players. The plaintiffs failed in their claim. So far, the courts have not accepted any arguments as to the competitiveness of a team. Legally, a ticket holder is purchasing the opportunity to watch the games without any expectation to the outcome.

Player Holdouts

In 1999, Ottawa Senators hockey star Alexei Yashin held out for the third time in a five-year period. In his final season of a four-year contract, Yashin failed to honor the last year on the contract and was subsequently suspended by the team. He missed the entire 1999-2000 season. A Senators season ticket holder filed a lawsuit against Yashin for interfering with the contractual relationship between the fans and the Senators ("Yashin," 2000). The complaint argued that the holdout decreased the value of the season tickets. The fans purchased the tickets with the understanding that the players under contract would play, unless injured. Although a trial court ruled that the fan had a legal right to sue the player, an Ontario Superior Court threw out the case, reasoning the plaintiff did not establish a contractual right requiring Yashin to be on the roster.

Strike/Replacement Players

Many labor disagreements between players and management have disrupted sports seasons. In the past 30 years, labor unrest has postponed or cancelled games in the NFL, MLB, NBA, and National Hockey League (NHL). These disagreements resulted in lawsuits. In 1983, the NFL had a labor disagreement that led to the cancellation of many games. In *Bickett v. Buffalo Bills, Inc.* (1983), a season ticket holder sued the Buffalo Bills, alleging breach of contract and warranty, fraudulent misrepresentation, unjust enrichment, and deceptive practices based on the failure of the Bills to play home games that the fan had purchased tickets to attend. Because the ticket is a revocable license, the team can revoke that license for any nondiscriminatory reason that it would like. This privilege extends to not playing the games themselves. The team would, however, be required to refund the ticket price for the games not played.

Team Relocation

Franchise relocation has become a common occurrence in the sport marketplace. Virtually every professional sport league has seen a team moved to a new market in the last 20 years. In response, cities have unsuccessfully brought lawsuits against the franchises in order to force them to remain playing in the city. Individual season ticket holders have also brought lawsuits against the teams to compel them not to move. After the 1994 NFL football season, the Los Angeles Rams moved their franchise to Saint Louis, Missouri. Larry Charpentier, a season ticket holder in Los Angeles, claimed breach of contract and that the team defrauded him when it moved (*Charpentier v. Los Angeles Rams Football Company, Inc.,* 1999). The court held the team did not breach any contract with the individual because any such contract would give the purchaser the opportunity to buy the seats at the local venue ahead of other perspective purchasers. Once the team moved, there were no seats to purchase, so the plaintiff's contractual rights left with the team.

The Cleveland Browns (now the Baltimore Ravens) were in a similar situation when they moved the franchise from Ohio to Maryland. A class action lawsuit representing 40,000 season ticket holders claimed that the team's owner breached the season ticket holders' contractual right to renew their tickets for the following year (Apperson, 2001). More specifically, the plaintiffs claimed that the team's move deprived the season ticket holders of their right of first refusal to purchase 1996 season tickets. This case was settled out of court, whereby each season ticket holder would be eligible for $50 per seat and given the option of either taking cash or donating it to charity.

LEGAL ISSUES RELATED TO STADIA MATTERS

There have been numerous lawsuits by season ticket holders due to stadia issues. Typically, these issues are the result of construction and relocation of seat assignments. Because of the new configuration of the stadium, many seat locations change and often result in a less desirable location for the season ticket holder. For example, many seats are lost due to luxury box construction. The ticket holders for those seats need to be relocated and often are placed in less popular sections.

Seat Relocation Related to New Stadium Construction

Stadium construction is an area that results in many lawsuits against the sport organization. Because the new stadium is configured differently, many seat locations are worse in the new stadium than they were in the old one. Often, the ticket sales department is in the crosshairs of angry fans. A lawsuit stemming from the Cincinnati Bengals' move into Paul Brown Stadium was brought by season ticket holders unhappy with their new seats (*Reedy v. Cincinnati Bengals, Inc.,* 2001). Because the team and Hamilton County were partners for the stadium construction, the settlement from

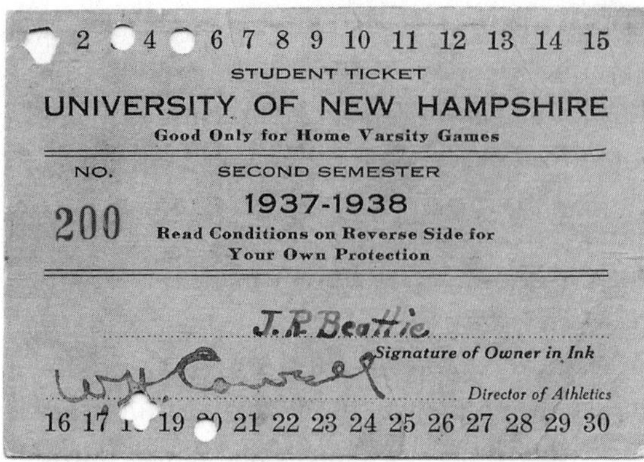

the lawsuit cost the taxpayers of Hamilton County more than $2.5 million. The settlement included refunding the cost of PSL for fans that paid for a license in one section but received seats in another section. The county paid 10% interest on the money refunded to the fans because the cost of the PSL depended on the location of the seats and fans paid a higher price than their seat location required. Some fans were frustrated with the circumstance and took a full refund, while others wanted the tickets and the refunded difference between the seat locations. Also, some fans were able to be moved into a more desirable location when those seats became available.

While preparing to move into the new Raymond James Stadium, the Tampa Bay Buccaneers had to create new seat assignments for their season ticket holders. Because the new stadium held 8,000 seats less than the old Houlihan's Stadium, many fans had their seat locations moved to a different location (Reese, 2004). The Houlihan's Stadium had a concentration of seats between the 30-yard lines. In the new stadium, the seats were more evenly distributed throughout. Also, the Buccaneers reserved 400 seats in prime locations to be used for team VIPs. Many fans threatened to sue based on their new locations. However, the team had established a protocol for designating the seat assignments based on when seat deposits were made, the length of time as a season ticket holder, and previous seat location in Houlihan's Stadium (Reese). The team offered to discuss the new location with any aggrieved fan and offered a refund to any fans wishing to give up their tickets (Reese). Although the lawsuit did not go to trial, the Buccaneers put themselves in an advantageous position by creating and following that policy.

In *Yocca v. Pittsburgh Steelers Sports, Inc.* (2003), the Pittsburgh Steelers faced a lawsuit from fans when they moved into Heinz Field from Three Rivers Stadium. At least four fans were upset that they paid for a PSL based on a color-coded map distributed by the Steelers. The fans were surprised that their seat locations fell in a location less desirable than indicated on the map. A trial court dismissed the lawsuit, stating the map was an artist rendering of the new stadium that did not indicate any number of seats or any location of rows of seats. However, if the map had contained references to actual seat locations, the case might have gone to trial.

Stadium Renovations

Not all stadium issues arise with new stadia. In the late 1990s, the Dallas Cowboys made renovations to Texas Stadium. During these renovations, the team installed a Row A in the upper deck in front of the previous front Row 1. A season ticket holder in Row 1 brought a lawsuit against the team for breach of contract, fraud, and misrepresentation, arguing that their tickets should be the first row of the section (*Chaussee v. Dallas Cowboys Football Club,* 1997). The court ruled in favor of the team because the Cowboys promised Row 1 tickets and delivered Row 1 tickets. The team did not promise front row tickets.

CHAPTER SUMMARY

As this chapter described, there are many potential legal implications to the selling of tickets. Because many tickets are highly desirable, the possession of season tickets could be a commodity. But courts have routinely denied plaintiff claims for future expectation of the season tickets, thus the legal ownership of the future tickets remains with the team and not the season ticket holder. The season ticket holder purchases a revocable license to the current season's games only.

LEARNING ACTIVITIES

1. How closely should the marketing, ticketing, and legal departments work? Should all marketing collateral be reviewed by the ticketing department?
2. How can a ticketing department decreases the potential risk of a lawsuit from fans?
3. In 2009, the University of Toledo held a "home game" against Ohio State University at Browns Stadium in Cleveland. Toledo was given 58,000 seats to the game, while the much larger Ohio State University was allocated 12,500. Toledo began to sell their tickets to the game to Toledo season ticket holders and donors to the athletic department. It is believed that many of the Toledo season tickets were purchased by Ohio State Buckeye fans that were looking only to use the Cleveland game tickets. Would an alumnus from Toledo who was unable to purchase a ticket because it sold out have a claim against Toledo, Ohio State University, or against Ohio State ticket purchasers?
4. A long-time season ticket holder claims to have received his ticket application two weeks after the completed applications with deposit were due. The team has already moved another person into those seats. Does the season ticket holder have a claim against the team?

10

Policy Development

Shelley Binegar

LEARNING OBJECTIVES

Upon completion of this chapter, students will have gained a familiarity with common policies, an understanding as to why policies are important, and an appreciation of the thought process involved in creating said policies. Students should feel confident writing a policy that would be approved by supervisors, be enforceable, and be applicable to the majority of situations.

KEY TERMS

accessible seats, holds, lap seat, loyalty points, transfers, wait list, will call

INTRODUCTION

Writing policies is usually one of the least favorite activities of any ticket director, but also the most important. Having firm, clear, well-known policies can make a ticket director's job infinitely easier. Conversely, not having policies can make it infinitely harder. There are two main rules that should be followed when creating policies: 1) policies are guidelines, not absolutes, and 2) supervisors should sign off on all policies before implementation.

Regarding the first rule, there will always be exceptions and extenuating circumstances for every policy. Flexibility is the key when dealing with the public in a customer service capacity. A ticket director will need to use his/her best judgment at times but having written policies will help guide those decisions. Policies should be thought of as a type of safety net. Being able to show an upset fan or patron a written policy and explain that that policy is simply being followed and implemented in a particular situation is an extremely powerful tool. People tend to respond in a more reasonable manner when they can be shown that there is, in fact, a policy and that policy is being followed. Problems occur when there is not a written policy. Fans can feel like they are being treated unfairly if the decision appears to be one of judgment and not policy. It is also harder for a supervisor to support an employee's action if it is based on judgment.

The second rule is equally important. The ticket office is almost always the front line to any event or facility. Most fans will only ever interact with the ticket office. They will more than likely never meet upper management. Therefore, the ticket office staff must have full confidence that when they follow a policy and the customer continues to complain, they will be supported by their supervisors. This is not to say that rule one should be discarded, but the policy should be followed the majority of the time, and the ticket office staff must feel confident in enforcing said policies. It is extremely important that, before any policy is implemented, any and all supervisors have signed off on the policy. There are few situations worse than enforcing a policy, having it go to the next level, and having supervisors say they were not aware of the policy and do not agree with it.

Below are some standard ticket office policies. Although not comprehensive, they will provide a solid foundation on which to build.

HOLDS

Creating a policy for the use of "hold" tickets is extremely critical. Hold tickets are what keep a game or event from ever being a sellout. They are seats that are never put on sale to the general public but rather held for internal use. The hold category is one of the most important and often most overlooked. It is also an area that can get a department or team into the most trouble. Without a firm policy on who has access to these tickets and in what ways they can be used, hold tickets can easily be overlooked or lost track of, and can cause auditing nightmares. In the ticketing world, when a venue announces the game is sold out, they are simply saying there are no tickets available to the general public to purchase. A ticket director knows there is no such thing as a game or event ever being completely sold out. A ticket director needs to plan on last minute requests and problems; expect the unexpected. This is where hold tickets come into play. More likely than not, these tickets will end up in the comp ticket category when all is said and done, but sometimes they are used for last-minute purchases by VIPs.

There are several questions one should ask and answer before setting a policy on hold tickets.

1. **How many tickets per game are going to be put on hold?**

   The general rule of thumb is to hold 5% of the capacity of the facility. For instance, if a basketball arena seats 10,000 people at capacity, 500 seats should be held. If a football stadium holds 80,000, then 4,000 should be held. However, this is just a starting point. The number of seats that are held each game depends on the type of event, what the use of these tickets will be, who has access, the anticipated attendance, and how many have been needed historically. It does not make sense to hold 500 seats in the basketball arena mentioned above if the anticipated attendance is only 2,000. Remember, these tickets will likely end up being used as comps. The more a team holds, the less revenue generated through ticket sales. If an event is "sold out" and there are 1,000 seats on hold and only 500 were used, 500 went unsold. That means there are

NO REFUND
NO EXCHANGE

500 empty seats that could have been sold at full value. A supervisor is not going to be happy when he realizes that the tickets could have sold and increased revenue.

Ticket directors walk a fine line when deciding how many seats to hold. If a team holds too many and seats go unused, then the team loses revenue. If a team holds too few, it runs the risk of not being able to accommodate a last-minute request from a VIP or not being able to handle a problem adequately during the event. Turning a large donor or VIP away because the team did not have enough tickets on hold can result in the loss of revenue through a donation instead of ticket revenue. The best way to determine how many seats to hold is to look at historical data. How many have been used in the past? In this situation, the past is often the best predictor of the future. If the team does not have historical data, it should err on the side of holding too many, keep detailed records of how many are used per game, and adjust as needed.

2. **Where will the hold ticket seats be located?**

Hold ticket seats should be located in a variety of sections and areas. There should be a handful of hold tickets at all price levels, including the highest and the lowest. However, it is recommended that the bell curve (Figure 10.1) be used as a guideline in this situation; meaning, if there are nine price levels and level one is the most expensive and level nine is the least expensive, the majority of the hold tickets will be in level five.

Hold ticket seats should also be in different "blocks." If 20 are on hold in Section A, they should not all be right next to each other. Divide the seats up into blocks of two, four, six, and eight. Rarely will a team ever need a single hold ticket or enough tickets for a group larger than eight. Most people who request large blocks of tickets expect that they will not all be seated together.

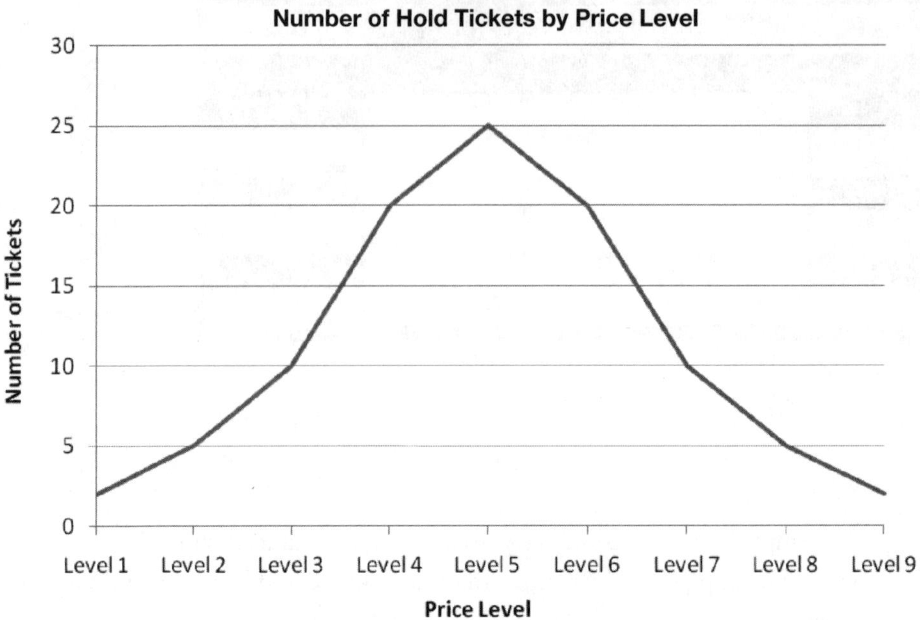

FIGURE 10.1. Ticket Hold Bell Curve

3. **Who has the authority to release/use hold tickets?**

   Although the ticket director will typically be the one with access to the hold tickets, this does not always mean that person will have the authority over their use. It is important to know who has this authority to use or sell the tickets, so as to avoid complications. It is recommended that only a few people have access to these tickets, again to avoid unnecessary confusion and complications. In a collegiate athletics department, the Director of Athletics and the Ticket Director should both have access, as well as the Ticket Director's immediate supervisor if it is not the Director of Athletics. The fewer people with authority , the easier it will be to control. As the date of the event gets closer or a game becomes sold out, people will begin asking for "favors." A clear policy on who can authorize the use of holds will make things much simpler. A request form can help in this area. A sample form is in Figure 10.2 (Policies and Procedures Handbook, 2006). When writing a policy on hold tickets, make sure it is clear about who can request hold tickets and who can approve the hold tickets. Written requests also help track the use of hold tickets and provide backup for auditing purposes.

Ticket Request Form

Tickets Requested By: ______________________ Date Requested: ________

For Which Event: ________________________ # of Tickets: ___________

Purpose/Use of Tickets:

____

____

____

____

If tickets are to be mailed, list address: ______________________________

____

____

____

Request: ☐ Accepted ☐ Denied

Authorized By: ____________________________ Date: _______________

Office Use Only

Delivery Method: Date Mailed ________ Will Call

Payment Method: Check Cash Credit Comp

Credit Card #: _________________________________ Exp. Date __________

Seat Location: ____

FIGURE 10.2. Sample Ticket Request Form

4. **For what purposes can a hold ticket be used?**

   There are many uses for hold tickets; a sample list is below. These are recommendations only. Each department should determine its own list and remember that there will always be exceptions to the rules and that flexibility is necessary. Hold ticket uses include:

   - Donors/development purposes
   - Staff requests
   - VIPs/dignitaries
   - Relocations for problems the day of the event

DUPLICATE TICKETS

It never fails that fans or patrons will forget their tickets at home, throw them away by accident, never receive them in the mail, or that the tickets will be stolen. A ticket office has to be prepared to handle these and many other situations with the best customer service possible while ensuring the integrity of the event. A standard duplicate policy is below ("Lost/Stolen Ticket Policies," 2009):

> The ticket office will provide duplicate tickets for single game tickets at the request of the original purchaser at no cost should the tickets become lost, stolen, or destroyed. Duplicate tickets will only be issued if the ticket office has record of the seat location. For instance, tickets purchased over the counter through the walk-up sales feature are not sold onto individual accounts; therefore such tickets cannot be duplicated. Duplicate tickets will not be mailed and can only be picked up at Will Call on the day of the game. If someone other than the original purchaser is going to pick up the tickets, it must be noted in advance. A photo ID and signature are required to pick up the duplicate tickets. Although there is no charge for this service, the ticket office reserves the right to discontinue duplicating tickets on a particular account should this policy be abused. In order to duplicate a set of season tickets, the ticket office must receive a signed letter from the original season ticket purchaser.

The ticket office should note that duplicate tickets were issued in the person's account and keep a log. If a pattern begins to appear in an individual's account, further review and action may be necessary. Unfortunately, not every customer is honest; some will claim to have lost their tickets in order to get additional tickets for free. With today's technology, this is becoming harder to do, but it is still possible. The use of barcodes has added an additional security level. Instead of issuing a duplicate pass, typically tickets can now be reprinted, which deactivates the original barcode so that in case someone tries to use the original tickets on game day, they will be stopped at the gates.

WILL CALL

Will Call is the ticket window or booth on game day where patrons can pick up preordered tickets. As a general guideline, all tickets that are left at Will Call should be paid for in full with no balance due. A Will Call window is generally not set up to accept payments. Tickets should only be released to the original purchaser unless the name has been changed by the original purchaser prior to the day of the game. A photo ID and signature should be required to pick up tickets (Brown, 2005). The signed envelope, form, or receipt should be kept in the game folder in case there is ever a question as to why tickets were released to a person and to whom they were released. Also, all tickets left in Will Call that were not picked up should be kept in the game folder. Fans will call asking for a refund citing they never received their tickets when,

Courtesy of iStockphoto.com

in fact, they were left in Will Call and never picked up. As a general guideline, tickets ordered within two weeks of an event should automatically be placed at Will Call. It is too risky to mail tickets that close to a game unless using an express mail system.

A ticket office will need to determine whether they will accept third party will call. Third party will call is when Fan A drops off tickets for Fan B at the Will Call window on the day of the game; the envelope did not originate in the ticket office. If accepting third party will call, make sure it is clear who dropped the tickets off and who is authorized to pick them up.

LAP SEAT

Lap seat policies are designed to define who needs a ticket when entering the event. Many fans will ask how old a child must be to require purchasing an additional ticket or seat. There are two schools of thought regarding a lap seat policy. First, it is easiest and eliminates the need for any judgment decisions to be made if a ticket office simply states, "Every person entering the facility must have a ticket regardless of age." ("Football Game Day," 2009) The second option is that children under a predefined age (typically under the age of two) do not need a ticket if they are going to sit on the lap of an accompanying adult.

The first is easy for everyone to explain and to understand. Event staff is never put in the position of having to guess or debate the age of a child. However, it is not viewed as the fan-friendly version. Fans often complain and question why they have to pay for a ticket for a child that is not going to technically use a seat because they are too little to sit by themselves. Below is a sample lap seat policy:

> Children who have celebrated their third birthday are required to have a ticket to gain admittance. Children under three years of age are not required to have a ticket provided they sit on an adult's lap. As a courtesy to all fans and to comply with fire regulations, children should not sit in the aisles or walkways. ("Ticket Policies," 2009)

TRANSFERS

Transfer policies vary greatly from ticket office to ticket office. Some offices have very detailed policies outlining specifically to whom tickets can be transferred and during what time period, while other offices simply state that transfers are not allowed. When deciding on a policy, the culture surrounding the event is very important, as is the supply and demand of the tickets in question. Below are a set of questions to consider when setting a transfer policy.

1. **Can ticket holders transfer their seats to anyone or are there restrictions?**

   If a team is going to allow transfers, it can either allow the original ticket holders to transfer to whomever he/she would like or it can limit who is eligible to receive the transfer. This decision is largely based on the demand for the seats in question. A facility that is in a sold-out situation typically limits to whom tickets can be transferred, if transfers are allowed at all. This is to protect long-time season ticket holders and fans from being "skipped" by new fans. For instance, say Fan A has been a season ticket holder for 20 years and has retired from his job and is moving to Florida. His seats are located at the 50-yard line. Fan A would like to "give" or transfer his tickets to his neighbor, Fan B, who has never been a season ticket holder but has used Fan A's tickets over the 20-year period when Fan A was not able to attend. Fan C has also been a season ticket holder for 20 years but has seats on the 10-yard line. Is it fair or right for Fan B to become a season ticket holder on the 50-yard line in front of Fan C? Does it make a difference if Fan B is Fan A's brother instead of neighbor? Should a fan be able to transfer to only blood relatives or should spouses and domestic partners also be considered? What sort of documentation, if any, is required to verify the relationship (e.g., birth certificate, marriage license, power of attorney forms, death certificate)? Would it make a difference is the venue was not sold out? What if there are plenty of good seats available to new season ticket holders?

2. **Can a business transfer to an individual and vice versa?**

   Oftentimes when people have had season tickets for numerous years through their business and they retire or leave the company, a company will allow individuals to transfer the tickets into their personal names. Dilemmas occur when the person authorizing the transfer from the company to the individual is, in fact, the individual. An example would be that the President of Company A has sold the company to Company B. Before leaving the company, the President of Company A contacts the ticket office and authorizes the transfer of the seats to his personal name. When the new President of Company B takes over, he discovers the company no longer has seats. A clear cut policy should be developed in regards to who in the company has the authority to authorize the transfer of seats.

3. **Can seats be transferred at any time of the year, or is there a specific designated transfer period?**

   If transfers are going to be allowed, a team may want to consider limiting the time period during which requests are accepted. For instance, a good time to transfer seats would be during the off-season or a down time of the year. This allows for proper follow-up with the involved parties.

4. **Is there a charge for the transfer of tickets?**

   There is work involved in transferring seats. Charging ticket holders may discourage people from transferring without legitimate reasons. A team can expect up to 10% of season ticket holders in a sold-out venue to request a transfer each year. For a facility that holds 80,000 people, this could be 8,000 seats that need to be transferred each year. Divide that by, on average, four seats per account and a team is looking at 2,000 transfer requests per year. This can legitimately take up a full-time employee's time.

5. **Are only seats transferrable or are parking passes and loyalty points also transferrable?**

   Typically parking passes and loyalty points are tied to a ticket holder's donation level and are considered benefits of a particular giving level and, therefore, are non-transferrable. Each ticket office will need to make its own determination, but allowing parking passes and loyalty points to be transferred is highly unusual.

ACCESSIBLE SEATS

Accessible seating policies are more than simply an adherence to the ADA regulations. The number of accessible seats required in a particular venue is predetermined by federal regulations. However, the number of seats is limited, and therefore, a policy needs to be developed. If a patron already has regular tickets but is now in need of accessible seats, the ticket office should exchange the seats at no charge. A problem arises when the patron has more than two seats. Due to the limited nature of accessible seats, a venue will typically limit a patron to one seat for the person with accessible needs and one for a companion; however, this is one area in which exceptions are made for special circumstances ("Wheelchair Ticket Policies," 2009).

TICKET EXCHANGE

The exchange of tickets refers to a patron who has already purchased tickets for a particular event and wants to exchange them for either different seats for the same event or tickets for a different event. If the patron is in need of accessible seats, then follow the accessible seat policy. As a general rule, ticket offices should not allow exchanges, as it has accounting implications (Binegar, 2005). If the money was deposited and accounted for in one event and the patron wants to exchange tickets for a second event, the money would need to be moved in order to maintain accurate financial records. Although this can be done, it should be an exception, not the rule. This includes not allowing ticket upgrades or buying back tickets from patrons. As with many policies, exceptions are inevitable.

CHANGE OF ADDRESS

When ticket holders needs to update their address or contact information, it is important to have a process in place to ensure accuracy and limit errors. The standard policy requires the change of address request be in writing (emails qualify) and list both the current and new address. Fans can also update their contact information on a renewal form, or for those organizations that offer online account management options, fans can update their address online. The ticket office should keep the written request as backup in case clarification is ever required. A standard change of address form is in Figure 10.3 ("Policies and Procedures Handbook," 2006).

Ticket Office Change of Address/Contact Information Form

Account # ________________ Date ________________

Change From:

Name: ________________

Address: ________________

City: ________________

State: ________ Zip: ________

Phone: ________ E-mail: ________________

Change To:

Name: ________________

Address: ________________

City: ________________

State: ________ Zip: ________

Phone: ________ E-mail: ________________

For Office Use Only: Change made by: ________________

Date: ________________

FIGURE 10.3. Sample Change of Address Form

SECONDARY MARKET/COUNTERFEIT TICKETS

As technology evolves in the ticketing industry and barcodes becomes the standard, it is becoming more and more difficult to counterfeit tickets. However, there are still those fans who believe they can buy tickets for a sold-out event or at a lower price online or from a person on the street. In the unfortunate event that this happens, a policy must be in place so as to minimize the damage. There are multiple ways to handle these types of situations. There are two main questions a team needs to answer before deciding on a policy:

1. Will the team take legal action against the person who purchased the counterfeit tickets?
2. Will the team give the fan that purchased the tickets the opportunity to purchase real tickets for the event?

The answers probably depend on how prevalent the counterfeiting problem is at the venue. There is a delicate balance between protecting the organization and providing great customer service.

WAIT LIST

A wait list is created when the demand for tickets significantly exceeds the supply. How the wait list is managed is extremely important. Those fans that put their names on the wait list are typically the most die-hard and loyal fans. If this list is mismanaged, it can cause bad public relations. The policy needs to be clearly communicated and fair. A wait list policy can be as simple as first come, first serve or can involve a more complex loyalty point system. Either way, fans that have their names on the list should be clearly communicated with regarding where they are on the list, how they will be notified, how they can move up, and what their options will be once they are contacted. For instance, if Fan A wants to add his name to the wait list for season football tickets, how would he go about doing this? Is there a form? Can he do it online? Who will follow up with him letting him know where he is on the list and the approximate wait time? If tickets do become available, is there a limit to how many he can purchase? If Fan A needs four tickets for his family but only two become available and he declines them, does his name remain on the list? Does he move to the bottom or stay where he is? How will the team contact the people on the wait list? By phone? By mail? What if the team leaves a message? Is there a time period in which Fan A needs to call back? If the ticket office never hears from Fan A, is Fan A removed from the list? Whatever the decision and policy is, make sure all communication and efforts are documented with dates and times. Depending on how long the wait list is, a ticket office may want to consider sending a certified letter with a firm deadline for response.

LOYALTY POINTS

As introduced in Chapter 5 (Ticket Pricing), loyalty points—sometimes called priority points—are becoming more and more common, specifically in the college athletics realm. Loyalty points allow a ticket office and department to quantify the fan's relationship with the department. Loyalty points can be as simple as one point per $100 donation to the department or an extremely complicated formula that involves multiple factors. Below is a list of questions a department should consider and discuss when creating a point system:

- Should a person receive points for being an alumnus?
- Does being a former student-athlete or varsity letter winner count in the point total?

- Are donations made to the university in general counted or just donations to the athletic department?
- Are historic donations weighted the same as donations made in the current year?
- Is there a difference between annual donations and donations to a capital campaign?
- Does the number of season tickets purchased factor in, or does the person simply have to be a season ticket holder?
- Does a person have to have been a season ticket holder for a minimum number of years before the individual begins accumulating points?
- Does a person receive points for each season ticket held? For which sports?
- Are all loyalty points active or must the person have donated in the current year?

These are simply some basic questions to get a department thinking. Each school will have unique criteria based on traditions and the culture of that institution. For instance, does being a member of the student support group count? What if students had to purchase season tickets; do those years count as being a season ticket holder? There is no perfect system that works for everyone. The best way to decide on a system is to run a test on the list of donors or season ticket holders and see if, when the point system is applied, they rank in the way that is expected. If not, go back to the drawing board.

Once the system is in place, how and when the point system is used should be clearly communicated to all fans. For instance, loyalty points can be used for seat upgrade requests, post season tickets, away game allocations, and parking locations. Whatever the case is, make sure it is public knowledge and that the system is followed. There are few things worse than saying a point system will be used and then not using it. Fans are becoming more and more savvy when it comes to knowing where they rank and to what they are entitled. They do talk to one another and will figure out exactly where their seats should be located. When questioned by a fan, it should be easy to defend the team's position by simply pulling up the point system and showing the fan exactly where he/she ranks. A sample loyalty point system can be seen in Table 10.1.

SEAT RELOCATIONS

Each year, an organization will receive numerous requests from current season ticket holders to move or upgrade their seat locations. If a loyalty point system is in place, it can be used to decide who receives priority and moves to the top of the list. If an organization does not have a point system, the process needs to be clear and fair for fans. Typically a first come, first serve method is used. Although this will take care of the basic requests to move closer to the 50-yard line or to move to an aisle, there are always special circumstances that need to be handled delicately. Below are a few real life situations that have occurred. How would you handle these? A person wants to move seats because

- water is dripping from the balcony above;
- the person sitting next to the fan constantly arrives to the game intoxicated;

TABLE 10.1. Sample Loyalty Point System

Factor	Points
Current year donations to the booster club	10 points per $100 donated
Consecutive years of donating	10 points per year
Historic donations to the department	10 points per $100 donated
Consecutive years of season tickets	10 points per year
Alumnus	One-time allocation of 50 points
Former letter winner	One-time allocation of 100 points

- the people behind the fan kick the seat;
- the people in front of the fan like to stand for the majority of the game;
- a person recently got a divorce and does not want to sit next to former in-laws anymore;
- it is difficult to hear the public address announcer from where the seats are currently located; or
- the person next to the fan has extremely bad body odor.

COMPLIMENTARY TICKETS

Complimentary tickets are a large and complicated category in any ticket office. They also create another hot spot for auditing concerns. A defined complimentary ticket policy must be developed and followed. When used properly, complimentary tickets are an excellent public relations and recruiting tool; however, misuse can result in extensive loss of revenue, as well as administrative and NCAA sanctions. The transfer or resale of complimentary tickets should be strictly prohibited. All complimentary tickets should be distributed by the ticket office and should be signed for by the recipients unless there is a need to ship the tickets. The ticket director should coordinate the accounting and distribution of all complimentary tickets and ensure that each individual receiving complimentary tickets understands and abides by the rules and regulations set by the department and any or all governing bodies.

The next sections cover the basic complimentary ticket categories: department staff, coaches, entertainment, student-athletes, prospective student-athletes/recruits, and charities. A detailed, specific policy should be developed for each category. Suggestions have been given, but each venue will have its own constituency groups and categories that will need to be addressed.

Department Staff

Tickets can be used as perk for those who work at the particular venue, facility, or with the team. There are no hard costs for the organization, but it can be considered an added value to any employee's contract. Before issuing complimentary tickets to a staff member, IRS regulations should be considered. Currently, the value of a complimentary ticket is not considered additional income unless the event is sold out. However, this interpretation is subject to change and should be monitored regularly. The number of tickets given to each staff member can depend on rank of the employee, number of members in the employee's immediate family, whether tickets are specified in the employee's contract, and how many tickets are available. If tickets are available, it is recommended to offer each employee complimentary tickets to all regular season home games equal to the number in their immediate family or four, whichever is greater.

Coaches

Complimentary tickets have become a standard item in a head coach's contract. Make sure the ticket director knows how many tickets and in what locations they were guaranteed in an official contract. A copy of the contract should be kept on file for auditing purposes. The number of tickets guaranteed can vary greatly from school to school or team to team. For associate and assistant coaches, tickets are typically tiered, with coordinators receiving more complimentary tickets than an assistant coach. Coaches typically receive more tickets for their sport than for other sports. For other sports, they can default to the same policy as department staff.

Entertainment

Special groups performing or making half-time or pre-game presentations may be issued complimentary tickets. In this type of situation, it is recommended that only the individuals actually performing be admitted for free. Guests of these individuals would need to purchase tickets. Bringing in groups is often part of the marketing and ticket sales plan. Make sure the marketing staff understands the complimentary ticket policy and does not over-promise.

Student-Athletes

Complimentary tickets for a NCAA student-athlete are highly regulated by the NCAA. The NCAA manual should be consulted to ensure compliance before setting a policy. Per current NCAA regulations, each student-athlete is allowed four complimentary admissions per event in his or her designated sport ("NCAA Division I Manual," 2009). Complimentary admissions are provided only by a pass list for the individuals designated by the student-athlete. "Hard tickets" are not issued, meaning the student-athlete is never in possession of an actual ticket, and recipients of the complimentary tickets cannot receive their tickets until the day of the game.

Student-athletes may not receive payment for complimentary admissions nor exchange them for any item of value. Student-athletes are allowed to transfer their allotments to another student-athlete if desired. For instance, if Student-Athlete A is not using his four complimentary tickets for this Saturday's game, he can allow one of his teammates to use them. The individual utilizing the complimentary admission must present identification to the person supervising the use of the pass list at the appropriate admission gate and sign the pass list. The individual is then provided with a ticket stub, directed to a specific reserved seating area, or treated as a general admission ticket holder.

Prospective Student-Athletes/Recruits

The NCAA has very specific guidelines for the issuing of complimentary tickets to recruits. The NCAA manual should be consulted prior to creating a policy. Currently, during the official visit to the university campus, complimentary admissions may be issued for the exclusive use of the prospective student-athlete and his or her family, guardian, or spouse. On an unofficial campus visit, a maximum of three complimentary admissions to a campus athletic event are allowed for the prospect and those accompanying the prospect. The guests of the prospect do not have to be the parent, guardian, or spouse as they do on an official visit.

All requests for complimentary tickets for a recruit should be submitted in writing. The request should specify the name of the recruit, the event he or she is to attend, whether the visit is an unofficial or an official campus visit, and whether the recruit is to be seated by general admission in the student section or by reserved seating. The request should be submitted to the ticket office at least 24 hours in advance of the scheduled event to allow ample time for preparation of the pass list, as all recruit admissions must be administered through a pass list and not through hard tickets, similarly to student-athlete complimentary tickets.

Charities

A ticket office will receive numerous requests to donate tickets. Requests can range from elementary school carnivals to cancer research auctions. A formal policy should be developed. For auditing purposes, requests should be submitted in writing and kept on file. A sample form is shown in Figure 10.4 ("Request," 2009). Forms can be tailored to fit specific organizations. If working in college athletics, a compliance officer should sign off on any donation requests prior to approval in order to avoid any potential NCAA violations. When developing a policy, consider limiting the number of tickets donated per year to charities, being consistent with how many are donated per request, limiting the location to general admission, and issuing a voucher versus hard tickets.

NIU

Print Form | Submit by Email

REQUEST FOR ATHLETIC MEMORABILIA

Event Sponsor Information:

Event Name ____ **Contact Person** ____ Contact Phone# ____

Address (city,state,zip) ____

Date & Time of Event ____ Location of Event ____

Organization/Recipient:

☐ NIU ☐ Charitable ☐ Educational/School ☐ Community Service/Non-Profit

Memorabilia Request:

☐ FOOTBALL ☐ BASKETBALL ☐ W. BASKETBALL Other ____

Type of Memorabilia (Please note: a $30 invoice will be sent to organizations requesting an autographed game ball. Please add a self-addressed stamped envelope for schedule card requests).

◯ Autographed Game Ball ☐ Poster (free) ☐ Season Tickets ☐ Single Game Tickets ☐ Schedule Card (free)

Please answer the below questions:

1. For what type of activity will this item be used? ____
2. Will money be raised and who will the proceeds benefit? ____
3. What is the deadline for receiving the item? ____
4. Will there be any commercial sponsorship or co-sponsorship for your event? ☐ YES ☐ NO
5. Will there be any advertisement or promotion of a commercial agency? ☐ YES ☐ NO

IF SUBMITTING THIS FORM AND REQUEST BY FAX, PLEASE FAX TO: NIU ATHLETICS @ 815-753-8887

Recipient Reminders:

Recipients of any donated item are required to send a letter to NIU Athletics acknowledging the donation was received and the amount of money the item raised. Thank you in advance for your willingness to cooperate with this request. Please note: proceeds may not benefit a high school or a high school athletic program (including students in the 8th grade).

PLEASE FAX THIS LETTER: **NIU MARKETING, Amanda Benzine @ 815-753-0639 or email: abenzine@niu.edu**

Approval Signatures:

FOR ATHLETIC DEPARTMENT USE ONLY

Signature of Senior Associate Athletic Director: ____ Date ____

NCAA Bylaw 12.5.1.1 Institutional, Charitable, Educational, or Nonprofit Promotions: A member institution or recognized entity thereof (e.g., fraternity, sorority, or student government organization), a member conference, or a noninstitutional charitable, educational, or nonprofit agency may use a student-athlete's name, picture, or appearance to support its charitable or educational activities or to support activities considered incidental to the student-athlete's participation in intercollegiate athletics, provided: The student-athlete receives written approval to participate from the director of athletics.

Signature of Director of Athletics: ____ Date ____

FIGURE 10.4. Sample Donation Request Form

INCIDENT REPORTS

Although we like to think that events will occur without incident, that rarely happens. A ticket office often becomes the place where fans and patrons will go with questions, problems, or concerns. It is usually a centrally located area that everyone is familiar with and that is staffed throughout the event. Incidents can range from a lost child to someone who has fallen and is injured. Whatever the incident, a process must be in place on how to handle situations. More than likely, an event management staff member will need to be called to handle the situation. However, the ticket office can assist with knowing the correct steps to take. Having an incident report form readily available will help a staff member gather the correct information. A sample form is in Figure 10.5 ("Event Incident Report," 2009).

EVENT INCIDENT REPORT

DATE OF EVENT:____________________ **TIME OF INCIDENT:**__________**am/pm**
ON-SITE SUPERVISOR:____________________ **VENUE:**____________________

SPORT:	BSE	BB-m	BB-w	CC	Cheer	FB
	GO-m	GO-w	GYM	SB	SOC-m	SOC-w
	TN-m	TN-w	T/F	VB	WR	

EVENT TYPE:	Camp	CHAMPS	Clinic	Competition
	Fundraising	Practice	Rental	Other__________

Incident(s) and action taken:______________________________

Relevant names and contact information:______________________________

Follow-up action needed:______________________________

REPORT COMPLETED BY: ____________________ **TITLE**____________________
SIGNATURE____________________ **DATE:**____________________
CONTACT INFORMATION PHONE: (_____)__________ **EMAIL**____________________

Submit the completed form to the event manager

Figure 10.5. Sample Incident Report Form

CHAPTER SUMMARY

Creating and writing policies for any ticket office, whether it be for a theater, professional team, or intercollegiate athletics team, requires more than simply putting something in writing. It requires looking at multiple factors from multiple perspectives and addressing as many of those factors as possible before implementing any policy. Taking time in the creation process will eliminate problems during the implementation stage.

Although not every possible scenario has been addressed in this chapter, nor every policy, students should now at least have a sense of what goes into creating policies.

LEARNING ACTIVITY

1. In theory, a loyalty point system should reward the most dedicated fans. Read the bios of the three fans below and rank in order who should get the tickets for the BCS Championship game.

   Joe Fan – Joe has been a football season ticket holder for 10 years. Each year, including the current year, he makes the minimum $500 donation to the booster club to maintain his seats and parking location. He played football at the institution but never received his degree.

   Jane Fan – Jane has been a women's basketball season ticket holder for 20 years. She is an alumna of the institution and donates $1,000 each year, including the current year, to the booster club. She donated $5,000 to the women's basketball locker room renovation project five years ago to get her name on one of the lockers.

   Jim Fan – Jim is an alumnus of the institution and has just recently purchased season tickets. This will be his second year as a season ticket holder, but he has purchased season tickets for football, men's basketball, and women's basketball. His first year as a season ticket holder he donated $500 to the booster club. The second year he increased to $1,000. However, he has also made a pledge on the new football end zone facility for $100,000.

   Now, use the sample loyalty point system from this chapter and calculate the points for Joe, Jane, and Jim. Did you reach the same conclusion? What if only one of them could get tickets? Is the system fair?

11

Internships and Job Preparation

Vicky Martin and James T. Reese, Jr.

LEARNING OBJECTIVES

Upon completion of this chapter, students should be able to discuss strategies for a successful career in ticket operations, develop and write an effective cover letter and résumé, develop a database of contacts through effective networking, secure an internship and a job interview, and use professionalism within sport.

KEY TERMS

cover letter, follow-up letter, jobs, internships, interview, portfolio, résumé

INTRODUCTION

Finding an internship or full-time job in ticket operations is a demanding task but, once achieved, can prove to be extremely rewarding and fulfilling. This chapter will introduce barriers that may be faced, as well as specific tools and techniques that will help increase a person's marketability within ticket operations. Furthermore, it will provide techniques for how to write an effective cover letter and résumé, develop a networking database, secure an internship and job, and communicate what the industry requires regarding professionalism within the sport industry.

The recommended strategy for success in ticket operations is to fully understand the position and the specific skill requirements. Being diligent enough to research each position and the requirements for that specific position is important. Having sales experience and a professional appearance is also becoming extremely important to success within ticket operations. Other skills imperative to success are excellent verbal and non-verbal communication skills; sales experience; computer and organization skills; and having maturity, energy, and enthusiasm for the position.

To fully prepare for a job or internship within the sport industry, students must start planning early. The building of a résumé is crucial. Volunteering for a variety of sport-related jobs will enable a student to effectively build a résumé. Remember that experience will yield an internship, and the internship will aid in obtaining a job. To be effective in ticket operations, sales experience is a must. If a person can sell, he/

she will always have a job. Being able to sell will help a person get a foot in the door. In addition, a career in ticket sales provides significant income earning potential. The remainder of the chapter will provide information on how to be successful in a search for an internship or job position within ticket operations.

HOW TO WRITE EMPLOYMENT DOCUMENTS

The cover letter and résumé are personal marketing tools and are often the first glimpse that a prospective employer will have of a person. They reach the employer's desk long before the person gets the chance to make a personal impression, so the person must be sure that he/she shows himself/herself in a positive light. Employers spend, on average, 15 seconds looking at a résumé; therefore, the résumé must quickly catch the employer's attention. Even if the applicant has a limited amount of work experience, appeal can be accomplished through effective visual design and strategic inclusion of relevant skills, awards, and activities.

A person should develop and maintain a base résumé and cover letter, then use a filing system and update the résumé a few times a year. Every time a person does something career related (e.g., conference attendance, volunteer opportunities) a note should be placed within the file so he/she will remember to update the résumé and cover letter.

Cover Letter

The cover letter must be informative and professional and should enhance, but not be identical to, the résumé. Each cover letter should address the specific requirements of the organization for which the person is applying. A person must ensure that the cover letter is addressed to a specific individual with his or her official business title and address. If this information does not appear on the application form, the title and address can be found through research by either a telephone call to the organization or through the Internet. In an effective cover letter, there must be an introduction, a body of content, and a closing paragraph. A person should always list what is important and why and provide information about qualities and experience that the company is seeking in a prospective employee, not the information that the person wishes to provide. Attention to detail is critical; a cover letter must be well written and error free.

Résumé

The résumé is a personal marketing tool which allows a person to make contact with a prospective employer and may, therefore, help in obtaining an interview and possibly a job. By today's standards, a résumé is typically one page in length. As mentioned earlier, a résumé is often the first glimpse that a prospective employer will have at an applicant. On average, 15 seconds is spent looking at a résumé. Even if there is a limited amount of work experience, a thorough, well-written résumé will open doors. Any error on the résumé could cause it to end up being thrown away. Figure 11.1 illustrates a few résumé tips, while Figure 11.2 provides a sample résumé (Liberty University Career Center, 2010f).

434-592-4109
careers@liberty.edu
www.liberty.edu/career

Key Points: **Employers spend an average of 15 seconds looking at a resume.**

- Make resume professional, attractive, and easy to read.
- Place most important information first.
- **Bold,** *italicize*, CAPITALIZE, or underline critical facts.
- Stress results, skills and accomplishments rather than performed duties.
- Use the correct tense when describing past/present activities.
- Proofread for misspelled words and grammatical errors.
- Use your resume to market yourself and get an interview.
- Choose headers to highlight your individual strengths. (Leadership Skills, Computer Skills, Relevant Coursework)
- Begin sentences with action words.
- Avoid personal pronouns (I, me, my).
- Always include a cover letter when submitting a resume.
- Customize your resume each and every time you apply so that you highlight the jobs, skills, volunteer work, and additional experience that are relevant to the job you seek.

BUILDING YOUR RESUME

Heading
- Include your name, address, phone (include area code), e-mail address, and homepage or online portfolio link (if applicable).
- Make sure to use the same style heading for all pages of your resume packet: cover letter, resume, references.

Objective or Profile
- An objective is a brief summary statement of who you are and what your purpose is. Clearly, you're looking for a job so don't state the obvious. Instead, use keywords from a specific job description that you are applying for or skills that define you so this stands out.
- A profile can be a bullet point list or summary paragraph that lets the reader know your top skills and abilities from the very top of the page. This allows you to target specific areas toward a specific job or incorporate certifications or coursework in which you've been trained.
- How do you choose which one? You don't need both so look at what the job is seeking and identify what skills you have that most align with what the employer wants. Use the one that seems to best fit the job you're applying for.

Education
- Name of School, City & State, Years attended (or anticipated graduation date), Degree, Major, Minor, Specialization.
- Summarize your educational achievements (colleges attended, locations, graduation dates, certificates, academic majors, minors, and course concentrations). You may include international study experience here or in an "International Experiences" section.
- Start with most recent degree awarded and work backwards.
- Do not list high school or earlier education unless exceptional or relevant in some way.
- GPA is optional. Recommend 3.5 or higher, which can either be a cumulative GPA, major GPA, or both.
- Include any relevant coursework (specific to your objective) or training (laboratory techniques, computer skills). This may also be included in your Professional Profile above.

Experience
- Name of Employer/Company, City & State, Dates Employed, Job Title or Meaningful Job Description.
- You may summarize any experience relevant to your stated job objective, whether paid or unpaid, with a summary statement.
- Highlight/Bullet Point skills developed, achievements and accomplishments, or quantifiable results. Action words are always good!
- Begin with your most recent experience and work backwards. This can be in one section or divided based on relevancy.
- Focus on skills (communication, analysis, teamwork, research, leadership, management) and accomplishments.

Activities & Community Services (Optional)
- Emphasize any significant activities you participate in outside of work (community service, extra-curriculars). Quantify what you do with the role you play, hours involved, personal investment, or other ways to show an employer more about your character and personality.
- List activities that demonstrate: leadership ability, initiative, good communication skills, and perseverance. Highlight leadership roles.

Honors and Awards (Optional)
- If award or organization is well known, listing honors/ awards may be sufficient; if not, write out identifying information/qualifications.

Languages (May also be under Professional Profile or Education)
- If you include languages (either under "skills" or "languages" sections), be sure to accurately represent skill level:
- Basic ability – completed coursework in language. Literate – can read and write language. Conversational – can speak language. Proficient – can read write and speak understandably. Fluent - can read, write and speak with similar skill to native speaker.

References
- Generally, you DO NOT need to state "references available upon request". If employers want your references, they will ask.
- You will need to create a separate reference page that should include the person's name, title, address, email, and phone number.

FIGURE 11.1. Résumé Tips

Susie Sample
123 Liberty Lane
Lynchburg, Virginia 24501
Phone: 434-582-2000 Email: ssample@liberty.edu

PROFESSIONAL SKILLS PROFILE: Advertising & Public Relations

- Conducted market research to create advertising campaigns.
- Performed statistical analysis of research data for communication campaigns.
- Studied professional communication and methods for utilizing media in advertising.
- Trained in the principles of direct marketing communication and advertising design.
- Proficient in Microsoft Work, EXCEL, PowerPoint, Adobe Indesign, and Photoshop.

PROFESSIONAL INTERNSHIP & FIELD EXPERIENCE

Selah Yearbook (August 2008–May 2009) at Liberty University

Marketing Team (January-May 2009): Part-time position in the practicum class as part of the marketing team. Worked in collaboration with eight student peers to develop marketing campaigns to promote yearbook sales. Actively contributed to the development of promotional materials and scripts. Team produced record sales for the school.

Copy Writer (August–December 2008): Volunteered part-time to research, interview, and write creative stories that accurately depicted campus events and people. Managed all aspects of story production while adhering to strict deadlines. Contributed more than 10 articles and submissions for inclusion in the 2009 publication.

Prototype Advertising Intern (Summer 2008): Full-time temporary internship position accumulating more than 360 hours of hands-on training under professional staff. Developed ad campaigns for local businesses.

EDUCATION

Bachelor of Science (BS) in Communication Studies, Liberty University, Lynchburg, VA, May 2008. Specialization in Advertising and Public Relations.

EMPLOYMENT EXPERIENCE

Assistant Manager, Chick-fil-A, Lynchburg, Virginia, 2004 to Present
Promoted from cashier to Assistant Manager, coordinating operations and personnel throughout high-volume operation to ensure consistently high-quality customer service.

Source: Liberty University Career Center

FIGURE 11.2. Sample Résumé

Thank-You Letter

Once the interview is completed, it is imperative that the applicant write a letter of thanks to the organization. The letter should be handwritten and should cover areas of interest that were covered during the interview. Taking the time to write a thank-you letter will not only demonstrate your consideration for the interview process but will

Lee Thompson
1908 Morrie Street
New York, NY 02858
May 20, 2010

Ms. Marsha Robinson
Vice President, Strategic Development
XYZ Corporation
8000 West Broadway
New York, NY 02888

Dear Ms. Robinson:

It was a pleasure meeting with you on Monday, May 18th to discuss the Director of Business Development position. I appreciated the time you spent discussing your preliminary business development plans. I was impressed with the professionalism of your organization and the strategies currently in place.

As we discussed, I am extremely confident that I can make a substantial contribution to your strategic development efforts based on my past accomplishments:

- Successfully developed and implemented strategic marketing plans
- Developed strategic partnerships resulting in $24 million in revenue
- Opened international markets
- Managed a team of 10 with only 4% turnover over 5 years

Together, I believe we can achieve the company objectives within your time frame. With the outstanding products of XYZ, your dynamic team, and my experience, we can lead XYZ toward a prosperous future. Enclosed is an additional copy of my résumé for your convenience. If you have any questions, please feel free to contact me any time. I look forward to your positive response.

Sincerely,
Your signature here
Lee Thompson

FIGURE 11.3. Sample Interview Follow-Up Letter

also demonstrate that you are serious about the desired position for which you interviewed. The thank-you letter will also serve to reinforce qualifications and interest in the position advertised. Figure 11.3 illustrates an example of an acceptable thank-you letter.

List of References

Providing a list of references (see Figure 11.4) would also serve you well. It is much more convenient for the employer to see a list of references, so that he/she can easily access the names and telephone numbers. It is more time consuming for the employer to contact the interviewee after the interview for a list of references if all that was stated on the résumé was that "references available upon request" (Liberty University Career Center, 2010d).

Steven Z. Sample

Local: 2003 Riverside Dr.
Lynchburg, VA 24502
434-555-0555
ssample@liberty.edu

Permanent: 1102 West Street
Seattle, WA 77777
206-777-0777
sample@aol.com

References

Mr. John Dees
Vice President
Ross Brothers
1111 Main Street
Lynchburg, VA 24502
434-222-2222

Mr. John Haire
President and CEO
Maxwell Corporation
3333 Maxwell Drive
Seattle, WA 77777
206-888-8888

Mr. Mark Hine
Vice President of Student Life
Liberty University
1971 University Blvd.
Lynchburg, VA 24502
434-582-2000

Dr. Janet Smith
School of Business and Government
Liberty University
1971 University Blvd.
Lynchburg, VA 24502
434-582-2000
(Liberty University Career Center, 2010c)

FIGURE 11.4. Sample References List

THE IMPORTANCE OF CREATING A PERSONAL PORTFOLIO

A personal portfolio is considered to be a living and changing collection of documents that will reflect accomplishments, skills, experiences, and attributes. A portfolio will not take the place of a résumé but rather highlight accomplishments and skills that a person can offer in the chosen field. A portfolio allows a person to set himself/herself apart from other applicants by providing the opportunity to be more personal and creative in expanding on and exhibiting skills, knowledge, projects, and experiences. The goal of a portfolio is to highlight specific skills and abilities in the classroom, workplace, and extracurricular activities.

Key tips for a successful portfolio:

- A portfolio is a helpful addition to any field, as it can take the experience a person has gained and visually show an employer that specific experience.
- A portfolio should be visually appealing and easy to read because it will be judged partially on the overall look and layout.
- Decide which items to include in the portfolio; consider its purpose and value in communicating the intended message. Ensure that all documents that are placed in the portfolio are relevant to the interview and will help sell the applicant to the employer.
- Customize the documents to highlight proficiencies in the required skills of the job sought.
- Include only samples of the finest work.
- A portfolio will never expire; a person is able to add to and edit it for as long as he/she has a career.

Suggested contents of a portfolio (Liberty University Career Center, 2010d):

- Table of Contents
- Résumé
- Official copy of a transcript; scholarship letters; standardized test scores; writing samples; computer and software skills; PowerPoint presentations; letters of commendation/appreciation; etc.
- Conferences and workshops attended; websites created; events organized and worked; samples of flyers; completed class projects; newsletters or brochures.
- Completion of project by a deadline; joining a new organization; running for an office; leadership recognition; recommendations from teachers/supervisors; school transcripts showing good attendance; certificate of appreciation for a service learning project; extracurricular activities; personal quality skills verification that the person works well with peers and supervisors in making sound and critical decisions, which add value to the workplace.

- Evidence of work readiness skills, through a paying job or volunteer work. Examples of experience to include are business cards from past employers, a list of skills relating to jobs, descriptions of projects completed, and/or pictures of the person on the job.

There are two kinds of portfolios: electronic and paper. Below are some key tips on portfolio building from the Liberty University Career Center (2010d) that will help a person set himself/herself apart from other applicants:

- Have a professional case to hold the portfolio
- Put loose papers in paper protectors
- Use good-quality paper (preferably bright glossy white or professional résumé paper)
- Keep it organized; don't make it cluttered
- Keep it short, no more than 25 pages
- Include a résumé
- Use dividers to separate sections (a person is able to be extremely creative here)
- Pick only the best work for the samples, whether writing samples, ads, graphic arts, photographs, school projects, group presentations, etc.
- Include recommendation letters and references
- Include any awards and honors given
- Include transcripts and degrees or licenses and certificates (when appropriate)
- Include any military records, awards, or badges (if applicable)
- Take it to the Career Center and have them look over it
- Never leave the portfolio. No matter if they want to show it to someone else, give them a copy or the website address of an electronic portfolio
- Tell the employer you have brought a portfolio during the interview so that you can show them
- Make sure to schedule enough time in an interview to present the portfolio

IMPORTANCE OF PROPER COMMUNICATION

Today's communication is dramatically different from the more traditional forms of communication (letters and telephone calls). Other forms of communication have now been added. Email has generally replaced letter writing, and text messaging is being used in place of telephone communication. How people communicate with prospective employers is crucial to their success within the industry.

The ability to communicate effectively through all resources is becoming a critical aspect of the ability to correspond on a business level. One of the most hazardous elements of communication is the inability to communicate expression or tone. A message can often be misinterpreted, even though no offense was intended. By using proper language, a person will definitely convey a professional image.

Appropriate Voice Messages

Remember to have an appropriate voice message, either on a cell phone or home phone. Using slang, swearing, or inappropriate music will send an unsavory message to the caller about who a person is before the caller has met the person. This may, in some instances, cost the person an interview with that company. If people share a residence, they should be sure to let others know an employer may be contacting them. How roommates respond to phone calls could affect a person in the hiring process.

Grammar and Spelling

Proper grammar and spelling in email messages and letters demonstrates early on that a person is a professional within the field. Below are some keys to effective email etiquette (Reese, 2009):

- Be aware of who the audience is (business or friend).
- Always state the purpose of the email.
- Remember to be concise and to the point; answer all questions asked.
- Do not write paragraphs using all capital letters; this is considered bad email etiquette.
- It is imperative that proper spelling, grammar, and punctuation are used.
- Always read the email and check grammar and spelling before sending it.
- Acknowledge receipt of an email in a timely fashion (in fewer than two days).
- Remember not to forward jokes, personal items, and inappropriate content via email.
- Always show respect.

THE TELEPHONE INTERVIEW

A job interview is an organized meeting used to evaluate a potential employee by a recruiter for prospective employment at a company. Most job interviews last about one hour. Job interviews are usually preceded by the evaluation of a résumé and a phone interview.

A common initial interview is the telephone interview. This form of interview is common when candidates do not live near an employer or when an employer does not have sufficient resources to interview many candidates face to face. Telephone interviews have the advantage of keeping costs low for both the employer and the candidate. Most phone interviews last for fewer than 30 minutes and feature a mix of questions about competency, the résumé, work experience, and education.

It is important to adequately prepare for a telephone interview. Practice is always beneficial, especially if a person has not worked in an office setting before. It is also important to find out as much as possible about the organization and job role before any type of interview. Potential interviewees should visit the organization's website and competitor websites and keep up to date on industry specific issues. They should also research the size of the company, its structure, products and services, markets, competitors, and future plans. Planning for possible questions that may be asked in the telephone interview is also important. Also, a person should spend time thinking up questions to ask the interviewer. Asking questions shows interest in the company and position. Finally, interviewees should make sure to keep a copy of the résumé, cover letter, application form, and any other notes they may have made on the company in question.

Telephone interviews are typically conducted by a member of a firm's human resource department or outsourced to a specialist organization. Questions will usually focus on résumé, work experience, academic history, motivations for applying to the firm in question, the particular industry and job role, knowledge of the firm itself (e.g., competitors, global reach, future plans), skills, qualifications, and competencies (Liberty University Career Center, 2010a).

Examples of possible interview questions:

- Tell me about yourself.
- Tell me about your background and accomplishments.
- What are your strengths? Weaknesses?
- How would you describe your most recent job performance?
- What interests you about our company?
- How do you stay professionally current?
- What outside activities are most significant to your personal development?
- What do you know about our company?
- Why are you looking to change positions?
- Where do you see yourself in five years?
- What are the best and worst things your boss would say about you?
- What five adjectives best describe you?
- What concerns do you have regarding this position?
- Why should we hire you?

The day the telephone interview arrives, the candidate needs to be as professional and presentable as one would be in a face-to-face situation from the moment the interviewer calls. Wearing interview-style clothes may also help. The interviewee should find a quiet place to answer the phone and study some relevant material on the company and industry before the scheduled call so that he/she is focused on the interview. Remember never to use slang in the interview. A telephone interview begins from the moment a person answers the telephone and ends only when the conversation, questions, and goodbyes have been completed. Remember, the interviewer does not want to be interrupted during a telephone interview. A person must charge his cell phone on the day of the interview. If the phone cuts out or starts beeping during the conversation, there is a risk of irritating the interviewer or losing a train of thought. Do not be worried to take a little time to consider a question or response before answering.

Part of the reason why firms choose to conduct a telephone interview is to find out how interested candidates are about working at their company. It is important to be enthusiastic throughout a telephone conversation. The interviewer may be able to tell a candidate at the end of the conversation if the interviewer would like to see the candidate for a face-to-face interview. If the interviewer does not, there is no harm in the interviewee asking them when he/she might hear from the company regarding the next interview. Then the interviewee needs to thank the interviewer and ask for further details, such as when, where, and with whom a subsequent interview will be; if there is anything the interviewee should bring to the interview; what the interview format will be; how many people will be competing for the position; and a summary of the crucial skills and competencies that the employer is looking for in an employee.

THE IN-PERSON INTERVIEW

Before the interview, the following tips will make the process less stressful and give a person confidence for the future interview:

- Prepare and practice in advance of the scheduled interview with friends or professors.
- Do a mock interview at the university Career Center.
- Prepare questions to ask the employer.
- Prepare interview materials (e.g., resume, portfolio, letters of recommendation).
- Confirm date, time, and location of interview a few days before the scheduled interview.
- Request the name of the person who will be conducting the interview.
- Travel the route a day before to account for time, parking, and directions.
- Research the company. Important things to know are (Liberty University Career Center, 2010a):
  - The sport organization's name, products, services, and a brief history of the team or athletic department.
  - The job description of the position for which the applicant is being interviewed.
  - When the day of the interview arrives, be sure to have a professional attitude all day.

THE DAY OF THE INTERVIEW

- Get enough sleep to be fully awake during the interview, and wake up early enough to have adequate time to dress unhurriedly.
- Always arrive seven to ten minutes early. Travel the route one day before the interview to become familiar with the amount of time that it will take to get to the interview.
- Eat beforehand so that your stomach does not growl during the interview.
- Rehearse opening and closing statements. Always use the interviewer's full name, and pronounce the name correctly. If you are unable to sell yourself, the interviewer may not believe you will have the ability to sell tickets.
- Dress professionally for the interview.
- Greet the interviewer with a smile; be polite and friendly. A firm handshake is required.
- Bring extra copies of the résumé, transcript, references, and examples of previous work/projects or sales performance.
- Look alert and enthusiastic. Make sure the good impression at the beginning of the interview remains just as good throughout and at the end. Many will remember the beginning and end of events better than the middle.
- Rehearse your voice. Dropping it at the end of sentences gives an air of confidence and credibility.
- Maintain eye contact throughout the interview.
- Be professional in all that is done and said.
- Be respectful of the interviewer's time. Try to find out information through research.
- Respect the interviewer's point of view, even if you do not agree. Try to stay neutral or welcoming to all perspectives.
- When the interviewer prompts a questions, be prepared with carefully thought-out answers.
- Take time to formulate concise answers to the questions asked. Avoid long rambling answers.
- Some interviews take place over lunch. This may serve as a test to view your behavior in ordering of food and how your table manners are in a public setting. During the interview, it is advisable that you do not smoke, chew gum, drink alcohol, or eat anything messy or with strong flavors (e.g., garlic), regardless of what the interviewer is doing. Always try to let the person paying for the meal order first, therefore leaving the option to order a dessert if they do.

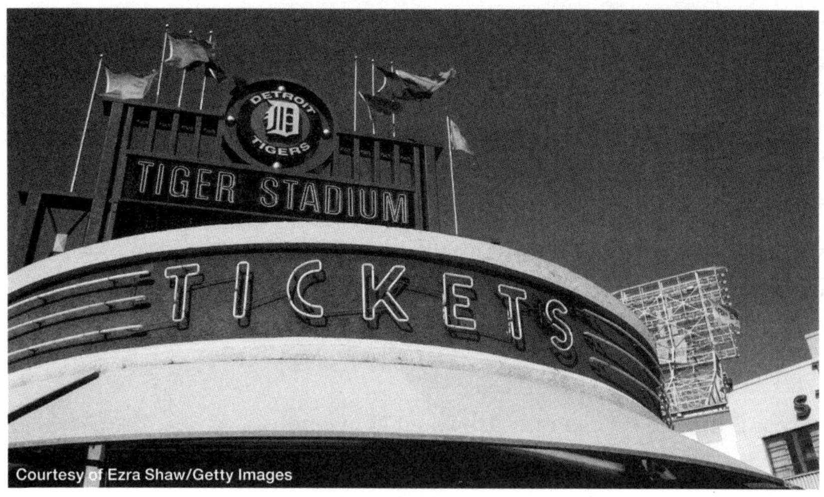

Courtesy of Ezra Shaw/Getty Images

- After a successful interview, be sure to send a handwritten thank-you note to the interviewer within 24 hours. (Liberty University Career Center, 2010a)

THINGS TO AVOID DURING AN INTERVIEW

- Arriving just in time or late.
- Using slang, text language, or profanity.
- Chewing gum or yawning during the interview.
- Fidgeting, playing with hair, or biting nails.
- Criticizing past supervisors or employers.
- Discussing intimate personal issues.
- Cracking jokes and using first names (unless asked to).
- Answering questions using "you know," "like," "umm," etc.
- Appearing desperate in wanting the advertised position. (Reese, 2009)

WHAT EMPLOYERS ARE NOT SUPPOSED TO ASK DURING AN INTERVIEW

In a perfect world, this is not something anyone would need to worry about. Unfortunately, not all people involved in the interview process are properly trained. There are a few very specific things potential employers are not supposed to ask during the interview process. Questions related to the following topics should not be asked (Doyle, 2006):

- Religion or religious affiliation.
- Ethnicity or nationality. (e.g. Where were you born? What is your native language?)
- Race.

- Marital or family status. (e.g. Do you have any children? Are you planning to have children? Will you keep working if you get pregnant? Do you have a boyfriend or girlfriend?)
- Military Service.
- Age, unless trying to determine if the applicant is an adult.
- Physical condition. May not ask about any physical or mental illnesses, disabilities, drug or alcohol rehabilitation, trips to hospital, worker's compensation claims, or whether you smoke or consume alcohol.
- Sexual preference.
- Arrest record. Employers can only ask about convictions.
- Financial status. May not ask if you have ever declared bankruptcy, if your wages have been garnished, whether you own or rent, etc. However, potential employers may ask financial questions if they are specifically relevant to a respective position.

If you are asked one of the above questions, you should try to always answer the intent of the question or you can try tactfully to change the direction of the conversation. Another option, in order to avoid the question, is to change the topic of the conversation (Doyle, 2006).

There is one additional thing to keep in mind during a job interview. Although potential employers may not ask questions about the topic areas identified above, they may ask follow-up questions on these topics if the interviewee brings them up during the interview or lists them on a résumé. In other words, if the door is open, the interviewer may legally walk through it.

SAMPLE QUESTIONS TO ASK AT AN INTERVIEW

Be prepared to ask questions! Most interviews end with the interviewer asking, "Do you have any questions?" Ask intelligent questions that show you are informed and well prepared (Liberty University Career Center, 2010g).

- Would you describe a typical work day and tasks I would be completing?
- How will I be trained or introduced to the job?
- Why is this ticketing position open?
- How often has this position been filled in the past five years? What were the main reasons previous employees left?
- What would you like the next person who fills this position to do differently?
- What are some objectives you would like to see fulfilled in this job?
- What is most pressing? What would you like to have done in the next three months?
- What are some of the long-term objectives you would like to see completed?

- What are some of the more difficult problems one would have to face in this position? How do you think these could best be handled?
- What type of support does this position receive in terms of people, finances, etc.?
- What freedom would I have in determining my own work objectives, deadlines, and methods of measurement?
- What advancement opportunities are available for someone who is successful in this position and within what time frame?
- In what way has this organization been most successful in terms of services and various ticket packages over the years?
- What significant position duties changes, company infrastructure changes, or ticketing policy changes do you foresee in the next year?
- How is one evaluated in this position? What are the opportunities for growth and promotion in the ticket office and within the organization?
- What accounts for success within the company? Season ticket renewal rate, overall ticket sales, etc?
- I want this job. Would you consider hiring me for a 30-day trial period so that I could prove myself both in a sales and administrative capacity?
- What could I say or do to convince you to offer me this job?

These questions are presented only as interviewing guidelines. They are meant to help prepare for an interview. Some questions may or may not be appropriate for the particular interview situation. Remember to relax, go with the flow, and before you know it, you will be in your next job.

As a follow up to the interview, it is appropriate to ask the employer when he/she expects to make a decision. Be sure to alert listed references that you have gone for an interview, as well as sending the specifics about the job and a résumé. This will enable them to know how to answer questions if called by the company for a reference. It is important at this stage to be patient because the hiring process is usually longer than the employer expects. While waiting to hear whether you have the position, continue to job hunt. If you do not receive the position, do not burn bridges, as this is another opportunity to continue to develop your networking database.

PROFESSIONAL DRESS

A good image produces a strong first impression. First impressions are extremely important, so an interviewee has to consider what impression he/she wishes to make. Professional dress for men is a white or striped shirt and tie with a dark suit. For women, suits are best, but a professional dress is also acceptable. Even though the company's environment may be casual, for the interview, it is recommended that people always dress using the conservative approach.

The following is considered unacceptable dress for the interview process:

- Wrinkled clothing, golf shirts, shorts, rope belts, baseball caps
- Heavy cologne/perfume (no cologne or perfume is best)
- Scuffed-up shoes, flip flops, sneakers
- Any form of seductive wear
- Heavy makeup, excessive jewelry
- Unshaved face, messy or uncut hair

RESOURCES FOR TICKET INTERNSHIPS AND JOBS

Websites

- TeamWork Online: www.teamworkonline.com
  - This website provides links to jobs with sports teams.
  - Under "Career Help," you will find sample job titles and descriptions and links to career fairs.
- Sports Careers: www.sportscareers.com
- Women's Sports Jobs: www.womensportsjobs.com
- SR Sports Jobs: www.srsportsjobs.com
  - This is a site you must pay to access.
- Work in Sports: www.workinsports.com
  - This is a site that you must pay to access (weekly or monthly).
- Game Face: www.gamefacesportsjobs.com
  - This is a site you must pay to access.
- International Ticketing Association (INTIX): www.intix.org
  - INTIX provides job announcements with paid membership.
- Jobs In Sports: www.jobsinsports.com
  - This is a site you must pay to access.
- Individual team organization websites.

CHAPTER SUMMARY

Being prepared and displaying professionalism from the initial phone interview to a face-to-face meeting with a prospective employer is crucial to securing a full-time position. What one says will speak volumes about integrity and professional stature in the field. We are all salespeople, marketing our chosen profession to the public every day of the week. Therefore, completing your degree requirements with excellence and continuing your education will only strengthen your future employment opportunities. Additional information can be found from your university career center, as well as a wealth of information found on the Internet allows for research possibilities so that you will never be unprepared for the interview process. Remember to effectively and efficiently research, as this will be critical to your success in securing a job in the field of ticket operations or related sport management fields.

LEARNING ACTIVITY

1. Modern technology allows people to prepare for job and internship interviews in ways not convenient in the past—for instance, most cellular phones now have video capability. In preparation for a job or internship interview, your task for this learning activity is to conduct a mock interview with a friend or colleague. Make the environment as realistic as possible by preparing a list of interview questions in advance. You each may see the questions. The purpose of this exercise is not to surprise each other with certain questions but to force you to think on your feet under a stressful situation. Even if you know the questions in advance, if done properly, answering the questions in a structured environment will likely be more challenging than expected. Your goal is to make your mistakes when practicing and not in the actual interview. Dress for the mock interview just as you would for a real interview to make the environment as realistic as possible. Tape the mock interview and review the tape, taking notes and looking at the footage from the perspective of a hiring manager. Make any appropriate changes necessary to give you the best opportunity for a successful interview.

12

Securing a Job in Ticket Operations or Ticket Sales

James T. Reese, Jr. and Vicky Martin

KEY TERMS

close the sale, cover letters, informational interviews, networking, personal branding, practice, product knowledge, references, relationship building, résumé building, sales skills, sales training,

LEARNING OBJECTIVES

Upon completion of this chapter and after successfully implementing the recommendations, students will have developed the skills necessary to secure a job in ticket operations or sport ticket sales.

INTRODUCTION

This chapter is designed to provide readers with the information needed to develop the skills, attitude, and confidence necessary to successfully secure a position in ticket operations or ticket sales. Research indicates that ticketing and sales hiring managers look for similar traits when searching for sales staff (Reese, 2008). Positions in ticket operations are primarily administrative and customer service based, while those in sales deal with ticket distribution. Regardless of position type, those looking to break into ticket operations and ticket sales can use the information in this chapter to prepare for the interview process to gain a competitive advantage over other candidates.

REQUIRED SKILLS

The sport industry is one of the most difficult professions in which to succeed. Many people around the world have a passion for sports, which leads to more applicants for jobs in sports than opportunities. By default, this function of the law of supply and demand results in lower entry salaries and longer hours in sports jobs than entry level positions in many other industries. Breaking into sports is just the first hurdle. Remaining in sports long enough to earn a salary high enough to live on long term or support a family is the real challenge.

Professional sports teams and sport organizations in general use the market to their advantage when searching for employees. The high demand for jobs in sport provides sport organizations with the luxury of a constant pool of potential candidates in the form of interns. Some sport organizations are more organized than others in regard to the search process. Those with established human resource departments utilize training programs, orientations, relationship building techniques, etc. Those choosing to evaluate staff in a more economical way, especially in sales, may place 15 to 20 sales interns in a room full of office cubicles, provide them with a phone and call sheet, then turn them loose to make 100 or more calls a day to see who generates the highest sales volume. Students must be prepared for organizations that are unstructured or perhaps chaotic when looking to break into sports. Those who are ultimately successful in ticket operations or ticket sales typically exhibit some or all of the following 10 skills:

1. **Multi-tasking** – Unfortunately, many jobs in sport and entertainment are understaffed, overworked, and underpaid. This creates an environment where the staff is forced to learn multiple positions and tasks, many of which need to be performed simultaneously. For example, depending on the environment, an employee may be working on an important project for a supervisor or team owner, need to answer the phone, and have a customer at the counter with a question about licensed merchandise. Employees must learn to be constantly interrupted and provide superior customer service with a smile, without it affecting job performance. Research indicates that sport organizations look for entry level candidates who are multi-dimensional and were active in extracurricular activities in college. This demonstrates that they are able to manage multiple tasks and a busy schedule.

2. **Coachable** – The profession of sales has been around for millennia, and there are a variety of different sales training techniques. Research indicates that some hiring managers for sales positions are looking for salespeople they can train to buy into their specific style of sales training (Reese, 2008). Others are interested in salespeople with previous experience to accelerate the learning curve. Regardless of what level of sales training employees bring to a position, they must remember to adapt to the environment and learn the respective sales system at the organization.

3. **Competitive** – Research also indicates that hiring managers are looking for salespeople with a competitive nature (Reese, 2008). This makes sense because sales offices are competitive environments. Some hiring managers specifically look for former athletes when reviewing résumés. Have you ever been told you are too competitive? If so, ticket sales may be the profession for you. Be sure to include any previous athletic participation on a résumé. Mentioning a competitive background may also help in an interview setting.

4. **Pleasant Personality and Fearless** – Extroverts are not the only people successful in sales; however, those who generally enjoy working with people will have a higher probability of success. Fearlessness involves having the ability to deal with constant rejection. Hitters in baseball are considered exceptional if they succeed 30% of the time. The success rate in sales is occasionally much lower. It is sometimes as little as 10%. Salespeople must be able to deal with the roller coaster of emotions that accompanies the sales process. Always remember the anonymous but very powerful saying "every no is one step closer to a yes."
5. **Good Listener** – Developing good listening skills will benefit employees in more than just their careers. One of the biggest mistakes salespeople make is to talk too much and listen too little. Talking during the sales process should be strategic. The goals are to:
   a. determine the needs of the customer in order to present the appropriate product or service;
   b. connect and build a long-term relationship with the customers; and
   c. answer questions and close the sale (i.e., get the customer to buy).

   Remember that employees must learn to balance the amount of time they spend with each customer. If they are spending too much time with customers, they will likely lose sales to colleagues. However, if they spend too little time, they may not build an adequate relationship. Salespeople who are skilled at building long-term relationships and can generate constant repeat business are the people who are typically the most successful in sales.
6. **Poise and Confidence** – Everyone has met people who carry themselves with poise and confidence. Everyone has also met those who are considered confidently obnoxious. There can be a fine line between confidence and arrogance. The goal is to carry oneself in a way that communicates one is good at one's job and genuinely cares about the customers. These are things the employee can control. Remember, customers buy from people they like and trust. The more employees practice and study, the more success they will have and the more confidence they will develop.
7. **Ability to Overcome Objections** – Salespeople are constantly bombarded with objections from customers when attempting to close a sale. The biggest mistake made by young salespeople is the desire to end the sales process after being presented with an objection. This is a natural response in an effort to not push someone past a perceived boundary, which could anger them. However, salespeople must remember that not all objections are legitimate. Some are smokescreens by customers. It is the job of salespeople to ask the right questions to determine if objections are legitimate. Even then, there may be a creative solution to close the sale. For example, price could be an objection

provided by a customer. It is the job of the salesperson to ask the right questions to determine if the correct ticket package is being presented. Otherwise, a salesperson could lose a sale even though there is a package available within the customer's price range. Price may also be presented as an objection, when in reality the person is just too busy to speak. Asking the right questions and demonstrating poise and patience will allow a salesperson to navigate through smokescreens and overcome objections.

8. **Practice Makes Perfect** – Just as athletes spend hours honing their skills on a court or field to become proficient, salespeople must practice a variety of skills to master their craft. The easiest way to accomplish this is through role playing. Role playing, or pretending to make sales calls with colleagues, accomplishes a variety of things. First, it adds an element of stress to an environment, especially when done in front of a group or class. The more people practice their craft in stressful situations, the better they become. When the use of video is incorporated, the process is enhanced further because participants can analyze their performance at the conclusion of the training. Many people are amazed when they watch themselves on tape and can make immediate positive corrections to speech, body language, posture, etc.
9. **Passion for Sports** – Just because a person enjoys playing sports or watching sports on television does not mean he or she is cut out for a career in sports. A job in sports requires a significant number of sacrifices. These sacrifices may be a longer than normal path for career advancement; financial inconvenience; or time away from family on weeknights, weekends, or due to travel. It is important to remember that working in sports or entertainment requires people to work while others are recreating. Those with a true passion for sports and a willingness to make necessary adjustments in lifestyle have the greatest chance of long-term success in the industry (Reese, 2008).
10. **Product Knowledge** – Studying does not end upon graduation—every employee will need to apply the same skills used in high school and college to their careers. As stated earlier, people buy from those they like and trust. By building a base of product knowledge, an employee communicates confidence and competence to customers. Product knowledge will ultimately happen with experience. However, the faster employees learn the products, the more immediate success they will have in sales (Reese, 2008). It is acceptable to ask questions. Just try to ask them once and take good notes. Colleagues will be happy to assist through the learning curve, but no one likes to answer the same questions over and over.

BUILDING A RÉSUMÉ

Perhaps the biggest mistake students interested in working in sports make is not properly building their résumés. As previously mentioned, the field of sports is extremely competitive. Sport organizations routinely receive in excess of a thousand résumés for an entry level position. Keep that in mind when applying for jobs. An applicant cannot fail to meet minimum requirements provided on a position announcement and still expect to be competitive for a position in sports. There are just too many other qualified, and sometimes overqualified, candidates. Students should begin building their résumés as soon as possible. Beginning to gain sport-related work experience as a freshman is not too early.

Many students do not know in which specific area of sports they wish to work early in their academic careers (e.g., sales, marketing, operations, media relations). The best way to determine in what direction a student would like to take a career is to try a variety of sport positions. Be sure to do everything possible to get sales experience. Outside sales (i.e., outbound phone calls or appointments) is best, but even inside sales (e.g., retail) can be valuable as well. Also, the sales experience does not need to be in sport. Many with sales experience in non-sports professions successfully transition to sports. Why is it important to have sales experience on a résumé? Take a look at the majority of position announcements for jobs in sport. One will consistently find that the majority of entry level positions in sport are in the discipline of ticket sales.

Most interscholastic and intercollegiate athletic departments do not have the revenue to adequately staff their departments. This creates an abundance of volunteer opportunities for students to build their résumés. Students should make a list of the areas in which they are most interested and then contact local high schools and colleges to see if any opportunities exist in those areas. They should be sure to give each activity an adequate amount of time in order to experience it fully. If that position does not ignite a passion, they should continue volunteering for a variety of areas until they identify one that interests them. Do not feel that volunteering for activities that are ultimately decided against is a waste of time. It is not. At a minimum, each time a student volunteers for an area he/she is not interested in, it narrows the student's focus and brings him/her closer to finding the right fit for a future career. Sound familiar? "Every no is one step closer to a yes."

In order to adequately test a variety of different areas, this process must begin as early in a student's career as possible. Waiting until junior or senior year may be too late. Building a résumé as a student leads to an internship. The internship should lead to a job. Earlier in this chapter, we discussed the mentality of sport organizations when they recruit prospective employees. These organizations take advantage of a flooded market of candidates willing to do an internship, many times unpaid, in order to break into sports. Students should put themselves into the position of the sport organization for a moment. The hiring manager for a professional sports team has an internship available in ticket sales. There are 1,000 applications from students for the position. Hypothetically, let's say 500 applicants do not have any sport experience whatsoever, 300 applicants have some sport experience but no ticket sales experience, and 200 applicants have ticket sales experience. If the student was the decision maker, likely in an office that is overworked and understaffed, which group would be looked to for highly qualified candidates who could step into the workplace and make an immediate positive impact on the organization? Most hiring managers would throw the 800 résumés with no ticket sales experience in the trash and focus on the remaining 200. What does that say about how one must build a résumé to be competitive for a job in sports?

In summary, students should start building a résumé as early as possible. They should volunteer for as many different areas as possible until finding an area about which they are passionate. Then they should focus on obtaining as much experience as possible in that area in order to be competitive for an internship. If students perform well in their internships, they have a high probability of securing a job. If they perform well in their internships and no job is available at the internship site at the conclusion of the internship, their supervisors will likely assist in any way possible to help them transition into the industry. This may include contacting other organizations, which may have employment opportunities available, on students' behalf. If the students' performance is average, or below average, in their internships, job assistance may not be available from the internship site. If they perform poorly, or if they end up not liking the internship focus, they may have to complete another internship to break into the industry. Therefore, proper planning in the form of résumé building and outstanding internship performance is crucial to an efficient transition to the workforce. Chapter 11 covers the application and interview process in detail.

PERSONAL BRANDING AND PROFESSIONALISM

Merriam-Webster (2010) describes professionalism as "the conduct, aims, qualities that characterize or mark a profession or a professional person." A profession is a body of persons engaged in a calling or a livelihood. Why is professionalism important? We all will be evaluated on what we do and how this will influence other people. In their book *Professionalism Public Perception and Profit,* Exline and Hyde (2006) list the five keys of being a professional:

1. Character – who you are and what you stand for.
2. Attitude – your mental outlook. Attitude is everything. A positive attitude is an essential component of professionalism (Hurst & Reding, 2000; Kramer, 2003).
3. Excellence – your commitment to quality.
4. Competency – your degree of expertise.
5. Conduct – how you deal with others (Hurst & Reding, 2000).

Displaying professionalism takes time and attention to detail. One question that students can ask themselves is: How do I wish to be perceived? We are all evaluated based on a variety of criteria including ethics, beliefs and morals, job performance, appearance, communications skills, and character (Reese, 2009). By what standards do you wish to be evaluated?

Just as products such as soft drinks, automobiles, and entertainment options are "branded" to attract consumers, students must realize that they convey their personal brand to those around them. Here are a few tips for creating a personal brand that will further, not hinder, professional advancement:

1. **You Are Always on Stage** – The way you communicate, dress, behave, and present yourself is constantly being evaluated by someone. Whether you realize it, you are constantly being evaluated in one form or another by friends, colleagues, faculty, supervisors, family, and even strangers. This includes not just in the workplace but in your personal life as well. What are you communicating to others by your choice of clothing, the way you speak, or by the photos and language on your preferred social networking site? Are you conducting yourself in a way that will lend itself to receiving a positive recommendation from your supervisor at work or a faculty member that may be able to assist with securing an internship? Many human resource managers and sport administrators openly admit they use social networking websites to obtain information that may assist in narrowing candidate pools. What does your personal brand say about you?
2. **Addressing People** – How do you address a person in authority you have just met? Do you use his/her first name? Be careful not to take anything for granted. It is always best to address people in authority (e.g., hiring managers, supervisors, educators, physicians, upper level administrators) in a formal way until given permission to address them informally. Do not give the impression you are trying to get too close to someone too fast. How you communicate, whether verbal, written, or electronic, is very important. Is your speech littered with swearing and/or slang words? If so, both give the impression you are less sophisticated. Think about the voice message people hear when they call your home, office, or cell phone. What impression are you communicating?
3. **Respect** – Many make the mistake of not respecting a person's time or opinions. If you are going to be late for a meeting, or need to cancel, call ahead to let the person know. Arriving 20 minutes late or not showing up at all, without advance notice, communicates a complete disregard for that person's time, which may be limited. Always try to arrive five to ten minutes early for appointments and meetings. In regard to opinions, remember that you can respectfully agree to disagree on a variety of issues. You will not agree with everyone in the workplace on things like social issues or politics. Although you can choose not to socialize with people with whom you may disagree, you still need to help facilitate a productive workplace. In order to avoid the possibility of creating a hostile environment, never try to force your ideology on others.
4. **Alcohol Consumption** – Intentionally placing prospective candidates in a social environment is an evaluation technique sometimes used by organizations.

Do not make the mistake of making a fool of yourself in social situations; it could hinder your chances to secure a job. If you choose to use alcohol, do so in moderation. Never use illegal drugs. The sport industry is a very small circle, and people talk. The industry is difficult enough to get into without limiting your chances further.

5. **Manners** – What would others say about your manners? Do you open or hold the door for someone in your group or for people walking behind you, or do you just close the door on them? Do you know which fork to use for different meal courses? When at dinner with a potential employer, do you let the person who is paying for your meal order first, so that you will know what the expected cost of the meal will be? Or do you just order steak or seafood and dessert, regardless of price, because it is a free meal? You are likely being evaluated by others when in these situations. If you are not familiar with proper manners, dinner etiquette, etc., do some research to prepare yourself for these important situations.
6. **Confidence** – You should be confident in your abilities without being arrogant. Walk with good posture, give firm handshakes, and look people in the eye when you speak to them. Remember to listen more than you speak. Carry yourself with the confidence and belief that you deserve to be in your current job position and can compete with anyone in the room, regardless of their position in the organization. Be the type of person that has a presence about him/her and is noticed positively when in social or business environments. People gravitate toward leaders.
7. **Work Ethic** – How hard you are willing to work can take you a long way in the sport industry. Be the first person into the office in the morning and the last one to leave. Work weekends if there is a need. If you are the type of person who looks forward to punching out at 5:00 p.m. each day and having weekends off, the sport industry may not be for you. Whatever your tasks are, be the best at them. Find a niche or task no one wants to do and claim it as yours. Your goal should be to make yourself an indispensable employee. Find out if there are times when senior administrators work. After others have gone home, try to get some time alone with them so they get to know you. For example, if the chief operating officer works every Saturday morning from 8:00 a.m. until noon, offer to come in and work on Saturday morning to help your office catch up on anything that needs to be done.

NETWORKING

The word networking is constantly thrown around in everyday conversation, but few take the time to define networking or explain how the process works. Cuneen and Sidwell (1994) define networks as "groups of people bonded by like interests and similar goals that are social or professional" (p. 19). The popularity of social and professional networking sites such as Facebook, MySpace, LinkedIn, and Plaxo are excellent examples of the power of networks.

In addition to enjoying working with people and dealing with rejection, salespeople must be fearless in regard to meeting new people. People who can walk into a room where they do not know anyone and still walk away from the event with a pocketful of business cards are ideal for a career in sales. If you are not confident enough to handle such a task, practice. Networking is definitely a skill that can be learned. It should become part of your everyday routine until it becomes second nature. Networking is simply building long term relationships.

© iStockphoto.com/lisegagne

For example, a great way to assist networking at social events is to avoid standing with people you already know. From a networking perspective, you already have them in your database and do not need to spend too much time with them. If you stay around people you already know, you may never step out of your comfort zone and meet anyone new. If necessary, make networking a game. Compete with friends or colleagues to see who can collect the most business cards at a networking event. After returning home, add all of the business cards to your computer database and email each person to thank them for taking time to speak with you. If you have not joined an online professional networking group such as LinkedIn or Plaxo, do so immediately. Then invite all of your new contacts to join your group.

Use this same strategy each time you go to a conference, workshop, or any event where you can meet new people. Salespeople call this "working the room." Please keep in mind when you are working the room that you cannot just walk around the event asking for business cards and expect to build relationships. You must be genuine, listen, and take the time to get to know people. As in the actual sales process, be sure not to talk too much or spend too much time with any one person or group of people. Otherwise, you will walk away with fewer contacts than you could have. Also, please understand there are certain times when openly networking, or working the room, is not appropriate or should be done with discretion (e.g., family events, organizational events with professional athletes). As previously mentioned, the sport industry is a very small circle. You are usually two to three phone calls from almost anyone. The more legitimate contacts you add to your network, the more effective you will be in securing a job in sport. Always remember that many jobs in sport are never advertised; they are filled by word-of-mouth or networking.

Keys for effective networking include the following (Liberty University, 2010c):

1. Decide that you want to build and develop a network. This will allow you to put your energy and efforts into effective network management.
2. Make a list of all your contacts; this could start with your family, friends, neighbors, and then colleagues, bosses, former co-workers, and people you meet at workshops or conferences.
3. Set a goal of adding five or more new contacts every week, and be sure to follow up with these contacts.
4. Communicate regularly and stay connected with people, especially in your industry.
5. Share resources with your contacts.
6. Keep track of all your contacts, where they are, and what they are doing.
7. Be sure to inform your network that you are currently seeking employment and specifically what position you are seeking so that they will be able to help you with your search. Remember to always write a thank-you note to those who assist you in getting an interview or securing a position.
8. Pay attention to corporate politics, and never burn a bridge.

The earlier you begin building your network, the sooner it has a chance to yield dividends. Remember, everyone has a network in place to some extent. You just have to know how to use it. Below are some Internet links to help you become more familiar with networking:

- Networking to Enhance Your Job Search

http://www.rileyguide.com/network.html

- Successful Job Search Networking

http://jobsearch.about.com/cs/networking/a/networking.htm

- Do social networking sites improve your ability to network in real life?

http://computer.howstuffworks.com/internet/social-networking/information/social-networking-sites-improve-your-ability-to-network.htm

- Job Networking Tips: Learn from professional résumé writers about eight networking tips to use in your job search.
  http://www.enetsc.com/jobsearchtips14.htm

SECURING A POSITION IN TICKETING AND SALES

As previously mentioned, you may be competing with up to 1,000 other applicants for an entry level position in sport. Therefore, you must take a sales approach from the very beginning. The harsh reality is very few hiring managers will take the time to look through a pile of résumés that large. More often than not, organizations will accept sales candidate recommendations from people they trust through their word-of-mouth network. To ensure an interview, you must put your personal network to use.

Do any of your friends, colleagues, professors, etc. know someone who works for the organization with which you are trying to interview? If so, forward them your résumé, and ask that they share it with their contact. Your goal is to use your network to ensure that your résumé is reviewed and that an interview is scheduled. If you are fortunate enough to get an interview, you must then earn the position on your own by being prepared, having adequate experience for the position, and demonstrating that you are the best candidate for the position.

A basic guideline in sales is to always try to deal with the person who can sign the check. In other words, always try to deal with a decision maker. The same approach applies for the hiring process. Your goal is to interact with the person who decides which candidate gets the position. Salespeople have been finding ways around "gatekeepers" for decades. Schedule informational interviews with the decision makers to get their advice on how to break into the business. Of course, be sure to have a résumé on hand to share just in case they happen to have any positions available. Many executives arrive at the office early, work during lunch, and leave for home in the evening. Therefore, applicants should schedule phone calls for before 8:00 a.m., during lunch, and after 5:00 p.m., when gatekeepers are typically not in the office.

EXPECTATIONS OF JOB SITES

What do job sites look for in potential candidates? Let us take a look at it from the perspective of a hiring manager or senior administrator. Some of the basic requirements are simple but often overlooked or ignored. Examples include the following:

1. Come to work on time.
2. Arrive to work with an adequate amount of sleep and not under the influence, or residual influence, of any substance. In other words, arrive in a condition that allows you to maximize effectiveness and performance.
3. Have a superior work ethic. Do more than the minimum required. Demonstrate a passion for the sport industry and a desire to advance within the organization. Do not be the type of person who is first in line to punch out at 5:00 p.m. Those individuals do not last long in the demanding sport work environment.
4. Take a big picture approach to doing business. For example, if the organization belonged to you and your personal finances were on the line, how would you approach the allocation of funds? How would you spend money on business trips? Approach customer service? What additional revenue streams do you foresee in the future? If you take this business approach, your decision making will likely be well received by those to whom you report.
5. Finally, understand that everything you say and do, on business time as well as personal time, can reflect on the organization.

If you follow these simple guidelines, you will no doubt be on your way to moving up quickly within your respective sport organization.

CHAPTER SUMMARY

This chapter is designed to provide students with recommendations necessary to successfully secure a job in sport. Because the sport industry is so demanding and difficult to gain access to, a list of required skills was provided to ensure that entry level employees are able to handle the fast-paced and stressful work environment. Because sport organizations receive many more inquiries and résumés than there are opportunities available, readers were recommended to begin building their résumés as early as possible to become competitive in the résumé review process. Next, recommendations for personal branding, or controlling one's image, were provided, as well as suggestions for professionalism. The importance of networking, or building a base of contacts with similar interests, was discussed. Finally, recommendations for setting up an actual interview and successfully navigating the interview process were provided.

LEARNING ACTIVITY

1. Because networking is one of the most important activities in securing a job in sport, your task in this learning activity is to add to your personal network by scheduling an informational interview with a person employed at a senior level in the sport industry. To successfully complete this activity, select a person in a position similar to the job you wish to pursue after graduation. The sport and title of the executive is up to the student but should be taken seriously and not just chosen out of convenience. The person you select may be a coach, administrator, corporate executive, etc. depending on your career ambitions. Contact the person you select, asking for approximately 30 minutes of his/her time. As a courtesy, set the appointment around the other person's schedule. Create a list of questions that inquires about his/her experience, how he/she broke into the sport industry, and what recommendations he/she has for you in your effort to establish a career in the administration of sport. Take a few résumés along in case there is an offer to assist you in your endeavor. Also, be sure to ask for the contact information of the person with whom you meet so you may add that information to your database of contacts.

References

§67.306 R.S. Mo. (2009).

11 Del. C. §918 (2009).

4 P.S. §202 (2009).

4 P.S. §211 (2009).

520 MA ADC 8.01 (2009).

720 ILCS §§375/1.5 (2009).

A&E Television Network. (Producer). (1996). *Modern marvels: Baseball parks* [DVD]. Retrieved from http://shop.history.com/detail.php?p=68325&v=history_education_k-12_product-categories_modern-marvels

Adelman, M. L. (1986). *A sporting time: New York City and the rise of modern athletics, 1820-70.* Chicago, IL: University of Illinois Press.

Ala. Code §40-12-167 (2009).

Alabama Public Act 2009-568 (2009).

American heritage dictionary (2nd ed.). (1982). Boston, MA: Houghton Mifflin.

Appeals No. 01CA0693 (Colo. 2002).

Appenzeller, H. (2005). *Risk management in sport: Issues and strategies.* Durham, N.C.: Carolina Academic Press.

Apperson, J. (2001). *Modell, Browns fans reach deal on lawsuit.* Retrieved from http://www.baltimoresun.com/sports/ravens/bal-modell040501,0,6075242.story

Araton, H. (1998). *Sports of the times: Striking back at the Marlins.* Retrieved from http://www.nytimes.com/1998/05/24/sports/sports-of-the-times-striking-back-at-the-marlins.html?pagewanted=1

ARCHTICS ticketing system. (2008). Retrieved from http://archtics-ticketing-system.software.informer.com/

Ariz. Rev. Stat. §13-3718 (2009).

Ark. Stat. §5-63-201 (2009).

Arkansas Public Act No. 573 (2009).

Ballena Technologies. (2012). Seat upgrade system. Retrieved from http://seats3d.com/seat-upgrade-system.php

Basketball ticket system rewards the loyal. (2005, October 25). Retrieved from http://www.pittnews.com/vnews/display.v/ART/2005/10/25/435daf105d78b

Bayton, E., & Edwards, N. (2011, September 12). *Anti-counterfeit plan can prevent damage to team's reputation.* Retrieved from http://www.sportsbusinessdaily.com/Journal/Issues/2011/09/12/Opinion/From-the-Field.aspx.

Bebawi, S. G. (2011). Definition of online education as distance learning. Retrieved from http://www.sabri.org/EDTECH-01/Definition.htm

Belson, K. (2011, January 14). As economy sagged, online sports ticket market soared. *The New York Times.* Retrieved February 18, 2011, from http://www.nytimes.com/2011/01/15/sports/15tickets.html?_r=1.

Berman, J. (2005). The secondary marketplace: A first person perspective from StubHub. *The Migala Report,* Article 5. Retrieved from http://www.migalareport.com

Bickett v. Buffalo Bills, Inc. 472 N.Y.S. 2d 245 (1983).

Binegar, S. M. (2005). *Ticket office policies & procedures manual.* Florida Atlantic University.

Boyd, D. W., & Boyd, L. A. (1998). The home field advantage: Implications for the pricing of tickets to professional team sporting events. *Journal of Economics and Finance, 22,* 169-179.

Branch, A. (2007). *NFL, Ticketmaster finalize secondary ticketing deal.* Retrieved from http://www.ticketnews.com/news/NFL-Ticketmaster-Finalize-Deal01271823

Branch, A. (2009, September 18). *Paperless ticketing slows down Bruce Springsteen show.* Retrieved from http://www.ticketnews.com/news/Paperless-ticketing-slows-down-Bruce-Springsteen-show9091871

Briggs, J. C. (1996). The promise of virtual reality. *The Futurist, 30*(5). 13–18.

Brinkhaus, Coppage, Coppage, and CAMAS, Inc. v. PDB Sports, Case No. 96 CU 43 Div. 5 (Dist. Ct. Col. 1996).

Brown, W. (2005). *Michigan State athletic ticket policies.* Michigan State University.

Burbach, C. (2009, October 1). *Concert ticket headaches.* Retrieved from http://www.omaha.com/article/20091001/NEWS01/710019928

Burns, K. (Producer). (1994). [Television series]-The first inning: Our game 1840s-1900 [Baseball: A film by Ken Burns]. PBS Distribution.

C.R.S. 18-4-416 (2009).

C.R.S. 6-1-718 (2009).

Cal. Penal Code §346 (2009).

Cavoto v. Chicago National League Ball Club, Inc., 222 Ill.2d 569 (2006).

Charpentier v. Los Angeles Rams Football Company, Inc., 75 Cal. App. 4th 301 (1999).

Chaussee v. Dallas Cowboys Football Club, No. 05-9600429-CV (TX Ct. App., 5th Dist. December 2, 1997).

Chicago Cubs franchise history. (2010). Retrieved from http://en.wikipedia.org/wiki/Chicago_Cubs_franchise_history#Chicago_White_Stockings.2FChicago_Colts

Cleveland Forest Citys. (2010). Retrieved from http://www.baseball-reference.com/teams/CFC/

College Sports Scholarships (2001). The historical origins of wrestling: Facts and information. Retrieved from http://www.collegesportsscholarships.com/history-wrestling.htm

Conn. Gen. Stat. §53-289c (2008).

Coronel v. Chicago White Sox, Ltd., 595 N.E. 2d 45 (1992).

Costa v. Boston Red Sox Baseball Club, 809 N.E. 2d 1090 (2004).

Courty, P. (2003). Some economics of ticket resale. *Journal of Economic Perspectives, 17,* 85-97.

Cuneen, J., & Sidwell, M. J. (1994). *Sport management field experiences.* Morgantown, WV: Fitness Information Technology.

Davies, T. L., Lavin, A. M., and Korte, L. (2009). Student perceptions of how technology impacts the quality of instruction and learning. *Journal of Instructional Pedagogies, 1,* 2–16.

Denver Broncos ticket office. (1996). Post-season checklist. Denver, CO.

Denver Broncos ticket office. (1997). Post-season lottery post card. Denver, CO.

Denver Broncos ticket office. (1998). Season ticket relocation postcard. Denver, CO.

Denver Broncos ticket office. (2005). Reserved seat season-ticket assignment form. Denver, CO.

Denver Broncos. (2001). *Denver Broncos media guide.* Denver, CO: A.B. Hirschfeld Press.

Dolezalek, H. (2004). Pretending to learn. *Training, 40*(7), 20–26.

Donald W. Reynolds Razorback Stadium football game day ticket policies. (2009). Retrieved from http://www.nmathletics.com

Doyle, A. (2006). Retrieved from http://www.yourjobinterview.com/Questions_Employers_Can%27t_Ask.html

Doyle, A. (2010). *Successful job search networking: How to use job search networking to find a job.* Retrieved from http://jobsearch.about.com/cs/networking/a/networking.htm

Drayer, J. (2011). Examining the effectiveness of anti-scalping laws in a United States market. *Sport Management Review, 14*(3), 226-236.

Drayer, J., & Martin, N. T. (2010). Establishing legitimacy in the secondary ticket market: A case study of an NFL market. *Sport Management Review, 13*(1), 39-49.

Drayer, J., & Shapiro, S. L. (2009). Value determination in the secondary ticket market: A quantitative analysis of the NFL playoffs. *Sport Marketing Quarterly, 18*(1), 5-13.

Drayer, J., Stotlar, D. K., & Irwin, R. L. (2008). Tradition vs. trend: A case study of team response to the secondary ticket market. *Sport Marketing Quarterly, 17*(4), 235-240.

Driscoll, K. (2008). The history of thoroughbred racing in the USA. Retrieved from http://ezinearticles.com/?History-of-Thoroughbred-Racing-in-the-USA&id=481513

Duffy, D. (2006). Ticket scalping (Report No. 2006-R-0761). Retrieved from http://www.cga.ct.gov/2006/rpt/2006-R-0761.htm

Dwyer, T. (1991, June 26). Nevada's probe into free tickets hardly complimentary of Tarkanian. *The Baltimore Sun.* Retrieved from http://articles.baltimoresun.com

Elfenbein, D. W. (June 30, 2006). *Do anti-ticket scalping laws make a difference online? Evidence from Internet sales of NFL tickets.* Retrieved from http://ssrn.com/abstract=595682

Event incident report. (2002). Northern Illinois University facilities and game operations.

Exline, D. D., & Hyde, S. J. (2006). *Professionalism public perception and profit: The 4 P's of running a successful business.* Retrieved from http://www.wfps.org/files/AMUW09/Handouts/Sunday%20-%20Exline%20-%204%20Ps%20(150).pdf

Fisher, E. (2005). Secondary ticketing [electronic version]. *SportsBusiness Journal.* Retrieved from http://www.sportsbusinessjournal.com/article/47662

Fisher, E. (2010, May 31). Ticketing's change up. *SportsBusiness Journal.* Retrieved from http://www.sportsbusinessdaily.com/Journal/Issues/2010/05/20100531/SBJ-In-Depth/Ticketings-Changeup.aspx

Fitzgerald, D. (2009). UConn football attempts to waive liability for pat-down procedures. (2009, Sept. 30). Retrieved from http://ctsportslaw.com

Fla. Stat. §817.36 (2009).

Flandez, R. (2007, August 14). Enterprise: Firms go online to train employees; Virtual classes, videos give workers flexibility and save owners money. *Wall Street Journal,* p. B4.

Flash Seats FAQs. (2011a). Flash Seats. Retrieved from http://www.flashseats.com/FAQsDetails.aspx?ss=0&a=1#g1

Florida Atlantic University Ticket Office. (2005). Player pass list.

Foley, R. J. (2008). Brewers pitch bill to catch ticket scalpers. Retrieved from http://www.breitbart.com/article.php?id=D9D5K2L00&show_article=1

Frank, R. H. (2002). *Microeconomics and behavior* (5th edition). New York, NY: McGraw-Hill Irwin.

Futrell, A. (2006). *The Roman games.* Malden, MA: Blackwell Publishing.

Ga. Code Ann. §§43-4B-25 (2009).

Ga. Code Ann. §§43-4B-28-30 (2009).

Ganey v. New York Jets Football Club, 146 Misc. 2d. 302, 550 N.Y.S. 2d 566 (1990).

Geraghty, M. K. and Johnson, E. (1997). Revenue management saves National Car Rental. *Interfaces, 27*(1), 107–127.

Glantz, D. J. (2005). For-bid scalping online?: Anti-scalping legislation in an Internet society. *Cardoza Arts & Entertainment Law Journal, 23,* 261-287.

Goldberg, N. (Producer), & Wincer, S. (Director). (2004). NASCAR: *The IMAX experience.* [Motion picture]. United States: Warner Bros. Pictures.

Graham, S., Goldblatt, J. J., & Delpy, L. (1995). *The ultimate guide to sport event management & marketing.* Chicago, IL: Irwin Professional Publishing.

Green Bay Municipal Code 6.12 (2009).

Heidrick v. PDB Sports, Ltd., Court of Haw. Rev. Stat. § 440-17 (2009).

Hurst, B., & Reding, G. (2000). *Professionalism in teaching.* Upper Saddle River, NJ: Prentice Hall.

In Re: Platt v. Boston Red Sox Baseball Club, 292 B.R. 12 (2003).

In Re: Warren Liebman, 208 B.R. 38, (1997).

In Re: William Harrall v. Phoenix Suns Limited Partnership, 73 F.3d 218 (1995).

Ind. Code §25-9-1-26 (2009).

Industry insider: Sales panel (2011). *Sport Marketing Quarterly, 20*(2), 69–74.

Jacobs, M. (2010). Student ticketing: The next generation. Unpublished manuscript.

Job networking tips: Learn from professional résumé writers about eight networking tips to use in your job search. (2010). Retrieved from http://www.enetsc.com/jobsearchtips14.htm

Johnson, T. F., & Reese, J. T. (2011). Ticketing (packaging, quantity, re-selling, sales). In L. E. Swayne & M. Dodds (Eds.), *Encyclopedia of sports management and marketing,* (Vol. 4, pp. 1556–1559). Thousand Oaks, CA: SAGE Publications, Inc.

Kieran, J., and Daley, A. (1973). *The story of the Olympic Games.* Philadelphia, PA: J. B. Lippincott Company.

Kirkman, C. P. (2008–09). Note: Who needs tickets? Examining problems in the growing online ticket resale industry. *Federal Communications Law Journal, 61,* 739–763.

Kohne, E., Ewigleben, C., & Jackson, R. (2000). *Gladiators and Caesars: The power of spectacle in ancient Rome.* Berkeley, CA: University of California Press.

Kramer, P. A. (2003, Fall). *The ABC's of professionalism: To develop a strong sense of professionalism, a teacher must focus on the critical elements of attitude, behavior, and communication.* Kappa Delta Pi Record.

Kreps, D. (2009, Feb. 4). *Bruce Springsteen "furious" at Ticketmaster, rails against Live Nation.* Retrieved from http://www.rollingstone.com/rockdaily/index.php/2009/02/04/bruce-springsteen-furious-at-ticketmaster-rails-against-live-nation-merger

Kully v. Goldman, 208 Neb. 760, 305 N.W. 2d 800 (1981).

Ky. Rev. Stat. §518.070 (2009).

La. Rev. Stat. §4:1 (2009).

Las Vegas Municipal Code 10.52.030 (2009).

Lease Agreement, Wisconsin Rapids, Draft (2009). Retrieved from http://www.wirapids.org/egov/docs/1260889379_394226.pdf

Lee, S. Y., & Mohl, B. (2007). *MLB, StubHub ink resale deal.* Retrieved from http://www.boston.com/business/globe/articles/2007/08/02/mlb_stubhub_ink_resale_deal/

Lefton, T. & Lombardo, J. (2003). Stern's NBA shows its transition game. *Street & Smith's SportsBusiness Journal.* Retrieved from http://www.sportsbusinessjournal.com/index.cfm?fuseaction=search.show_article&articleId=30263

Liberty University Career Center. (2010a). *Interviewing preparation.* Retrieved from https://www.liberty.edu/index.cfm?PID=2034

Liberty University Career Center. (2010b). *Mock interview questions.* Retrieved from https://www.liberty.edu/media/1103/pdf/SampleInterviewerQuestions.pdf

Liberty University Career Center. (2010c). *Networking: In person networking vs. online networking.* Retrieved from http://www.liberty.edu/index.cfm?PID=17235

Liberty University Career Center (2010d). *Portfolio help.* Retrieved from https://www.liberty.edu/index.cfm?pid=2088

Liberty University Career Center. (2010e). *Reference page sample.* Retrieved from http://www.liberty.edu/media/pdf/careercenter/CareerCenter_ACF15E1.pdf

Liberty University Career Center. (2010f). *Resume tips.* Retrieved from http://www.liberty.edu/media/1103/redesignsummer2010/Resume%20Tips.pdf

Liberty University Career Center (2010g). *Sample questions to ask in an interview.* Retrieved from http://www.liberty.edu/media/1103/pdf/SampleIntervieweeQuestions.pdf

Liberty University Career Center. (2010h). *Sample resume.* Retrieved from http://www.liberty.edu/index.cfm?PID=153

Light, J. F. (1997). *The cultural encyclopedia of baseball* (2nd ed.). Jefferson, NC: McFarland & Company, Inc.

Lisle, B. (2000). Elysian Fields. Retrieved from http://xroads.virginia.edu/~HYPER/INCORP/baseball/origins.html

Lowry, P. J. (1992). *Green cathedrals: The ultimate celebration of all 271 Major League and Negro League ballparks past and present.* Reading, MA: Addison Wesley Publishing.

M.G.L.A. 140 §185D (2009).

Marquez, J. (2005, Aug. 1). Faced with high turnover, retailers boot up e-learning programs for quick training. *AllBusiness.com.* Retrieved from http://www.allbusiness.com/management/3494923-1.html

Masteralexis, L. P., Barr, C. A., & Hums, M. A. (2009). *Principles and practice of sport management* (3rd ed.). Sudbury, MA: Jones and Bartlett Publishers.

Md. Code §4-318 (2009).

Merriam-Webster dictionary. (2010). Merriam-Webster, Incorporated. Retrieved from http://

www.merriam-webster.com/dictionary/professionalism?show=0&t=1283397226

Mich. Comp. Laws §750.465 (2009).

Michigan Stadium football games policies. (2009). Wheelchair ticket policies. Retrieved from http://www.umich.edu/stadium/access/ticket-policy.pdf

Minn. Stat. 245 §609.806 (2009).

Mint Museum of Art (2001). History of sports. Retrieved from http://www.ballgame.org/sub_section.asp?section=2&sub_section=4

Miss. Code Ann. §97-23-97 (2009).

Morris, P. (2006). *A game of inches: The stories behind the innovations that shaped baseball: The game behind the scenes.* Chicago, IL: Ivan R. Dee.

Moulas v. PBC Productions Incorporated, 570 N.W. 2d 739 (1997).

Mullin, B. J., Hardy S., & Sutton, W. A. (2007). *Sport marketing* (3rd ed.). Champaign, IL: Human Kinetics.

Muret, D. (2011, March 14). Cards skip test run, embrace dynamic ticket pricing for whole ballpark. *SportsBusiness Journal.* Retrieved from http://www.sportsbusinessdaily.com/Journal/Issues/2011/03/Mar-14/Facilities/Facilities-column.aspx?hl=muret&sc=0

N.C. Gen. Stat. §14-344 (2009).

N.D. Cent. Code 40-05-01.26 (2009).

N.J.S.A. 56:8-33-4 (2009).

N.M. Stat. Ann. §30-46-1 (2009).

N.Y. Arts&Cult. Aff. §25.08 (2009).

N.Y. Arts&Cult. Aff. §25.13 (2009).

NCAA Division I manual. (2009). Indianapolis: The National Collegiate Athletic Association.

NCAA Division I manual. (2009-10). Indianapolis: The National Collegiate Athletic Association.

NCAA Final Four–All session tickets. (2010). Retrieved from http://www.razorgator.com

Networking to enhance your job search. (2010, September). Retrieved from http://www.rileyguide.com/network.html

New England Patriots, L.P. v. Stubhub, Inc., 22 Mass. L. Rptr 717 (2007).

New York Yankees ticket policies. (2009). Lost/stolen ticket policies. Retrieved from http://www.yankees.com

New York Yankees. (2009). Relocation program guide for the new Yankee Stadium. Retrieved from http://newyork.yankees.mlb.com/nyy/components/ballpark/New_Yankee_Stadium_Relocation_Guide.pdf.

Noe, R. A. (2010). *Employee training and development.* (5th ed.). New York, NY: McGraw-Hill Irwin.

Ohio Rev. Code §15.48 (2009)

Ohio University ticket office. (2002). *Complimentary and consignment form.*

Ohio University. (2002). Ohio University Athletic Ticket Office.

Oklahoma City Ordinance § 7-132 (2009).

ORC Ann. 505.95 (2009).

ORS 646.608 (2010).

Overby, S. (2011, June 29). *For San Francisco Giants, dynamic pricing software hits a home run.* Retrieved from http://www.cio.com/article/685312/For_San_Francisco_Giants_Dynamic_Pricing_Software_Hits_a_Home_Run

Oxford dictionaries (2011). Vomitorium. Oxford University Press. Retrieved from http://oxforddictionaries.com/definition/vomitorium

Parker, M. (1996). The history of horse racing. Retrieved from http://www.mrmike.com/explore/hrhist.htm

Patel, H., & Cardinali, R. (1994). Virtual reality technology in business. *Management Decision, 32*(7), 5–12.

Paulsen, M. F. (2009). Successful e-learning in small and medium-sized enterprises. Retrieved from http://www.eurodl.org/materials/contrib/2009/Morten_Paulsen.htm

Pearson, J. (1973). *Arena: The Story of the Colosseum.* New York, NY: McGraw-Hill.

Pepe, A. (2008). The Colosseum. Retrieved from http://www.the-colosseum.net/idx-en.htm

Pittsburgh City Ordinance 726.01 (2009).

Pittsfield's 1791 Baseball Bylaw. (2006). Berkshire Athenaeum. Pittsfield's Public Library. Retrieved from http://www.pittsfieldlibrary.org/images/1791_bylaw.jpg

Policies and procedures handbook. (2006-07). University of Wisconsin Athletic Ticket Office Press.

Quennell, P. (1971). *The Colosseum.* New York, NY: Newsweek Book Division.

R.I. Gen. Law §5-22-26 (2009).

Rascher, D. A., McEvoy, C. D., Nagel, M. S., & Brown, M. T. (2007). Variable ticket pricing in Major League Baseball. *The Journal of Sport Management, 21*(3), 407-437.

Rayle v. Bowling Green State University, 739 N.E. 2d 1260 (2000).

Reedy v. Cincinnati Bengals, Inc., 2001 Ohio App. LEXIS 475 (February 9, 2001).

Reedy v. Cincinnati Bengals, Inc., 758 N.E.2d 678 (Ohio Ct. App. 2001).

Reese, J. T. (2004). Ticket operations in a professional sports team setting. In U. McMahon-Beattie & I. Yeoman (Eds.), *Sport and leisure operations management* (pp. 167–179). London: Thomson Learning.

Reese, J. T. (2005, April 24). Technological advances in ticket operations. Presented to faculty, students, and professionals at Beijing Sport University, Beijing, China.

Reese, J. T. (2007, Sept. 10-16). Program convinces students that attendance has its rewards. *SportsBusiness Journal, 10*(20), 14.

Reese, J. T. (2008, December 8). Sports organizations want to know if you've got personality. *SportsBusiness Journal, 11*(32), 20.

Reese, J. T. (2009, September 25). Professionalism in sport. Presentation to the Liberty University Department of Sport Management.

Reese, J. T., & Mittelstaedt, R. D. (2001). An exploratory study of the criteria used to establish NFL ticket prices. *Sport Marketing Quarterly, 10*(4), 223-230.

Reese, J. T., & Moberg, C. R. (2007, Fall). An exploratory study of the college transplant fan. *The SMART Journal, 4*(1), 27–46.

Reese, J. T., & Snyder, D. L. (2005). Legal implications of reselling tickets above face value. *Sport Marketing Quarterly, 14*(2), 123–124.

Reese, J. T., Dodds, M. A., & Snyder, D. L. (2009). Fans apply full-court press over reseating policy. *College Athletics and the Law, 6*(8), 7.

Reese, J. T., Nagel, M. S., & Southall, R. M. (2004). National Football League ticket transfer policies: Legal and policy issues. *Journal of Legal Aspects of Sport, 14*(2), 163–190.

Request for athletic memorabilia. (2009). Northern Illinois University Compliance Office.

Ronca, D. (n.d.). *Do social networking sites improve your ability to network in real life?* Retrieved from http://computer.howstuffworks.com/internet/social-networking/information/social-networking-sites-improve-your-ability-to-network4.htm

Ross, A., & Dyte, D. (2010a). The Capitoline Grounds. Retrieved from http://www.brooklynballparks.com

Ross, A., & Dyte, D. (2010b). The Union Grounds. Retrieved from http://www.brooklynballparks.com

Rovell, D. (2011, April 1). *Will paperless change the face of the ticket industry?* Retrieved from http://cnbc.com/id/42377582/

Ryan, T. (1996). History of the Colosseum and Forum Romanum. Retrieved from http://www.iei.net/~tryan/h-colfor.htm

S.C. Code Ann. §16-17-710 (2009).

S.D. Codified Laws 7-18-29 (2009).

San Diego season ticket account title policy (2011). Retrieved from http://sandiego.padres.mlb.com/sd/ticketing/sth/account_policy.jsp

Schultz v. University of Pittsburgh, Civil Action No. GD 05-7626, Court of Common Pleas (Allegheny County, 2005).

Show, J. (2009, Nov. 8). Ticketing. Retrieved from http://www.sportsbusinessdaily.com/Journal/Issues/2009/11/20091108/Technology-In-Sports/Ticketing.aspx.

Shuai jiao. (2008). Retrieved from http://en.wikipedia.org/wiki/Shuai_Jiao

Silva v. Mt. Bachelor, 2008 U.S. Dist. LEXIS 55942 (Dist. Ore. 2008).

Sitzmann, T. (2011). A meta-analytic examination of the instructional effectiveness of computer-based simulation games. *Personnel Psychology, 64*(2), 489–528.

Smith, B. C., Leimkuhler, J. F., & Darrow, R. M. (1992). Yield management at American Airlines. *Interfaces, 22*(1), 8–31.

Smith, M. (2011, Oct. 24). Colleges jump on secondary bandwagon. *SportsBusiness Journal.* Retrieved from http://www.sportsbusinessdaily.com/Journal/Issues/2011/10/24/In-Depth/Colleges.aspx?hl=secondary%20ticket%20market&sc=0

Stecklow, S. (2006, January 17). StubHub's ticket to ride: Web site conceived in school is now a leader in hawking access to sold-out events. *The Wall Street Journal* (Eastern edition), p. B1.

Super Bowl tickets being resold at record prices. (2009, January). Retrieved from http://www.espn.com

Swaddling, J. (1999). *The Ancient Olympic Games* (2nd ed.). Austin, TX: University of Texas

Tauber v. Jacobson, 293 A.2d 861 (1972).

Tenn. Code Ann. §39-17-1105 (2009).

Tessera. (2011). Retrieved from http://www.yourdictionary.com/tessera

The Capitoline Grounds. (n.d.). BrooklynBallparks.com. Retrieved from http://www.covehurst.net/ddyte/brooklyn/capitoline.html

The Internal Revenue Service. (2010). Taxable fringe benefit guide. Retrieved from http://www.irs.com

Ticket policies & information. (2009). Qwest Field. Retrieved from http://www.seahawks.com/qwest-field/stadium-guide/ticket-policies.html

Ticketmaster, LLC v. RMG Technologies, Inc., 507 F. Supp. 2d 1096 (2007).

Ticketmaster. (2007, Feb. 26). *Ticketmaster named official ticketing provider and official secondary ticketing provider of the NBA.* Retrieved from http://www.prnewswire.com/news-releases/ticketmaster-and-nba-sign-league-wide-pact-for-ticketing-and-ticket-resale-58081607.html

Topeka City Codebook §54-7 (2009).

Tryboski, T. K. (2005). *Exculpatory clauses–Do they work?* Retrieved from http://www.rsplaw.com/newsletter/Exculpatory%Clauses.html

UK president addresses ticket investigation. (2004, May). Retrieved from http://www.accessnorthga.com

University best practices: General ticketing success. (2009a). *TicketReturn Digital Ticketing.* Featured client: Elon University.

University best practices: Student ticketing success. (2009b). *TicketReturn Digital Ticketing.* Featured client: University of South Carolina.

Va. Code Ann. §15.2-969 (2009).

Weiner, J. (2009, June 18). Are the days numbered for the paper ticket? *SportsBusiness Journal.* Retrieved from http://www.sportsbusinessdaily.com/Journal/Issues/2007/06/20070618/SBJ-In-Depth/Are-The-Days-Numbered-For-The-Paper-Ticket.aspx

Welcome to the sports knowledge underground. (2011). Retrieved from www.nikesku.com/home.cfm

What makes Flash Seats different?. (2011b). Flash Seats. Retrieved from http://www.flashseats.com/Default.aspx?pid=135&ss=0

Winfree, J. A., & Rosentraub, M.S. (2012). *Sports finance and management.* Boca Raton, FL: CRC Press.

Wis. Stat. §42.07 (2009).

Wolohan, J. T. (2009, March). Uphill battle. *Athletic Business, 3*(3), 26-30.

Yashin lawsuit tossed. (2000, May 11). Retrieved from http://www.canoe.ca/HockeyOttawaArchive/may11_yas.html

Yates v. Chicago Nat'l League Baseball Club, Inc., 230 Ill. App. 3d 472 (1992).

Yocca v. Pittsburgh Steelers Sports Inc., 827 A.2d 1203 (2003).

Index

About the Editor

James T. Reese, Jr.

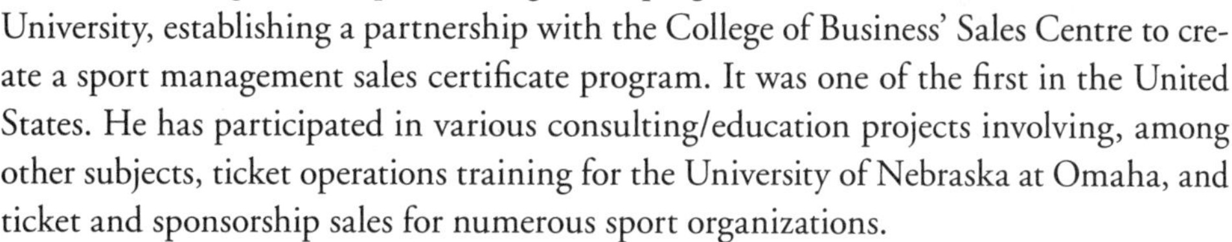

James T. Reese, Jr., EdD, is an associate professor in the sport management program at Drexel University in Philadelphia, Pennsylvania. Prior to his arrival at Drexel, he was an associate professor and graduate director in the Department of Sport Management at Liberty University in Lynchburg, Virginia. Before that, he served as an associate professor at SUNY Cortland in the Sport Management Department, and as graduate coordinator from 2006 until 2010.

Prior to his appointment at SUNY Cortland, Reese coordinated the undergraduate sport management program at Ohio University, establishing a partnership with the College of Business' Sales Centre to create a sport management sales certificate program. It was one of the first in the United States. He has participated in various consulting/education projects involving, among other subjects, ticket operations training for the University of Nebraska at Omaha, and ticket and sponsorship sales for numerous sport organizations.

Reese has a long history of involvement within the sport industry. From 2002–2003, Reese was the vice president of IFSA/USA (International Federation of Strength Athletes). Prior to that appointment, he worked as a ticketing administrator for the Denver Broncos Football Club for three years (1996-1999), assisting in the ticket planning of Super Bowls XXXII and XXXIII. Reese began his career in the sport industry with two years (1994–1996) as an assistant tennis coach and facility management assistant at Georgia Southern University and two additional years (1996–1998) as an assistant tennis coach and facility management assistant at the University of Northern Colorado.

Reese conducts research in the areas of ticket operations, ticket sales, ticketing-related legal issues in intercollegiate and professional sport, ethical issues related to sport, and facility and event management.

About the Authors

Shelley Binegar

Shelley Binegar is the associate athletics director at Northern Illinois University, where she oversees development, ticket sales, ticket operations, marketing, and licensing. She has a master's degree in sport administration from Ohio University.

Kristi Schoepfer Bochicchio

Kristi Schoepfer Bochicchio is an assistant professor of sport management and sport law at Winthrop University in Rock Hill, South Carolina. Her research interests include negligence in sport, emergency care, co-participant liability, hazing, and sport management internships.

Dexter Davis

Dexter Davis is a professor of sport management in the College of Hospitality and Tourism Management at Niagara University. His research interests include experiential learning in sport management, sponsorship effectiveness, and the role of corporate social responsibility in the sport industry.

Mark A. Dodds

Mark A. Dodds is an associate professor of sport marketing and sport law at the State University of New York, College at Cortland. His research interests include legal issues of sport, the use of sport in civic engagement, sponsorship activation, and sport brand equity.

Joris Drayer

Joris Drayer is an assistant professor of sport and recreation management at Temple University. His research interests include ticketing and pricing strategies in both primary and secondary markets as well as consumer behavior, particularly in relation to fantasy sport participation.

Flavil Hampsten

Flavil Hampsten has more than 10 years of work experience in the entertainment industry. He has worked to enhance and maximize revenue for several NHL, NBA, MLB, and MLS teams, as well as arenas. He currently works for the Charlotte Bobcats, where he has grown revenue by over 14%.

Peter Han

Peter Han is an assistant professor in the Sport Management Department at State University of New York, College of Cortland. His research areas include event and facility management, information technology in sport, Web/Internet marketing in sports, sport marketing, and international sports.

Kevin Heisey

Kevin Heisey is an associate professor at Liberty University in Lynchburg, Virginia. Prior to arriving at Liberty, he served as the graduate coordinator at the State University of New York, College at Cortland, where he was a faculty member from 2002 until 2011. Heisey competed in wrestling at the NCAA level as a member of the United States Air Force wrestling team. He was also an assistant coach at the college level and worked as an administrator and clinician for high school and youth clubs and clinics.

Katelyn Jacobs

Katelyn Jacobs is a graduate assistant in the Liberty University Ticket Office and a student in Liberty's Sport Administration master's program. She is a member of NACMA and her research interests include sport marketing, specifically the variety of benefits universities derive from supporting athletic programs; and the increasing integration of business principles into collegiate athletic departments.

Jim Kadlecek

Jim Kadlecek serves as director of the Mount Union Sport Sales Workshop & Job Fair and is actively engaged with the ticket sales efforts of professional teams and leagues. He is an associate professor of sport business at the University of Mount Union, where he teaches sales, sport marketing, and marketing research in addition to chairing the Department of Human Performance & Sport Business.

Vicky Martin

Vicky Martin is an associate professor at Liberty University in Lynchburg, Virginia. She has been a member of the Department of Sport Management faculty since 2005, and chair of the department since 2006. Prior to coming to Liberty, she taught in the Sport Management Department of Florida Southern College in Lakeland, Florida. Before moving to Florida, Martin taught physical education courses for both Peace College and Oral Roberts University.

Don Rovak

Don Rovak enters his fourth season as director of ticket sales and service with the Atlanta Falcons. In Rovak's first three years, his staff has been among the NFL leaders in new season tickets and group tickets. Previously, Rovak was vice president of marketing & ticketing for the Memphis Redbirds Triple A baseball team. Under his leadership, the Redbirds opened AutoZone Park and finished first or second in ballpark attendance each year.

Derek Thomas

Derek Thomas is a manager of corporate sales for the Denver Broncos and Sports Authority Field at Mile High. His career began in the Olympics and NCAA football, and he has 15 years of experience in the NFL with the Broncos working in ticketing, premium seating, marketing, and corporate sales.

Mark Washo

Mark Washo is a managing partner at Playbook Management International (PMI). Prior to PMI, he was the president, general manager, and primary board of governor of the Women's Professional Soccer League's Washington Freedom. Prior to joining the Freedom, Washo served as the executive vice president of the Chicago Fire Soccer Club, and before that, he was the senior vice president of the New York-New Jersey MetroStars (now New York Red Bulls). Washo joined the MetroStars after spending the previous five seasons with D.C. United as the team's senior director of ticket sales.